*The*
*Portuguese Economy*
*since 1974*

David Corkill

# The Portuguese Economy since 1974

EDINBURGH UNIVERSITY PRESS

Edinburgh University Press Ltd
22 George Square, Edinburgh

Typeset in Monotype Times Roman
by ROM-Data Corporation Ltd, Falmouth, Cornwall, England and
printed and bound in Great Britain by Page Bros Ltd, Norwich

A CIP record for this book is available from the British Library

ISBN 0 7486 0427 8

Map of Portugal, showing the country's regions, and major towns and rivers. (Drawn by the cartographers at the University of Portsmouth.)

PARA DINA, ALEX E SOFIA

# Contents

# List of Tables

# *Acknowledgements*

The idea for this book was first suggested during a productive and enjoyable sabbatical year spent as a visiting lecturer at Portsmouth Polytechnic (now the University of Portsmouth). It was colleagues and students in the School of Languages and Area Studies who pointed out the need for such a text, and I owe them a debt of gratitude for providing an environment in which research on the Iberian countries was encouraged and ideas could be discussed. My thanks go to the Department of English and History at Manchester Polytechnic (now Manchester Metropolitan University) for granting sabbatical leave in order to complete the project, and to the inter-library loans staff in the All Saints Library for their invaluable assistance. I would also like to thank Joseph Harrison and Ed Early for their helpful comments on the script, Tom Gallagher for his advice and constant encouragement, and Allan Williams and Fernando Rosas for stimulating discussion about Portugal. Finally, I would like to express my thanks to Dina and Alex for their support and tolerance while this book came to fruition, and to the Da Silva family, particularly Maria and Virgilio, for their hospitality during many visits to Portugal.

David Corkill

# *Abbreviations*

| | |
|---|---|
| AD | Aliança Democrática (Democratic Alliance) |
| AES | Acordo Económico e Social (Economic and Social Agreement) |
| AIP | Associação Industrial Portuense (Oporto Industrial Association) |
| CDS | Centro Democrático e Social (Social Democratic Centre Party) |
| CGTP-IN | Confederação Geral dos Trabalhadores Portugueses – Intersindical Nacional (General Confederation of Portuguese Workers – National Intersindical) |
| CIP | Confederação de Indústria Português (Confederation of Portuguese Industry) |
| CR | Conselho da Revolução (Council of the Revolution) |
| CSF | Community Structural Funds |
| EC 6 | The original members of the Community (France, West Germany, Italy, Belgium, Netherlands and Luxembourg) |
| EC 9 | The six plus United Kingdom, Ireland and Denmark |
| EC12 | The European Community after the addition of Greece, Spain and Portugal |
| EEC | European Economic Community, also known simply as the European Community since the late 1980s |
| EEZ | Exclusive Economic Zone |
| EFTA | European Free Trade Association |
| EMU | Economic and Monetary Union |
| ERM | Exchange Rate Mechanism |
| FEDER | Fundo Europeo de Desenvolvimento Regional (European Regional Development Fund) |
| FEOGA | Fundo Europeu de Orientação e Garantia Agrícola (European Agricultural Guidance and Guarantee Fund – EAGGF) |
| IAPMEI | Instituto de Apoio às Pequenas e Médias Empresas (Institute for the Support of Small and Medium-sized Firms) |
| ICEP | Instituto do Comércio Externo de Portugal (Portuguese Foreign Trade Institute) |
| IGT | Inspecção Geral do Trabalho (General Inspectorate of Labour) |
| IIE | Instituto de Investimento Estrangeiro (Institute of Foreign Investment) |

| IMF | International Monetary Fund |
|---|---|
| IPE | Instituto de Participações do Estado |
| MEP | Member of the European Parliament |
| MESS | Ministerio de Emprego e Segurança Social (Ministry of Employment and Social Security) |
| MFA | Movimento das Forças Armadas (Armed Forces Movement) |
| MFA | Multi-fibre Agreement |
| NIE | Newly industrialising economy |
| OECD | Organisation for Economic Cooperation and Development |
| OEEC | Organisation for European Economic Cooperation |
| OID | Operação Integrada de Desenvolvimento (Integrated Development Operation) |
| OPEC | Organisation of Petroleum-exporting Countries |
| PAC | Política Agrícola Comum (Common Agricultural Policy) |
| PALOP | Países Africanos de Língua Oficial Portuguesa (Portuguese-speaking African Countries) |
| PCEDED | Programa de Correção Estructural do Déficie Externo e de Desemprego (Programme for the Structural Adjustment of the Foreign Deficit and Unemployment) |
| PCP | Partido Comunista Português (Portuguese Communist Party; also APU and CDU) |
| PEDAP | Programa Específico de Desenvolvimento da Agricultura Portuguesa (Plan for the Development of Portuguese Agriculture) |
| PEDIP | Programa Específico de Desenvolvimento para a Indústria Portuguesa (Plan for the Development of Portuguese Industry) |
| PITIE | Programa Integrada de Tecnologia de Informação e Electronica (Integrated Programme for Information and Electronic Technology) |
| PRD | Partido Renovador Democrático (Democratic Renewal Party) |
| PS | Partido Socialista (Socialist Party) |
| PSD | Partido Social Democrata (Social Democratic Party; formerly PPD) |
| QCA | Quadro Comunitário de Apoio (Community Support Framework) |
| QUANTUM | Quadro de Adjustamento Nacional para a Transição para a União Económica e Monetária (National Adjustment Framework for the Transition to Economic and Monetary Union) |
| SEA | Single European Act |
| SEDES | Sociedade para o Desenvolvimento Económico e Social (Society for Economic and Social Development) |
| SIBR | Sistema de Incentivos de Base Regional (Regionally-based Incentives System) |
| SME | Small and medium-sized firms |
| UGT | União Geral dos Trabalhadores (General Union of Workers) |

# *Introduction*

This book was conceived to meet a need that became apparent when teaching undergraduate courses on the southern European economies in the contemporary period. It was difficult to recommend to students an accessible and up-to-date text on the Portuguese economy from the limited English-language literature available. It seemed that Portugal's belated integration into the European mainstream presented the ideal opportunity for an overview that would synthesise existing knowledge and identify the themes and issues that must be addressed in any re-evaluation of Portuguese economic development over the past two decades.

The aim is, therefore, to provide a concise general introduction to Portugal's economy. Inevitably, it amalgamates elements of various approaches and, where possible, makes a connecting analysis between the political and economic levels in order to furnish a comprehensible interpretation of the modern economy.

Naturally, it is necessary to acknowledge the groundwork and analysis carried out previously by Eric Baklanoff, Richard Robinson, Tom Gallagher, Allan Williams and Mark Hudson, and a growing number of excellent monographs by Portuguese economists and economic historians such as Fernando Rosas, João Cravinho, Jose M. Brandão de Brito, Jorge Braga de Macedo and many others. It is recognised that any attempt to distil the work of others is fraught with the dangers of omission and the impossibility of covering all aspects and developments. However, it is hoped that some compensation is offered by the comparative and non-Portuguese perspective.

It has often been said that 'Portugal has its head in Europe, but its feet in the Third World'. The feet were extracted from colonial entanglements in 1975 and the head turned irrevocably northwards when Portugal became a full member of the EC in 1986. Nevertheless, indicators of 'Third World' status are still evident in any assessment of the modern economy, and disagreement persists as to how precisely to classify Portugal's economic status. Usually it is ranked by international organisations either among the poorer First World nations or as being in the front rank of the developing countries. In the 1980s, the World Bank excluded Portugal from its group of 'developed market economies' in favour of a 'developing country' classification based on its per capita income (Lister 1988). The OECD frequently compares Portugal with other newly industrialising economies (NIEs), while recognising that, as a member of the EC, it also merits being categorised alongside the developed economies. Clearly, the confusion arises because, while the country is firmly within the European orbit, its economic structures require modernisation and it displays many characteristics of social underdevelopment.

A number of common themes and issues recur throughout the book:

- the search for national independence. For Salazar, it was maintained by pursuing a policy of economic nationalism and autarky; during the period 1974–82 through state intervention and control, while today the expectation is that greater influence and independence is likely to come from being part of a larger organisation, the EC;

- given the aforementioned emphasis on achieving independence, it is paradoxical that Portugal has often relied on outside help to extricate itself from crisis through an alliance with a more powerful partner, as was the case with the UK, or as head of a far-flung empire, or through an open world trading economy or, most recently, Europe;

- the wider context of southern Europe and the EC. An effort is made to analyse the Portuguese economy from a comparative perspective within the context of modern European developments. Unfortunately, this does mean that interesting topics such as relations with the Portuguese-speaking African countries (PALOP) and economic links between the autonomous regions of Madeira and the Azores and the mainland are not explored;

- continuity. Portugal's twentieth-century history is studded with turning points: 1926, 1974, 1986 and others. Yet, however dramatic and seminal events in these years might have been, the threads of continuity are often stronger and more persistent than change in any evaluation of the country's economic evolution;

- the struggle to initiate structural transformations despite political and economic diversions and constraints. Since 1974, the problem has been to make austerity compatible with a politically viable model of pluralist democracy. A conservative consensus gradually gained ground in economic policymaking as issues such as economic growth, unemployment and inflation took second place to concern for the external sector. It took until the second half of the 1980s before it was possible to switch the emphasis to economic growth, focus more on the internal market and initiate the much-delayed process of structural change. The premise is that four major formative and enduring influences shaped the contemporary Portuguese economy: half a century of authoritarian rule; the 1974 revolution and the problems encountered in the consolidation of a new democratic and economic order; the reorientation away from empire towards a closer relationship with Europe; and the accelerated structural change – as yet incomplete – initiated by the Social Democrat governments in the late 1980s. These themes are the axes for the book's organisational structure.

Chapter 1 examines the dictatorship, when, for long periods, economic development took second place to prudent, ultra-cautious economic management and a semi-autarkic strategy. Portugal's economic fragility was concealed by an expanding world economy and the captive colonial markets, but the contradictions had become transparent by the late 1960s. The structures, processes and practices bequeathed by Salazar to the post-1974 economy are outlined.

Chapter 2 covers the period from the late 1960s to the eve of Portugal's accession to the EC. The chronology begins in 1968, when Caetano took over the reins and embarked upon a modernisation programme based on rapid economic growth. The task of structural transformation was interrupted first by the internal opposition to the *Caetanista* project and then by the 1974 revolution that toppled the old regime. In the period of uncertainty that followed, market forces continued to play a subsidiary role in an economy dominated by state monopolies where economic decisions were determined principally by political considerations, both ideological and electoral. Balance-of-payments crises were the inevitable outcome as demand outstripped national income and the country grappled with inflation, foreign debt and public enterprise deficits. Any hopes of sustained growth were consistently hampered by a series of internal and external shocks and the stop-go policies that resulted.

Chapter 3 surveys the structure of the Portuguese economy with particular reference to elements such as human resources, the regions, the industrial, agricultural and service sectors, and natural resources. The problems confronting the contemporary economy are illustrated by focusing on specific sectors in more detail – ranging from textiles and clothing, shipbuilding and repair, to tourism and banking.

Chapter 4 outlines the continued search for development and influence within a larger entity through closer relations with Europe. How has a country often said to 'have its back to Brussels and Frankfurt' coped with this new challenge? Is it the case that once again an external stimulus – in this case entry into the EC – determined and shaped a coherent economic policy? The issues explored include the significance of EFTA as a 'halfway house', the impact of EC entry for industrial and infrastructure development, the emergence of the Iberian market, and attitudes to monetary union and the Single Market project.

The final chapter provides an interim assessment of the period 1985–91 when, for the first time since the revolution, political problems did not distract from the task of structural economic reform. This assessment of the economic record of the Cavaco Silva governments and the boom of the late 1980s examines policymaking in a number of vital areas including foreign investment, inflation, the public debt, tax reform and the labour laws. Finally, it is asked whether or not the period 1985–91 witnessed a unique confluence of factors that are unlikely to be repeated.

The research for this book was not archive-based and consequently did not confront the problems of access to and availability of historical records that have frustrated scholars in the past. It should be noted, however, that future prospects are looking brighter as archives from the Salazar era are opened up to researchers. This is not necessarily the case with regard to the statistical data for use by economic historians. Until recent improvements, national accountancy methods left a lot to be desired. After 1976, the National Statistics Institute (INE) abandoned the old system of drawing up accounts and relied on estimates provided by the Bank of Portugal and government ministries until the early 1980s. Since 1986, INE has had to conform to the EC calendar for the publication of major statistical series. However, the introduction of new procedures did not eliminate confusion and delay – the government was severely embarrassed when major discrepancies were found in the current account statistics after introducing supposedly simplified forms for trade reporting in 1989. Data, when it is available, is often slow to appear (the 1981 accounts were subject to a five-year delay) and is constantly revised. Moreover, because of frequent changes in the methods of calculation, the series are not strictly comparable and breaks often occur. When such imperfections exist for recent statistical data, longer-term historical sequences present enormous difficulties. In fact, Portugal is one of the few remaining European countries for which no series of national output data is available for the nineteenth and twentieth centuries. Encouragingly, a debate, as yet unresolved, is under way among quantitative economic historians in an attempt to reconstruct long-run growth series (Nunes et al. 1989). However, the accuracy of such estimates has been questioned, and it may be that they provide only 'a very rough guide' to the performance of the economy (Lains and Reis 1991).

Where possible, figures are quoted in dollars (US$), escudos or contos (1,000 Esc).

# CHAPTER 1

# *The Authoritarian Legacy*

Portugal languished as a backwater on the European periphery for three-quarters of a century, marginalised in economic and political, as well as geographical, terms. It remained an essentially small, agrarian country outside the mainstream while enduring Western Europe's longest-lasting dictatorship between 1928 and 1974. This chapter examines the economic legacy bequeathed by the Salazarist regime in the belief that the post-1974 economy cannot be understood without reference to the dictatorship. Indeed, many of the economic problems encountered since the 1974 revolution are attributable to the old regime which had shaped and determined Portugal's economic trajectory for almost half a century.

It is therefore necessary to understand the context in which economic policymaking operated during the 1920s and 1930s. Just as dictatorship or one-man rule was seen as preferable to the political upheaval experienced under the Parliamentary Republic (1910–26), so protectionist, semi-autarkic, socially congealed strategies were favoured as a means of escaping from economic dependence, underdevelopment and social upheaval. They emerged as solutions to a series of contradictions that were core features in Portugal's historical development and which, in crucial aspects, differentiate the country from its counterparts in the rest of southern Europe.

The first, and perhaps the most important paradox, was that while Portugal maintained a far-flung empire and refused to countenance withdrawal, it still performed a semi-peripheral, intermediary role as a broker or conveyer for the wealth generated by English industrial power. The relationship with the United Kingdom had important consequences. First, it severely delayed the industrialisation process in Portugal despite efforts made by, among others, the Count of Ericeira in the seventeenth century and Pombal in the eighteenth. Domestic industrial development was constrained by an alliance between English commercial interests and Portuguese agriculturalists. In return for protection against Spain, the Portuguese signed the Methuen Treaty (1703) which reopened the Portuguese market to English woollen cloth and manufactured goods in return for preferential duties on port wine exports. As a result, neither landowning nor commercial interests were willing to invest in risky industrial ventures. Second, Portugal's intermediary function between the advanced European economies and the colonies (first Brazil and then later Africa) and her sub-imperial role as a supplier of home-produced primary products, notably wine, meant that the direct exploitation of colonial wealth did not commence until the 1960s (Leeds 1984a).

Imperialism became a crucial plank in the nationalist ideology that Salazar inherited and then refined. It was founded on an emotive interpretation of Portugal's heroic past and the belief in a civilising mission. Such exalted views concerning the country's role in the world ignored the reality of its economic and political power. Whereas colonial possessions provided other nations with some of the basic requirements for their industrial development, for Portugal 'the empire ... was perhaps the greatest single factor contributing to decadence and stagnation' (Figueiredo 1975). Portugal became ensnared by its imperial role because its economic, human, administrative and military resources did not match such geographically dispersed territories, located in Africa, Brazil and India. Unable to compete with stronger European rivals, Portugal succumbed to humiliations like the 1890 British ultimatum which effectively arrested the extension of the colonial market and ended the dream of an African empire extending from Angola to Mozambique.

It is in the context of a backward, underdeveloped European nation that Portuguese colonial policy must be evaluated. For Europe's poorest economy, the empire assumed a disproportionate significance as its only claim to greatness. The empire, or *ultramar*, came to be regarded as an economic lifeline and a focus for development opportunities in the absence of alternative scenarios. The imperial 'holy grail' pervaded Portuguese policymaking throughout the twentieth century up until the collapse of the dictatorship. In 1951, the African territories became even more closely integrated into Portugal when they ceased to be colonies and were made provinces within the Lusitanian Community and an escudos area. It is curious but illustrative to note that Salazar never visited the overseas territories during his lifetime 'almost as though he needed them to remain a remote fantasy of imperial greatness' (Clarence-Smith 1985).

The second key factor in the formulation of Salazar's economic policy derived from the economic, political and social instability experienced under the First Republic (1910–26). There were no fewer than seven presidents, eight parliamentary elections, twenty-one governments and forty-five different cabinets in the sixteen-year period (Schwartzman 1989). In addition, 380 major strikes occurred during the first decade, the escudo's value plummeted, capital outflow and indebtedness reached alarming levels and there were high levels of emigration (1,000,000 emigrants left Portugal in search of a better life elsewhere between 1900 and 1914). These upheavals reduced the Portuguese economy to what Elizabeth Leeds describes as a form of 'crippled capitalism' (Leeds 1984a). Industrial development did take place in response to the stimulus provided by the First World War, but accompanying modernisation measures, which would have entailed expanding the domestic market and removing protection afforded to agrarian and industrial interests, floundered on the rocks of entrenched oligarchical resistance. Indeed, the consequences of the Depression, following hard on the heels of the chaotic Parliamentary Republic, served to reinforce demands for a conservative political project based on order, stability and social discipline.

The turbulent early decades of the twentieth century moulded Salazar's thinking and convinced him that two principles were of paramount importance: first, development is disruptive and involves social costs, and therefore future development must be limited, gradual and controlled. In order to achieve this, mechanisms were needed to diffuse, postpone and divert potential social conflict. Second, ways had to be found to unite divergent interests among the dominant domestic groups. Sammis (1988) argues that Salazar initiated a set of policies deliberately aimed at building a political and economic consensus among agricultural and industrial interests. These economic policies succeeded in bringing about an alliance that was 'a marriage between textiles and wine, chemicals and wheat'. The state encouraged cooperation between small, medium and large industrial interests and between landowners and industrialists. It prompted economic collaboration in policy areas such as agricultural modernisation, colonial development and controls imposed on the workforce. By ensuring a slow pace of modernisation and change, any potential conflict between these potentially antagonistic interests was minimised or postponed.

CORPORATISM

The nature of *Estado Novo* (New State) and the adoption of a corporatist system has spawned much sterile debate. Marxist historians have applied the label 'fascist' to the Salazar regime. They stress the similarities between the *Estado Novo* and contemporaneous fascist regimes elsewhere in Europe, particularly Mussolini's Italy. Hammond (1988) believes that although the regime was not based on mass mobilisation like German Nazism and Italian Fascism, 'it was structured to guarantee by its repressive nature the interests of the capitalist class'. Clearly, a country with a high level of illiteracy, a negligible working class and a pervasive rural conservatism did not require a mass party and other features common to fascist regimes. In an attempt to distinguish between north European fascism and its Mediterranean variant, Wiarda (1987) argues that Portuguese corporatism was 'an indigenous (Catholic and southern European) model based on [their] own history and traditions, rather than one imported from the outside'. This interpretation fails to find favour among historians of modern Portugal, who make a clear distinction between theory and practice. Corporatism is variously described as 'a facade' and 'formalistic' (Graham 1975), 'a theoretical showpiece' and 'a practical illusion' (Gallagher 1990) and at best 'a distant idea' (Robinson 1979). In fact, the corporatist structures established during 1933–5 stalled thereafter, and it was not until the 1960s that the full system comprising eleven corporations was finally in place.

### THE STAGES OF PORTUGUESE ECONOMIC DEVELOPMENT

It is useful to distinguish the phases in the development of economic policy under the dictatorship: the first 'restorationist' phase (1928–34); the *Estado Novo*'s semi-autarkic, cooperative strategy which predominated during the 1930s and 1940s; and the postwar era when, particularly after 1960, a major directional shift in favour of internationalisation and import-substitution in-dustrialisation took place. By the late 1960s, the contradictions and tensions inherent in the economic model had begun to emerge.

In a country with few trained economists, Salazar, an economics professor at Coimbra University, received a number of invitations to manage the economy before eventually agreeing to become Minister of Finance in April 1928. He gradually accumulated more and more power until, by June 1932, he was prime minister and the undisputed ruler of his country. While consolidating his authority, Salazar introduced stringent economies in an effort to balance the budget, stabilise the currency and reduce the national debt. His financial stewardship became a byword for parsimony throughout Portugal: housewives christened the spatula used for scraping every last ounce from the mixing bowl *o salazar*. Protectionist measures were introduced in order to guarantee the internal and colonial markets to domestic economic interests. The stabilisation programme provided a platform for economic growth and, fortuitously, the Depression of the 1930s did not make a deep imprint on the Portuguese economy. According to Rosas (1986), Portugal's economic underdevelopment provided insulation from the worst effects of the worldwide slump. The restricted internal market and low level of industrialisation, combined with the relative absence of competition in world markets for Portugal's principal exports, served to limit the damage to small and very specific areas. The worst-affected sectors can be gauged from the index of main exports by value for 1934 (1929 = 100): port wine 72.8, canned fish 72.6 and cork 62.7, while export earnings slumped thirty per cent, thirty-eight per cent and seventy-five per cent respectively. Where job losses did occur, the practice of dual employ-ment (mixing agricultural and industrial jobs) enabled the rural economy to absorb the unemployed while state expenditure cushioned the impact by providing credit, unemployment subsidies and promoting autarkic economic policies.

There is disagreement among historians about the origins and characteristics of economic policy under the *Estado Novo*. Rosas (1986) uncovered no eco-nomic plan or coherent project beyond the desire to maintain the values of traditional society and to safeguard rural and colonial interests. According to this interpretation, Salazar simply responded pragmatically to problems as they arose. In contrast, Leeds (1984a) argued that a set of clear-cut economic and political aims existed which amounted to a discernible economic model.

Although not immutable throughout the life of the regime, the model provided coherence and a 'continuous framework' which allows the regime and specifically its industrial policy to be analysed. It comprised a number of core components, including protection for agriculture and industry, controlled and guided economic development in order to limit the social consequences, a reliance on cheap labour and low production costs, the concentration of economic activity in the Lisbon-Setúbal axis in southern central Portugal, and a growing emphasis on colonial development to the detriment of metropolitan Portugal.

The *Estado Novo* established a political and economic basis for its longevity by combining a set of interlocking economic policies within an incomplete corporatist structure. Each element will be analysed briefly in turn:

- a wheat campaign;
- a colonial act;
- protectionism;
- industrial regulation (*condicionamento industrial*);
- public works; and
- a national Labour Statute.

### The Wheat Campaign

It is no coincidence that one of the first economic initiatives, the wheat campaign (*campanha do trigo*) targeted the agricultural sector. It reflected the influence exerted over the regime by the landowners but also consolidated the common interests they shared with the industrialists. Launched in 1929 and modelled on Mussolini's 'battle for wheat', the *campanha* aimed to stimulate wheat production, relieve the pressure on the balance of payments caused by imported wheat and revitalise the stagnant agricultural sector. However, it did little to boost cereal output, as government subsidies merely encouraged the extension of cereal-growing to unsuitable lands (Pintado 1964). New land was brought into cultivation only to suffer from soil erosion within a few years because of the over-zealous felling of trees, while the infrastructure and transport provision was so poor that often the silos and warehouses did not exist to store the produce. Nor did the price support system do anything to tackle the fundamental requirements of Portuguese agriculture – the need for investment in irrigation, the increased use of fertilisers, more mechanisation and the efficient use of labour. Interestingly, industrialists enthusiastically backed the campaign because agricultural subsidies raised production and generated demand for fertilisers, while mechanisation, albeit on a modest scale, benefited the metallurgical sector (Sammis 1988). In this manner, the larger and predominantly southern landowners and the monopoly industrialists shared mutual interests.

### The Colonial Act

Salazar's colonial policy was forged on the anvil of the imperial experience. Instead of providing expanded markets for metropolitan products and stimulating domestic industry, the colonies increased rather than reduced external dominance and subordination to foreign and, especially British, economic interests. It is no coincidence, therefore, that one of the dictatorship's earliest pieces of legislation was the Colonial Act (1930). The Act brought the colonies under tighter control from Lisbon and encouraged trade between the metropolis and the colonies by providing increased protection for Portuguese goods and by placing restrictions on the export of raw materials from the colonies. Imperial economic policy was based firmly on the premise that the colonies should furnish the raw materials while in return the metropolis supplied the manufactured goods.

Although the economic depression of the 1930s did not bite as deeply in Portugal as elsewhere, Clarence-Smith (1985) does note that it prompted a revised attitude towards the colonies. Reduced demand and falling market prices for Portuguese goods and the halt to immigration imposed by Brazil and the USA inevitably had a major impact on Portugal's balance of payments, reduced vital emigrant remittances and bankrupted banking and shipping companies. It was this crisis that convinced Salazar of the need for a strong currency and healthy foreign exchange reserves. Such a cautious and conservative strategy acted as an effective brake on anything but limited and constrained industrial development. Imported raw materials, fuel and technology would be required to pursue an import-substitution policy for manufactured goods. Devoid of other options, Salazar resorted to the economic exploitation of the colonies. Portugal's trade deficit was covered not, as in the past, by emigrant remittances but by hard-currency earnings from the export of colonial production such as Angolan coffee. After the Depression, colonial markets became increasingly important for Portuguese industry. The politically influential cotton textile manufacturers objected to competition from Africa, but in other sectors firms invested in colonial production, in many cases displacing foreign capital, particularly in plantation agriculture. Above all, it was the large firms created by Salazar's granting of monopolies which prospered from the exploitation of colonial resources and of the native population. Clarence-Smith estimates that the economic value of the empire to Portugal peaked during the 1950s, although imperial trade never exceeded twenty-two per cent of total trade. Moreover, the benefits that did accrue were obtained 'at the expense of a cumbersome and authoritarian system of state control, which generated a great deal of waste and inefficiency' (Clarence-Smith 1985). In addition, race relations deteriorated and the colonial peasantry suffered the deprivations of forced labour schemes, land confiscations and compulsory cultivation.

### Protectionism and Industrial Regulation

Salazar promoted the idea that Portugal should 'produce and save' by pursuing policies of self-reliance and protectionism encapsulated in the slogan '*orgulhosamente sós*' (proudly alone). A system of protective tariffs was put in place that effectively insulated indigenous industry, particularly the traditional industries located in the north, from external competition for a period stretching from the 1930s to the 1960s and, in certain instances, even longer. What began as a response to the Depression became an embedded feature of economic policy that endured for over thirty years, even though it was really only warranted for a short period after the Second World War during the import-substitution phase. Autarkic policies had long-term consequences: on the one hand, they allowed the treasury to build up a healthy surplus of gold and foreign currency reserves; on the other hand, they made a fetish out of the pre-Keynesian obsession with surpluses, insulated producers from both internal and foreign competition and reinforced the dependency on a pliant labour force, cheap raw materials and guaranteed markets.

The instrument used to control the pace, direction and impact of economic development was the Industrial Regulation Law (*Lei de Condicionamento Industrial*) of January 1931. It reflected 'the conservative and mercantilist' (Gallagher 1983) approach to development, shared with the elite, which viewed economic progress and technological change with suspicion and regarded it as a potential threat to morality, family life and industrial harmony. The law required government approval for the establishment of a new enterprise, the introduction of new technology and the transfer of ownership. The aim of this institutionalised intervention by the state was to establish an 'equilibrium of production' in the domestic market and to limit competition among small, medium and large enterprises. Only a few industries were reorganised during the 1930s to address overproduction problems. Over 100 flour mills were closed as surplus to requirements, and, in the most famous case of industrial reorganisation, outdated factories in the glass industry were obliged to merge to create Covina, the first modern enterprise in the sector. Workers were transferred to the new factory at Santa Iria de Azoa and received unemployment subsidies during the construction phase (Telo 1987).

The law protected the market shares enjoyed by existing firms, controlled the establishment and productive capacity of new enterprises and authorised the granting of monopoly concessions in the modern industrial sector. Key industries (*indústrias de ponta*) such as steel, metallurgy, chemicals and shipbuilding, were safeguarded against competition while small firms were secure from the predatory attentions of their larger brethren. Requests for changes were likely to meet stiff resistance, as they were vetted by the corporatist *gremios* (employers' guilds), which had a vested interest in limiting competition. In a detailed study of industrial regulation, Brandão de Brito (1989) uncovered a process characterised by delays, arbitrary decisions and opportunities for nepotism. He cites as an example a firm, Fábrica de Borracha Continental Lda, which requested permission to replace a piece of machinery in August 1956 and had to wait until January 1958 for approval. The emphasis on social stability led to careful scrutiny and sometimes rejection of industrial projects.

Job-creation was afforded a low priority. Business criteria were subordinated to legal and bureaucratic processes that imposed their own pace on decision-making. This system produced a cosy trade-off: small firms were secure in their existence and large firms could dominate the newer sectors.

The protection of small and medium-sized firms (SMEs) and the creation of large monopoly groups were not the only motives behind industrial regulation. Brazil had responded to the Depression by clamping down on immigration, thereby eliminating an outlet for Portugal's 'excess' population. The new system was expected to generate employment for some of the thousands of workers deprived of the opportunity to emigrate. In addition, the legislation served a political purpose by forming part of a policy armoury that included agricultural pricing, public works and controls over labour, which forged a community of interests among landowners, industrialists and commercial concerns which gave them a stake in the survival of the dictatorship. Nevertheless, it would be an exaggeration to assert that unanimity existed within the business community in favour of state intervention. Some found the corporatist structures, regulations and controls irksome but perhaps acquiesced initially because they overestimated the threat from the working class or underestimated the extent of state involvement (Schwartzman 1989). Later, they had either become so reliant on protected markets and competition-free activity, or learned to circumvent or to live with the worst bureaucratic features of the system, that criticism tended to be muted.

The relationship between the state and the *grupos económicos* (banking and industrial monopolies) was consolidated further by the provision of credits and subsidies. However, credit was not easily obtainable in the prewar period, and the government preferred to rely on tariff protection to encourage industrialisation. The limited stimulus on offer is revealed by the structure of Portuguese exports prior to 1945, which remained largely traditional in composition. On the eve of the Second World War, the breakdown in the commodity composition of Portuguese exports was as follows: foodstuffs fifty-one per cent, raw materials twenty-nine per cent and manufactured goods twenty per cent (Pintado 1964). Although industrialists began to campaign for the reorientation of government policy following the Depression (the Exhibition of Portuguese Industry held in 1932 is an example), it took until the end of the Second World War before official action was contemplated. The conflict highlighted the vulnerability of the Portuguese economy in a number of ways: traditional export markets were closed, there were problems for maritime transport, and the blockade severely limited the availability of raw materials, especially energy, along with intermediate goods and equipment. Unlike non-belligerents with a larger economy, who responded by adopting import-substitution strategies, Portugal's options were limited by her small internal market.

## Public Works

One of the principal areas in which the state became actively involved was infrastructure provision. A substantial public works programme provided assistance to the private sector, generated employment and allowed the regime to make propaganda out of its achievements. Some 6,500,000 contos were allocated under the 1935 Economic Reconstruction Law (*Lei de Reconstitução Económica*) for a fifteen-year programme of public building projects including post offices, schools and administrative premises (Saraiva 1983). Communications were improved through an investment programme in road- and rail-building and repair and, during the 1960s, airport construction. Hydroelectric projects, which included the building of three dams on the Douro river, were undertaken in a conscious effort to cut the mounting energy import bill. Port facilities at Lisbon and Leixões (Oporto) were upgraded in order to establish Portugal as an important ship repair and maintenance centre, and the national merchant fleet was expanded.

Robinson (1979) maintains that public works investment made a significant contribution to industrial development during the 1950s. Although this is undoubtedly the case, the benefits were very narrowly focused and the consequences for the economy were not altogether positive. The Law did not itself constitute a project aimed at stimulating economic development. In the first place, only two-thirds of the funds were actually spent, and defence swallowed two-fifths of the total spending (Loureiro 1991). As Gallagher (1983) notes, state contracts for the public works programme were awarded to a small, privileged group of enterprises in what Hudson (1989) labels 'a form of public financing in aid of private enterprise'. Moreover, public works investment took preference over social programmes in needy areas such as education and health. The result was to reinforce the position of an economic oligarchy with a conservative business mentality that preferred to eschew risk-taking in favour of the guaranteed profits to be made from state contracts.

## Labour Statute

From the 1930s onwards, the control, disciplining and exploitation of the workforce played an integral part in the Salazarian political economy. Independent trade-union activity was crushed by the state's repressive apparatus, and strikes were outlawed. Although the Labour Statute (1933) paid lip-service to social justice, harmonious labour relations and welfare benefits such as pensions, health care and paid holidays, it failed to deliver the most minimal provisions. In reality, the social security system failed to operate under Salazar. Far from improving, the proportion of GDP spent on welfare actually fell during the 1960s in comparison to the 1940s and 1950s (Williamson 1985). Nor did the network of *casas do povo* (people's community centres) and *casas dos pescadores* (fisherman's centres) allocate the welfare and educational benefits envisaged at their foundation. Coverage was very patchy throughout rural Portugal: in the mid-1960s, only 625 *casas* existed in a country containing 3,600 parishes (Williamson 1985). Instead of providing old age pensions, unemployment benefits and medical provision, they acted as a mechanism of social control.

Labour relations were regulated by Labour Courts, and, in practice, work contracts were imposed by the state bureaucracy. Collective negotiations under the corporatist structures served as a mechanism for holding down wages. A low-wage policy formed a key part of the government's strategy as profit-accumulation and investment was given priority over improved standards of living. This was achieved by controlling the trade unions and by maintaining an excess supply of labour (Thormann 1969). The *sindicatos* (official trade unions) lacked either political independence or bargaining power and were organised by occupation so as to cause the maximum fragmentation and reduce the possibility of workplace solidarity.

The state secured and guaranteed capital accumulation and consolidated the position of the dominant classes. The information that does exist on wages and salaries in the interwar period underlines labour's weakness in the bargaining process. Nominal industrial salaries rose by 800 per cent between the end of the First World War and 1944 while retail prices went up by around 970 per cent, indicating a fall in working-class purchasing power in the region of twenty per cent (Amaro 1987). This strategy paid handsome dividends during the Second World War, when conditions allowed huge profits to be made at a time when wages failed to keep pace with prices. According to Williamson (1985), labour's share of GDP stood at thirty-nine per cent in 1950, while profits, interest and rent took over sixty per cent. Labour's share did climb to reach fifty-two per cent by the early 1970s, but the improvement in real wages was restricted to a small portion of the workforce and did little to eradicate the extensive poverty suffered by large segments of the population.

STAGNATION OR ECONOMIC GROWTH?

It is commonplace to equate the *Estado Novo* with economic stagnation at least during the first two decades of its existence. This is often linked to the notion that the regime's policies retarded capitalist development in Portugal by interfering with its internal dynamics. Hammond (1988) declares that 'Portugal's economy remained stagnant for most of Salazar's rule' and that his policies 'prevented development'. In similar vein, Kayman (1987) writes about 'a retarded industrial development'.

It is true that Salazar shared with the elite a suspicion that economic and technological development was socially corrosive, politically dangerous and morally corrupting. It is possible to cite rhetorical evidence to support the thesis that Salazar sought, at least in the early years, to promote a pastoral ideology. Ministers often made statements confirming the existence of this line of

*Table 1.1*:    Annual Growth Rates 1914–73.

| Period | Real GDP | GDP per capita | Population |
|--------|----------|----------------|------------|
|        |          | (percentage changes in annual growth rate) | |
| 1914–21 | -7.1 | -7.2 | 0.1 |
| 1922–41 | 4.7 | 3.5 | 1.2 |
| 1942–5 | -3.8 | -4.8 | 1.0 |
| 1946–73 | 5.4 | 5.2 | 0.2 |

*Source*: Nunes, Mata and Valerio 1989.

thinking, but caution should be exercised when dismissing the regime as anti-capitalist and anti-industrial. Before long, the realities of a mass exodus from the rural areas undermined the pretence that a passive, isolated population could be maintained in the countryside. Certainly, Salazar's approach was non-developmental, and potential agricultural and industrial developments were neglected. Market forces were distrusted and distortions introduced into the labour market by making dismissals difficult. However, recent research by economic historians challenges the 'stagnation' and retarded capitalist development thesis when applied to the interwar period. Despite having to grapple with the problems of unreliable and inconsistent data, they prefer to use terms such as 'moderate and irregular' (Nunes et al. 1989) and 'slow' or 'relative' (Amaro 1987) to describe economic growth during the 1922–41 period while noting a certain upturn in the subperiod 1933–8. Given the combined effects of internal and external instability (transition to a new regime, the Depression and the impact of the Second World War) which did result in zero or negative growth, the rates are, in fact, quite impressive. Table 1.1 records average annual growth rates of 4.2 per cent for 1925–41 (3.7 per cent for 1932–9) which are only marginally inferior to the post-1945 performance.

In the 1922–41 period, there were only three years when GDP per capita actually declined, four when it stagnated and no less than thirteen when growth was registered. The employment figures reflect this modest growth. The industrial workforce expanded at an annual average rate of 2.3 per cent during the 1930s (rising from 478,000 to 602,000) and even more rapidly in the following decade (2.7 per cent) to over 750,000. Employment in manufacturing constituted twelve per cent of total employment in 1930, fifteen per cent in 1940 and nineteen per cent a decade later. However, although industrial growth did occur in this period (the industrial index rose at an annual average rate of 4.4 per cent between 1933 and 1945) and industrial investment was buoyant, it would be mistaken to conclude that it marked the start of a sustained industrialisation process. It is more accurate to speak of the reinforcement in the contribution of traditional sectors (mining, food and drink, textiles, clothing and footwear) to total industrial activity. The traditional industries only begin to cede ground to more modern industries in the post-1945 era. So, while it is an exaggeration to blame industrial regulation and state investment for restraining growth in the

Portuguese economy, it is unwise to take the revisionist argument too far. Protective tariffs encouraged some modest industrialisation but, on the negative side of the equation, discouraged modernisation, technological updating and vocational training. The Portuguese workforce remained predominantly unskilled, poorly remunerated and prone to emigrate in search of higher wages, better opportunities and tolerable working conditions.

The Second World War caused difficulties for a non-belligerent like Portugal but also presented opportunities. On the one hand, the energy shortage plunged certain industries, such as mining, into crisis. Likewise, the economic blockade and the disruption to maritime transport ensured that vital raw materials and intermediary goods and equipment were in short supply. The war interrupted the 'slow but sure' economic progress under way since the 1930s. However, it resolved the problem of overproduction in some traditional sectors, postponed necessary restructuring and, in some cases, encouraged a reversion to *indústria caseira* (artisan workshop activities) and compelled the use of obsolete technologies (Telo 1987). On the other hand, the war presented a chance to boost the industrial output. It left a home market bereft of competition from foreign goods and capital, in which price and quality constraints no longer existed – ideal conditions for making huge profits. An attempt was made to mobilise capital accumulated during wartime for investment in key sectors through the *Lei de Nacionalização de Capitais* (Nationalisation of Capital Law 1943), which reserved the home market for industrial investment. Also, Portuguese exports experienced an upsurge in demand (tin, wolfram, woollen goods, earthenware, glass etc.) and, although markets were limited, fetched high prices.

The war enhanced the state's already significant regulatory role in the economy. Raw material prices were controlled to keep down costs to the producer, wages were depressed (despite high inflation) and the working day extended. The authorities applied a generous tax regime to industrial profits and turned a blind eye to tax evasion and underdeclaration by firms.

In summary, the first stage in the process of economic development (1932–45) displayed a number of core features. In tandem with the promotion of ruralism and the primacy of agriculture, the authoritarian regime developed a tariff protection system and colonial policy to satisfy Salazar's supporters among the traditional northern industrial elites. The agriculturalists and traditional industrialists provided the political underpinning for the regime in the first phase. However, by 1945 their influence had begun to wane (the Ministry of Agriculture disappeared as an autonomous department during the Second World War), and the attempt to insulate Portugal from international economic currents was gradually abandoned after the Second World War. An indication that the priorities had shifted is provided by the *Lei de Fomento e Reorganização Industrial 1945* (Industrial Development and Reorganisation Law), which Brandão de Brito described as 'the only industrial project formulated during the whole period of the *Estado Novo*'. It gave the state powers to intervene when local firms could not meet the needs of the internal market. The intervention could take the form of enforced mergers and reorganisations or an insistence on investment in new technology. New industries were to be encouraged by offering inducements such as credits, tax exemptions and, crucially, the grant of decade-long exclusive concessions. The perceptible tilt in favour of credit provision to industry is revealed in figures from the Caixa Geral do Depósitos: in 1945, 42.5 per cent of the total credit allocated went to agriculture, while industry received 41.4 per cent; by 1949, agriculture's share had dropped to 29.6 per cent whereas industry took 68.1 per cent (Sammis 1988).

However, constraints still existed that kept Portugal at the bottom of the investment league in southern Europe. Pintado (1964) identified the obstacles to expansion as the small internal market, the lack of planning skills among industrialists and the government's obsession with price stability together with a preference for infrastructure investment over manufacturing ventures. Typically, when the economic transformation did take place, it was cautiously slow and reliant on exogenous sources for its dynamism – the result of political compromise between the conservative approach and strategies of industrial modernisation. During the early 1950s, decrees were issued that introduced some limited relaxation in the regulatory regime by removing *condicionamento* for some industries (cotton mills, oil presses), the abandonment of wartime rationing of rice and sugar and the liberalisation of the trade in products such as petroleum (Brandão de Brito 1989).

### A MORE OPEN ECONOMY?

The transformation from a protected, primarily agrarian economy into a more open, semi-industrialised one after the Second World War occurred gradually in a number of stages. During the first, proto-liberalisation phase (1945–60), industrial policy was still conceived within a regulatory framework. The impetus for import-substitution industrialisation that did take place derived as much from wartime shortages as from direct government policies; but, once under way, the sponsorship of new industries and the reorganisation of existing ones occurred within a framework marked by state intervention at all levels (Rosas 1989). After the war, Portugal benefited from the increase in world trade and the demand for Portuguese raw material exports (given a further boost by the Korean war), but structural deficiencies (poor productivity, the lack of skilled labour and a high import capacity) combined with government economic caution to set limits on the gains to be made from favourable external conditions. After the war, the authorities pursued tight monetary and fiscal policies because of fears that an economic boom might generate inflationary pressures. Portugal did share in the provision of US aid after 1950, but it failed to stimulate development to the same extent as elsewhere in Europe. Portugal received only US$516.7 million between 1945 and 1965 in US aid, and a substantial proportion of the total was devoted to military assistance. In contrast, Spain benefited from

US aid to the tune of US$1,863.9 million over the same period (Robinson 1979).

An industrial dimension was added to economic policy by Ferreira Dias (Subsecretary of State for Commerce and Industry 1940–4 and Economy Minister 1958–62), who subsequently became known as 'the father of Portuguese industry'. This former head of the National Electricity Board proposed the establishment of an industrial base through the installation of basic industries and the restructuring of existing ones. Nevertheless, pressure from the agricultural lobby concerned about rural depopulation, rising food prices and social conflict, allied to Salazar's continued preference for agriculture, applied a brake to the project. Clearly, the cornerstone of Portuguese corporatism – low salaries – could not be jeopardised. Yet the compromise (a freeze on agricultural prices to keep down industrial wages) condemned agriculture to decades of stagnation.

A further indication that the state wished to promote economic progress, albeit within strictly-defined parameters, is provided by the adoption of development planning. Economic planning can be traced back to the Economic Reconstruction Plan (1935), which encouraged long-term infrastructure projects. However, it was not until the 1950s that a form of indicative planning and a more technocratic approach common to other European countries came into being. Based on the French model, the First Development Plan (1953–8) recognised the need for industrial expansion but still betrayed the imprint of the landowning lobby. Significantly, between a third and a half of the funds were earmarked for the colonies. The Plan focused on medium-term infrastructure provision complemented by import-substitution projects aimed at reducing the import bill.

The first Plan did stimulate industrial development by building on traditional industries such as textiles, food-processing, wood and cork (Lewis and Williams 1985). The secondary sector registered historically high growth rates averaging around eight per cent per annum between 1953 and 1960, although GDP advanced only modestly (an annual average growth of 4.5 per cent during the 1950s) in comparison to the fast growth achieved elsewhere in southern Europe. The constraints quickly became apparent: the economy became highly import-dependent for iron, steel, chemicals and other products basic to industrial development. The transitional Plan in the mid-1960s introduced a social dimension, and the aims outlined in the Third Plan signalled some further advances by prioritising economic development and accepting the need for increased GDP growth, a more equitable distribution of income and the correction of regional disparities (Marques 1988). Although an advance on previous efforts, this exercise in corporative economic planning cannot be regarded as a success. The reasons for the disappointing outcome included the defective planning machinery, poor links to the private sector, the diversion of public funds for military purposes and the erosion of confidence caused by inflationary pressures (ILO 1979). A fourth Plan identified a number of growth centres but was scrapped following the April 1974 coup.

A question mark hung over the efficacy of the planning process. Did it promote development, or would that have taken place anyway if the plans had not existed? Certainly, the state looked to private enterprise to promote development, reserving to itself the role of creating optimum conditions for economic growth, particularly in the area of public works, planning and credit provision and the maintenance of low wage costs and cheap raw material prices.

The bottlenecks generated by postwar industrial expansion gradually nudged the regime towards the acceptance of liberalisation and closer integration into the international economy. Talk of 'a new era' (Morrison 1981) for the Portuguese economy must be tempered by the realisation that no wholesale conversion to liberal economics and the market economy took place. In certain respects, the distortions in the economy were reinforced and bureaucratic, regulatory controls strengthened. Nor did the pursuit of highly capital-intensive industrialisation do anything to alleviate the chronic unemployment situation (employment actually grew by a steady 0.5 per cent per year during the 1960s). Portugal did add the Cabo Ruivo oil refinery and the Seixal steelworks to its industrial inventory in this period, but domestic investment remained sluggish. The economy still relied on low-cost labour to maintain its international competitiveness, disregarding the negative effect of an unskilled workforce, poor productivity, low levels of technology and a cosseted private sector (Robinson 1979). Economic imperatives alone did not trigger the policy shift in the 1960s. The commencement of the African wars in 1961 involved the government in increasingly costly military expenditure in defence of the colonial interest. Such a commitment could only be financed out of higher levels of economic growth. In order to ensure that growth was sustained, Portugal depended heavily on foreign investment inflows to compensate for the drain on funds caused by a bloated defence budget. Despite these qualifications, the economy did experience uninterrupted growth throughout the 1960s, but the credit for the economic expansion must go overwhelmingly to exogenous factors.

TRADE PATTERNS AND CLOSER LINKS WITH EUROPE

The 1960s witnessed a fundamental reorientation in Portugal's trade patterns caused by closer integration into the international, and particularly European, economy. The change was influenced not only by membership of EFTA (Portugal was a founder member in 1958 along with Austria, the Scandinavian countries, Switzerland and the UK) but also by inclusion in international bodies such as GATT, the IMF and the World Bank in 1960. Membership of the non-EC European Free Trade Area became Portugal's chief link with its northern neighbours until the 1972 trade agreement with the EC 9 and eventual full membership in the 1980s. It brought distinct advantages: Portugal gained preferential access to EFTA markets with a population ten times larger than the domestic one. It was expected that EFTA membership would stimulate Portuguese industrial exports and diversify the export composition away from traditional foodstuffs, raw materials and low-technology manufactured goods. Relations with EFTA are discussed further in Chapter 4.

Portugal's export base did respond to external stimulus, and tourism emerged as a dynamic new factor. Northern Europe's prosperous and expanding economies supplied a growing volume of tourists while absorbing large numbers of emigrant workers whose remittances provided valuable foreign exchange. EFTA emerged as a major consumer of Portuguese exports to the detriment of the overseas territories, which absorbed a decreasing percentage. Traditional exports (cork, textiles, tinned fish and wines) were now supplemented by items such as machinery, metallurgical products, paper and pulp, chemicals, clothing and footwear (Baklanoff 1978). By 1973, a further shift had occurred: the EC 9 took forty-eight per cent of Portuguese exports and supplied forty-five per cent of the imports, while the colonies absorbed twenty per cent of the exports from the metropolis and supplied only ten per cent of total imports. The long-established links with the United Kingdom clearly influenced the decision to join first EFTA and then the Common Market following the enlargement in 1973. Inevitably, the logic of the imperial connection and economic nationalism had been progressively undermined by the changing economic realities of the 1960s and 1970s.

The second stage in Portugal's gradual and belated integration into the European mainstream came with the signing of a trade agreement with the European Economic Community in 1972. As with the earlier EFTA agreement, Portugal retained protective barriers for its own industry and concessions for some agricultural exports (wine, tomato concentrates). However, the Community was less generous with regard to some of the more dynamic exports such as cork, textiles and clothing (representing almost a quarter of exports to the EC 6 in 1972), which were placed on a 'sensitive products ceiling list' (United Nations 1974).

The second component in the liberalisation strategy related to the modification of attitudes towards direct foreign investment (DFI). Previously, DFI had been regarded suspiciously, with domestic capital given preference over foreign capital in order to minimise the extent of external control. Limitations were placed on the transfer into foreign ownership of national firms considered vital to the Portuguese economy, while exchange controls restricted the entry of foreign capital. A transformation began in the early 1960s, and the rules relating to DFI were relaxed in April 1965, although restrictions still surrounded sectors such as defence, public services, insurance and shipping. Foreign firms were encouraged to set up joint ventures and could repatriate profits and enjoy tax advantages. Partnership with local firms was preferable if only to enlist local knowledge in order to negotiate the labyrinthine complexities posed by the Portuguese bureaucracy.

The motives behind the more sympathetic treatment afforded to foreign capital are clear: a deteriorating trade balance, the need to extract maximum advantage from EFTA membership and the enlistment of support for the African wars. Within a few short years, inward investment had begun to transform the structure of the economy. Foreign multinationals set up subsidiaries in Portugal and established close links with the indigenous monopoly groups. They invested in infrastructure projects such as the Tagus suspension bridge and Faro airport on the Algarve. Timex, ITT and Plessey established subsidiaries, and Swedish capital was destined for the clothing industry. As a result, foreign investment in Portuguese industry rose from 1.5 per cent of the total in 1960 to twenty-seven per cent in 1970. The inflow of foreign capital, negligible prior to 1965, increased rapidly to reach US$85,000,000 by 1973, destined mainly for the export-oriented manufacturing sector (over a quarter of the total) and tourism (a fifth). The colonies also proved attractive to overseas investors, especially West Germans, Americans and Belgians eager to exploit Angola and Mozambique's natural resources. Between 1968 and 1973, a third of all investments in the empire were non-metropolitan in origin. It marked the beginning of the linkage between domestic development plans and external sources of finance and a belated attempt to exploit the raw material wealth of the overseas territories. Foreign capital was encouraged not by the size of the home market but by a combination of the more liberal DFI provisions and the labour costs (which for skilled and semi-skilled workers were among the lowest in Europe), supposed political stability, a docile, non-unionised labour force and the opportunity to export to EFTA countries free of duty.

Nevertheless, the new regulations should not be interpreted as marking a sea-change in attitudes towards foreign investment. Nationalist concerns did not suddenly disappear, and both Robinson (1979) and Clarence-Smith (1985) stress the policy continuities and the pragmatic approach adopted towards each DFI application. Indeed, the latter author downgrades the role played by the shift in government policy and prefers to attribute the growth in DFI inflows to the booming world economy and the re-equipment needs of Portuguese industry. Moreover, the reliance on DFI as a motor for economic development, while it introduced much-needed capital and technology, exposed flaws in the fabric of the economy. Foreign interests dominated the newer sectors of the economy such as vehicle assembly (United States), shipyards and ship repair (British and Dutch) and cellulose (Swedish). However, the bulk of the new investment was capital-intensive, and the impact on employment generation was consequently minimal. A gulf began to emerge between a modern, technologically advanced sector and the traditional, low-technology industries. Furthermore, the boom exposed regional imbalances, the unevenness of the growth process and the widening gap between industry and agriculture.

### PROGRESS DURING THE 1960s

On a purely statistical level, the Portuguese economy made impressive strides during the 1960s. GDP advanced at an annual average rate in excess of six per cent, while in the period 1968–73 Portugal achieved GDP per capita growth of 7.4 per cent, marginally below Greece's 7.5 per cent but superior to Spain's 5.8 per cent (Krugman and Braga de Macedo 1981). The industrial sector performed particularly strongly, averaging yearly growth rates around nine per cent, followed closely by the service sector buoyed by the tourist boom. Only agriculture, the perennial economic millstone, registered a disappointingly low 1.5 per cent increase in average annual output.

In response to the export-led growth strategy, the Portuguese economy was undergoing a substantial transformation in terms of output and the distribution of the labour force. An indicator of the growing internationalisation of the economy is provided by the strong surge in exports of manufactured goods, which increased at an annual average rate of 9.8 per cent between 1960 and 1972. Certain industries responded well to the new opportunities: clothing and footwear exported forty-one per cent of its production; machinery and equipment and pulp and paper each managed twenty-three per cent. Between 1960 and 1972, export growth was most pronounced in metallurgy, machinery and transport equipment (18.4 per cent), paper and pulp (17.5 per cent), clothing and footwear (15.4 per cent) and chemicals (11.7 per cent). The percentage of the working population employed in primary activities declined sharply between 1960 and 1973 from forty-four per cent to twenty-eight per cent, while both the secondary (including manufacturing) and service sectors increased their shares from twenty-nine to thirty-six per cent and twenty-eight to thirty-five per cent respectively. By 1973, the industrial sector's contribution to GDP was over fifty per cent (Baklanoff 1978).

It can be argued that in the late 1960s Portugal was about to enter the ranks of the middle-income, newly industrialising economies (NIEs) alongside countries such as Brazil, Taiwan and Hong Kong. They achieved high export growth by concentrating on labour-intensive manufactured goods produced by a semi-skilled labour force. Although on the surface the economic record for the 1960s appears impressive, it might have been even better but for some severe constraints and handicaps. The picture of growth and development is in many ways deceptive and disguises serious structural distortions that, rather than being dismantled, were in some cases reinforced. Portugal's structural problems can be analysed in the following, overlapping and interrelated, categories:

- the obsession with empire;
- concentration and the nature of Portuguese capitalism;
- migration and the labour market;
- the open economy and growing dependence; and
- agriculture, the Achilles heel.

### Portuguese 'Late Colonialism'

Post-1945 economic growth resulted in a realignment of the balance of political power within the authoritarian regime. Yet it is too simplistic to portray these developments in terms of a schism between the agriculturalists, who favoured a continuation of the old politics and corporatist arrangements, and the industrialists/monopolists, who pressed for import-substitution industrialisation and some measure of political liberalisation. If the conflicts of interest had been so straightforward, the regime might well not have survived as long as it did. In fact, as Sammis (1988) demonstrates, the differences did not follow strictly sectoral lines and are better classified as a split between colonialists and Europeanists. Salazar was able to sustain the alliance between agrarian and industrial groups because the families who headed the *grupos* also owned rural properties. In part, this is explained by the complementarity of economic activity, e.g. forests owned for wood pulp, but in many cases there was no direct connection. Hence the emphasis on colonial development appealed to the economic elite on a number of grounds: as a safety valve to provide an outlet for the excess population and minimise social disruption at home, and as a source of cheap raw materials and a captive market for metropolitan industrial production. This explains why the colonialists, comprising landowners, small and medium-sized industrialists and textile interests, were able to prevent the Europeanists, involving monopolists in alliance with foreign capital, from prevailing on the colonial issue. Of course, a price had to be paid for this compromise – political immobilism and an inability to extricate the regime from the quagmire of the colonial wars.

Fighting to retain its colonial possessions exacted an heavy economic cost. Defence expenditure, which consumed 28.7 per cent of the state budget in 1960, had risen to 41.8 per cent in 1971 (Kayman 1987), thereby depriving the economy of much-needed public investment funds. Military conscription (a quarter of the male population served in the armed forces) and voluntary exile in order to avoid the draft aggravated the problem of labour shortages. Nevertheless, the consequences were not entirely negative. Clarence-Smith (1985) argues that the wars acted as a catalyst for significant policy changes by providing 'a kind of forced Keynesian demand management'. Salazar was obliged to ignore some cherished principles and borrow abroad, seek foreign capital, encourage the growth of arms production and even run down the gold and currency reserves.

The impact could be seen in the colonies, where, for the first time, economic development was given priority. White settlement was encouraged by offering twenty-five-year government loans for new colonists. Evidence for the success of the colonisation policy is provided by the expansion in the number of settlers from 79,000 (1950) to 500,000 (1970) in Angola and a smaller but still significant increase in Mozambique. As Angolan and Mozambican industry expanded, the demand for metropolitan products declined, making the mismatch between the Portuguese and colonial economies even more apparent. However, the changing economic relationship with the metropolis did not prevent the overseas territories from enjoying a mini-boom during the 1960s. Angola in particular diversified its economic base, adding mineral exports (diamonds, iron ore etc.) to its mainstay coffee cultivation and initiating a process of rapid industrial development during which an average annual growth rate of nineteen per cent was registered in the manufacturing sector for the period 1961–73 (Neto 1991). Foreign investment played an important part in this process: the Belgian company, Petrofina, exploited Angola's oil reserves; the German company Krupp invested in iron ore and manganese extraction; and, in Mozambique, British and Japanese capital was responsible for the railways, while an international consortium built the Cabora Bassa dam (Duffy 1962). Yet although the colonies undoubtedly benefited from changed government priorities, the extent of the progress made requires qualification. In the first place, economic development tended to increase rather than diminish resentment at Lisbon's continued restrictive controls over the local economy and the favouritism afforded to metropolitan rather than colonial interests when awarding contracts. Second, the small, white elite benefited disproportionately from the expansion of the economy at the expense of the majority black population, who saw only marginal improvements and were still subject to forced labour. Third, the settlers were predominantly poor farmers from inland Portugal who lacked education and basic skills, and their privileged access to land and jobs stirred up racial tension.

## *Industrial and Financial Concentration*

When Portuguese industrialisation gathered pace after 1960, it bore the hallmarks of the conservatism and elitism that characterised the dictatorship. Industrial development became increasingly concentrated in economic and geographic terms. Monopoly concessions were awarded by the state to a small number of firms that were closely tied to the regime. This ensured that, although the social composition of Salazar's support base inevitably began to shift from agrarian-commercial to industrial-financial groups, they too were integrated into the existing power structures. Economic activity and investment was also geographically concentrated within the Lisbon-Setúbal coastal axis, thereby exacerbating regional disparities.

The genesis and growth of the vast financial-industrial consortia fashioned business structures with a number of distinctive features. First, there was a close, interdependent relationship between the government and the private consortia. An economic oligarchy, comprising a handful of people (the forty families), was able to enjoy state patronage and economic privileges. This proved politically advantageous, but became increasingly irrational and inefficient in economic terms. The interlocking relationship between the politicians and industrialists was probed by Makler (1979), who found that just under half of the industrial elite also held government posts. Williamson (1985) described how they circumvented official bureaucratic channels 'by recruiting top civil servants for executive posts with their consortia and by gaining public positions themselves'.

Portuguese corporatism acted as the 'benevolent guardian' (Williamson 1985) to the *grupos*, who in return offered uncritical support for the regime – something that might not have been forthcoming from a more heterogeneous business community.

Second, the consortia were involved across a range of industrial and financial activities including manufacturing, banking, agriculture and the media. These private economic empires were under the control of families such as the Champalimaud, Espírito Santo, de Melo, Quina and de Brito. An example of the diversity and range of interests involved is provided by the leading conglomerate, the Companhia União Fabril (CUF), owned by the de Melo family. Starting life as a soap-manufacturing enterprise, CUF grew to comprise 186 subsidiaries, employed 42,000 people and accounted for ten per cent of national production and twenty per cent of Portuguese industry (Baklanoff 1978). CUF's interests embraced shipping, textiles, mining, food, paper, cellulose, shipbuilding (Lisnave), electrical goods, petroleum refining, banking, insurance, supermarkets (Pão de Açucar) and hotels. The monopolies in soap, chemicals and tobacco combined with shipping and colonial interests to make CUF the largest enterprise in the Iberian peninsula and one of Europe's largest companies.

Third, the ownership of major banks and insurance companies served as the nucleus for extensive holdings. CUF's ownership of the Banco Totta e Açores, the inclusion of the Banco Pinto e Sottomayor in Champalimaud's inventory and de Brito's ownership of the Banco Intercontinental Português (BIP) served as the pivot for the consortia's industrial and commercial operations. The pillars of Miguel Quina's extensive economic empire consisted of three banks: Borges e Irmão, Banco de Crédito Comercial e Indústrial and the Banco do Alentejo.

Fourth, the *grupos* became closely associated with multinational capital. CUF established joint ventures with foreign capital in such areas as synthetic fibres (Japan), paper pulp (Sweden), mining (France) and shipbuilding (Netherlands/Sweden). Champalimaud enlisted Danish capital to develop its cement interests, while British and American investors jointly developed its pharmaceutical interests. Fifth, colonial interests figured prominently in the portfolios of the *grupos*. The ownership of sugar and coffee plantations, railways, shipping companies, manufacturing facilities and supermarkets enabled them to exercise vertical control over the production process from raw materials to retailing (Kayman 1987). This is exemplified by CUF's ownership of large peanut plantations in Guinea-Bissau and the Espírito Santo group's possession of extensive agricultural land as well as oil wells in Angola.

### Emigration and Remittances

Emigration figured prominently in the Salazar era, just as it has been a persistent feature of Portuguese life since the end of the nineteenth century. Leeds (1984b) argues that emigration was used as a conscious policy instrument for the maintenance of political and social stability by the Portuguese state. In fact, it served a triple purpose by controlling the supply and demand for labour, by making a positive contribution to the balance of payments through emigrant remittances and by buttressing the strategy of holding on to the empire. Ultimately, according to Leeds, emigration played a facilitating role in the industrial modernisation programme by reducing the need for labour-intensive development strategies. Therefore rapid economic growth was not required in order to absorb surplus labour because Portugal was exporting 'the stresses inherent in development' (Leeds 1984a).

There are three identifiable periods in the evolution of Portuguese emigration which relate to specific geographical areas: first, the long period from the 1880s to 1950 when Brazil was the predominant destination; second, the American period when Brazil was joined by the United States, Canada, Venezuela and Argentina as receiver countries between 1950 and 1960; and third, the recent period of European specialisation dating from the 1960s, when the demand for labour increased in the booming economies of Northern Europe. Apart from the 'pull' factors such as better job prospects and higher wages, the 'push' factors in the southern European rural hinterlands included high birth rates, stagnant rural economies, the dearth of job- and wealth-creating opportunities and the evasion of military service (King 1984). Emigration provided the opportunity to accumulate savings and to escape from the political repression associated with the authoritarian regime.

Around 100,000 Portuguese (three per cent of the active population) emigrated each year during the 1960s – a total that peaked at 150,000 annually in the early 1970s, by which time a quarter of the labour force was working abroad (King 1982). France took more than two-fifths of all legal emigration from Portugal in the two decades after 1960, and Paris became the city with the second-largest Portuguese population after Lisbon. A significant feature in the European phase was that the migrants originated in the industrial rather than the primary sector (Clausse 1984). This change is explained by the exhaustion of the potential stock of migrants from the north and interior of Portugal by 1970 (Chaney 1986). As a result of such intense international migration, Portugal earned the distinction of being the only country in Europe to undergo a net population decrease during the 1960s. The workforce declined from 3,130,000 to 2,930,000 between 1960 and 1973 (Baklanoff 1978). This meant that as the agricultural labour force contracted, the industrial and service sectors did not experience a commensurate increase in employment. In fact, labour shortages, especially among the ranks of the skilled and semi-skilled workforce, became an acute problem as emigration spiralled. Thormann (1969) observed that, prior to 1962, legal emigration involving workers from the secondary sector (manufacturing and construction) never exceeded a third of those emigrants in employment. By 1967, the proportion had climbed to just under a half. Industry responded to this challenge to sustained economic growth by switching to capital-intensive operations and found itself obliged to pay higher wages.

*Table 1.2*:    Level of Emigration: Legal and Clandestine 1961–74.

| Year | Legal | Clandestine | Illegals as % of total |
|------|-------|-------------|------------------------|
| 1961 | 33,526 | 1,270 | 3.65 |
| 1962 | 33,539 | 4,671 | 12.22 |
| 1963 | 39,519 | 14,451 | 26.28 |
| 1964 | 55,646 | 30,636 | 35.51 |
| 1965 | 89,056 | 27,918 | 23.89 |
| 1966 | 120,239 | 12,595 | 9.48 |
| 1967 | 92,502 | 13,778 | 12.96 |
| 1968 | 80,542 | 23,697 | 22.75 |
| 1969 | 70,165 | 83,371 | 54.30 |
| 1970 | 66,360 | 106,707 | 61.70 |
| 1971 | 50,400 | 100,797 | 66.67 |
| 1972 | 54,084 | 50,892 | 48.48 |
| 1973 | 79,517 | 40,502 | 33.77 |
| 1974 | 43,317 | 26,876 | 38.25 |

*Source*: Leeds 1984a.

Illegal emigration increased dramatically during the 1970s as a consequence of both draft evasion and the legal hurdles erected by the Portuguese authorities, who would only sanction emigration on the completion of military service. Estimates of the proportion of illegal emigrants vary, but Leeds (1984a) identifies the high point in 1971 when just over sixty per cent left illegally, and Clausse (1984) calculates that they comprised eighty-one per cent of all emigrants between 1970 and 1974. It is estimated that, in 1970, 87.4 per cent of emigrants chose Europe as their destination (three-quarters went to France); just under ten per cent went to North America; 2.6 per cent to South America and 0.8 per cent to other areas.

Did Portugal derive any economic benefits from such a high incidence of emigration? It is not easy to draw up a precise balance-sheet, and the literature reflects this difficulty. Baklanoff (1978) notes that, during the years when international migration was at its peak, Portugal registered accelerating rates of GDP growth. He contends that the exodus of workers to industrial Europe represented 'the equivalent of a huge effort in development assistance rendered by the countries receiving labour to those sending it'. In his view, it was these substantial capital transfers which enabled Portugal to minimise its levels of unemployment and underemployment and also spared the country the expense of investing in schools, infrastructure etc. (see also Morrison 1981). King (1984) disagrees and argues that migration constituted a form of development aid provided by southern Europe to the host countries. In theory, northern Europe benefited from cheap labour, and, in return, the source countries drew triple benefits: income from remittances, training received by emigrant workers when abroad and, as the rural areas became depopulated, a chance to transform outmoded agrarian structures by implementing land-consolidation programmes. On the debit side, remittances were often channelled into non-productive areas (consumer durables, housing, land purchase) in preference to productive investment. The typical emigrants tended to hold on to their land or make further purchases rather than relinquishing ownership, thereby forcing up land values and preventing agricultural restructuring (Bacalhau 1984).

Emigration on such a scale exacerbated Portugal's dependence on the developed economies and further exposed its vulnerability to downturns in the international economy. When just such a recession did occur in the early 1970s, the northern industrial countries tried to solve their own unemployment problems by dismissing foreign workers at a time when the supplier economies were least able to reabsorb the returnees. Whatever the long-term balance of advantage, emigration did make an important contribution to Portuguese economic development through financial remittances. Remittances represented around ten per cent of GDP by the late 1960s and early 1970s, thus offsetting the negative trade balance and covering forty per cent of the import bill. However, it was not until this period that emigrants' savings were tapped by the banks – a reflection of the underdeveloped banking system and the absence of networks outside the urban areas.

Foreign exchange earnings were also boosted by the rapid growth of tourism. The number of visitors grew from 353,000 (1960) to 4,000,000 (1972). State-sponsored development of the tourist infrastructure and facilities made possible a tripling of foreign exchange receipts between 1955 and 1963 (Lewis and Williams 1988). Portugal was to take advantage of the growing demand in northern Europe for foreign holidays by offering visitors the attractions of the Algarve, Lisbon and Madeira. The tourist industry featured in the development plans of the 1960s and 1970s, with capital investment prioritising hotel construction and upmarket tourism which stressed the interior destinations rather than the coastal zones.

*Table 1.3*:     Contribution of Emigrant Remittances to the Balance of Payments (millions of Esc).

| Year | Trade balance | Total remittances | as % of GDP |
|------|---------------|-------------------|-------------|
| 1964 | -6,162 | 2,270 | 4.8 |
| 1965 | -8,058 | 3,109 | 4.7 |
| 1966 | -9,785 | 4,537 | 5.6 |
| 1967 | -9,564 | 5,993 | 6.9 |
| 1968 | -8,705 | 7,548 | 7.3 |
| 1969 | -11,191 | 11,277 | 8.7 |
| 1970 | -14,340 | 13,875 | 9.7 |
| 1971 | -18,532 | 18,226 | 11.4 |
| 1972 | -18,294 | 21,831 | 12.1 |
| 1973 | -21,875 | 25,569 | 11.2 |

*Source*: Compiled from Leeds 1984a. Excludes colonies.

By the end of the authoritarian period, the economy relied heavily on remittances, tourism and foreign investment inflows to redress the trade imbalance. It made Portugal highly vulnerable to external forces beyond her control: migration could be abruptly reversed, as occurred in 1973–4, and tourism depended on a narrow range of markets for sustained tourist flows and for inward investment to finance hotel-building. Portugal illustrates the point that tourism assumes importance in small, open economies. Tourism also distorted regional development and exacerbated still further the coastal/interior schism by funnelling people away from rural areas into tourist zones. In addition, the employment impact varied: although labour-intensive, the industry is seasonal.

### Agriculture, the Achilles Heel

The growing disparity between the poor performance of the agricultural sector and the growth of the non-agrarian economy became particularly marked after 1960. The statistics demonstrate how agriculture lagged behind: while the economy grew at an average seven per cent annually between 1950 and 1973, the primary sector could barely manage even one per cent. Agriculture's contribution to GDP fell from thirty-one per cent in 1950 to twelve per cent in 1975 (World Bank 1978). Agriculture's share in total employment declined from just under half in 1950 to slightly over a quarter in 1975, and, despite the rapid decline, considerable underemployment of labour remained.

The causes of agriculture's poor performance are well known. A solution to the problems was not forthcoming because the political will did not exist. For the bulk of Salazar's period in office, agriculture did not possess its own ministry and was given low priority in the development plans (Gallagher 1983). The state adopted a passive attitude towards policy initiatives and innovations in the sector, preferring to regulate the market through a plethora of institutions and commissions set up to administer costly subsidies to privileged wheat, dairy and olive farmers. By maintaining artificially high prices for essential commodities, the government discouraged the adoption of new technologies and blocked the more efficient use of land and labour. As a result, the decline in agricultural employment was not accompanied by increased labour productivity such as occurred elsewhere in Europe. Moreover, it was not considered vital to provide technical help and credit facilities to the majority of farmers while the political

*Table 1.4*:    Share of Agriculture in Economic Development 1950–75.

| Year | GDP share (%) | Workers (million) | Employment (% share) |
|------|------|------|------|
| 1950 | 31.0 | 1.4 | 47.0 |
| 1960 | 24.0 | 1.3 | 41.5 |
| 1970 | 16.0 | 0.9 | 30.4 |
| 1975 | 12.2 | 0.8 | 26.8 |

*Source*: World Bank 1978.

climate discouraged their provision by grass-roots organisations. Consequently, the sector proved unequal to the task of satisfying internal demand for agricultural commodities resulting from changing dietary patterns (more meat, cereal and dairy products consumed), with the subsequent requirement that imports made up the shortfall.

The most important structural condition inhibiting agricultural development was the pattern of landownership. Land distribution (thirty-nine per cent of farmers owned less than one hectare each) ensured that subsistence farming became the norm for hundreds of thousands of smallholders on *minifúndios*, located principally in the northern regions where land fragmentation added to the problems. By contrast, in the south the large estates (0.3 per cent of the total number of landholdings, but accounting for forty per cent of the land farmed) predominated. The *latifúndios*, or farms of 500 hectares and over, employed largely landless labourers whose only escape from insecure employment and poverty was to emigrate to the urban areas or abroad. Poor land use exacerbated the problem: the 1968 census found that, on the larger farms, over half the arable land was left fallow. Crop yields were inferior to those achieved elsewhere in southern Europe, reflecting the insufficient use of fertilisers, pesticides and machinery – there were reputedly only 6,000 tractors in the whole of Portugal in 1958 (Anderson 1962). In their defence, landowners cited poor weather and soil quality, low prices and labour losses. Not surprisingly, they opposed closer links with Europe and the increased competition that would inevitably arise.

THE BALANCE-SHEET

This introductory chapter is premised on the conviction that some of the economic difficulties experienced after 1974 can be traced back to the distorted development that occurred under the *Estado Novo*. The legacy contained many contradictions and rigidities, of which some have persisted into the 1990s. They can be summarised in eight sections corresponding to the following paragraphs.

First, the fairly impressive growth rates achieved in the 1950s and 1960s on the back of the expansion in world trade disguised, but did not remove, a series of structural defects. Portugal undoubtedly moved from underdeveloped to semi-developed status, but economic growth was unevenly distributed and 'less solidly based' (Hudson 1989) than in Spain. Moreover, growth was probably much lower than could have been achieved if Portugal had exploited to the full all the advantages accruing to a late industrialiser.

Second, the old regime bequeathed a dualistic industrial structure in which a modern sector comprising a few oligopolies coexisted with a traditional sector made up of a large number of small firms. The large firms operated free from the straitjacket imposed by the corporative system and gave the regime support that might not have been forthcoming from a more heterogeneous business class. The close relationship was doubly damaging: the *grupos* could veto any proposal for change that might prejudice their interests, while their fortunes were closely tied to those of the regime. They had little to gain from a modernising project like that initially proposed by Salazar's successor from 1968–74, Marcelo Caetano.

Third, the dictatorship left a stagnant, neglected primary sector characterised by low productivity and a dualistic landholding structure desperately in need of reform. However, little support existed among the elite for a modernised agricultural sector. The post-revolutionary regime inherited a chronically weak sector unable either to respond to the food deficit as consumption began to rise or to satisfy the growing demand for raw materials from Portuguese industry.

Fourth, a cumbersome bureaucratic machine created to administer the *Estado Novo*'s corporatist structures remained in place. Thousands of functionaries applied rules and regulations, distributed raw materials and determined production targets in an attempt to manage and regulate the economy in the smallest detail. Any effort to navigate the Portuguese bureaucracy had to contend with red tape, corruption, inefficiency and sheer bloody-mindedness. There were other detrimental aspects: political influence and decision-making authority became overcentralised in Lisbon, to the disadvantage of the rest of the country.

Fifth, the maintenance of an empire during an era of anti-colonialism lay at the core of the *Estado Novo*'s economic and social policy and was closely connected to developments in continental Portugal. Much of Portugal's protected and uncompetitive industry was still dependent on a captive African market and was unprepared for the challenge of international competition. The policy of exporting white Portuguese to the colonies created major social and economic problems for the post-revolutionary governments as hundreds of thousands of settlers were uprooted and turned into refugees.

Sixth, the *Estado Novo* bequeathed a dependent economy highly sensitive to changes in the international economy and world trading conditions. The vulnerability was exacerbated by the high level of defence expenditure and a burgeoning commercial deficit caused by industrial development (oil imports, capital equipment) and agricultural shortfalls (wheat and other foodstuffs). In this context, tourism receipts and emigrants' remittances, both highly sensitive to recession, became doubly important. During the 1970s, the combination of shocks, both internal (the revolution) and external (oil prices, imported inflation), impacted on an economy ill-prepared to meet the challenge.

Seventh, Portugal adopted an equivocal attitude towards Europe, a product of an unresolved political stalemate between those pressing for stronger ties with Europe and isolationist interests still favouring imperial integration. EFTA membership proved to be a useful 'halfway house' in relations with Europe, but the brutal fact remained that Portugal would never attain full membership of the European Community as long as the political regime remained a dictatorship. In fact, the advocacy of Europeanist views became a means of expressing opposition to the regime as well as a symbol of modernisation and change.

Finally, the post-revolutionary regime inherited an array of social problems caused by years of official indifference and neglect. Portugal was the poorest and most backward country in Western Europe. When measured against the rest of Europe, the extent of the problems becomes apparent: a per capita income which stood at US$1,350 against an OECD average of US$4,500 (1973); a highly skewed distribution of income in both geographical and class terms; the highest infant mortality rate; the lowest educational levels (a third of those over fifteen years of age were illiterate, and education spending was proportionally the lowest); and an acute housing crisis (the lowest rate of housebuilding despite homelessness among a third of all families).

# CHAPTER 2

# From Political to Economic Crisis
## Portugal 1968–85

The limitations and contradictions inherent in the late Salazarist development model had become abundantly clear by the time the aged dictator, a stroke victim following a fall, gave way to his successor, Marcelo Caetano, in 1968. The fast growth fuelled by foreign investment, buoyant exports, booming emigrant remittances and tourism receipts could no longer be sustained. A number of factors account for this; the first was an acute labour shortage resulting from a combination of emigration, economic expansion and internal migration. Prior to 1962, less than a third of legal emigrant workers had employment experience in the secondary (manufacturing and construction) sector, but by 1965 the proportion had risen to just under a half. Consequently, Portugal suffered a highly unusual problem for a developing country with a large unskilled work-force, namely a growing number of unfilled vacancies. The second distortion relates to investment patterns during the late 1960s and the early 1970s. The 'strong and lopsided' (Bratenstein and Fischer 1975) investment boom worsened already existing imbalances within the economy. Investments displayed a worrying tendency to concentrate in manufacturing, building, transport and communications while the laggard sectors such as agriculture suffered a fall in the proportional share in total investment, down from eight per cent to five per cent between 1968 and 1972.

It became clear that Portuguese industry, cosseted and protected for so long, would struggle to maintain its competitive edge in a more open, liberal and closely integrated European economy. As Caetano duly acknowledged in a 1969 speech, economic autarkism had long since outlived its usefulness. Import-substitution development had reached its limits. Apart from the constraints imposed by such a small domestic market, the industrial growth registered during the 1960s sucked in imports, especially of capital goods, imposing severe strains on the balance of payments. Economic survival, therefore, depended on the restructuring of Portuguese industry and the adoption of an export-oriented strategy to take advantage of an expanding world economy.

THE NEW INDUSTRIAL POLICY

Caetano's new industrial policy (NIP) recognised that Portugal's economic structures had to be adapted to prevailing world market conditions in order to prepare them for greater integration into Europe. A new development model, based on the successful Japanese approach, was launched in which the state and the monopoly business groups were to cooperate in the implementation of a crash modernisation programme (Cravinho 1983). The necessary reform measures were formulated by a group of technocrats whose aim was to ensure that the country enjoyed accelerated growth in the future and 'relative prosperity in dependency' (Passos 1991). The NIP's aims were, first, to achieve higher economic growth rates. Although growth in the 1960s had been impressive, particularly in relation to the 3.7 per cent average for the period 1947–58 (Rocha 1985), still higher rates were essential if Portugal was to reduce rather than simply maintain the economic differentials with the industrialised countries. The second aim was to identify priority industries and channel resources to them. The criteria used to select industries for priority treatment included comparative advantages in world trade and the potential for expanded market shares. The planners hoped to maximise the advantages that accrued from the country's geographical position, its natural and human resources and productive structure.

The industries identified by the planners as priority areas for investment were petrochemicals, metal products, transport equipment, paper and pulp, glassware, construction, naval repairs and agro-industrial products. Implicit in the NIP was that sectors not chosen would be starved of resources and face certain contraction, and perhaps even extinction, unless they substantially modified their structures. It was also noticeable that the priority sectors were all large, capital-intensive industries in a country where the overwhelming majority of firms are small or medium-sized (SMEs). The strategy was based on the assumption that the faster growth achieved by the larger firms would pull along the SMEs in their wake as they expanded.

The technocrats espoused a new conception of the 'Portuguese economic space' (*espaço económico português*). For them, it was logical that the individual economies should be more closely integrated into their regional context – Portugal into Europe and Angola and Mozambique into southern Africa. This new division of labour implied the relocation of labour-intensive, less sophisticated and unprofitable production to the colonies. Portugal would assume the role of an exporter of capital and high-technology industrial goods, while the colonies would furnish raw materials and basic, low-technology products.

The NIP envisaged a considerable role for planning, but simultaneously with general economic liberalisation and a reduced state role in the market. Rather than offering protection, subsidies and myriad legal restrictions, the state gradually dismantled customs barriers, loosened its grip over the internal market and stimulated modernisation by encouraging economic concentration and technological development. It assumed a major role in the provision of an improved infrastructure. In a redefinition of its role, the state now helped the private sector to restructure and modernise the economy. A wages policy and a role for trade unions were core elements in the new strategy. The technocrats identified low wages as a major disincentive to the adoption of new technology. It was anticipated that, by easing the clamp-like restrictions on trade unions, pressures would be exerted for higher wages and improved working conditions. This in turn would force employers to substitute capital for labour in order to keep down their costs and product prices. Caetano's labour reforms were a key element in moves towards liberalisation. The 'Lisbon Spring' was a short-lived affair that introduced some cosmetic changes into political life. Press censorship was eased, the curbs on opposition activity relaxed and political exiles allowed to return. The opposition was able to mount a campaign for the 1969 elections and, more significantly, an element of democracy was introduced into trade-union elections. These measures heralded an upsurge in strike activity and the emergence of an Intersindical, to coordinate trade-union activities. Initially, Caetano believed that he could contain the new, independent labour confederation; but, once it fell under communist influence, the government imposed a ban in 1971. A year later, collective bargaining was suspended. In response, the movement simply went underground and helped to organise the growing number of workers involved in industrial action. In 1973, there were over forty major strikes.

## THE FAILURE OF THE CAETANISTA REFORMS

The failure of the reform strategy can be attributed to a combination of factors. First, the economic project lacked coherence and depended heavily on favourable political circumstances. Ultimately, Caetano's reforms were a political failure that exposed the regime's inflexibility. There could be no 'transformation from above' as occurred during the mid-1970s in neighbouring Spain. Caetano proved unable or unwilling to overcome the *duros* (hardliners), nor did he manage to mobilise new social groups in support of his 'renovation in continuity' project. In this respect, the Caetano interlude diverges sharply from the subsequent Spanish experience when a period of rapid economic growth overseen by a technocratic elite created the conditions for dismantling the old regime from within. By contrast, Caetano lacked the sizeable pro-democratic and pro-European middle class and business community that would buttress and underpin the reforms. That no such social base existed is a direct consequence of the deformed economic structures created by the Salazarian political economy. A few hundred individuals represented big business, and outside this small elite there existed only 'a disorganised collection of small businessmen who comprised a sort of industrial peasantry' (Bermeo 1987b). So, although Caetano did promote a small team of forward-looking young technocrats, prominent among them Rogério Martins, Xavier Pintado and João Salguiero (Secretaries of State for Industry, Trade and Planning respectively), they wielded far less influence than their Spanish counterparts. It is significant that they never attained cabinet rank and held subordinate positions in the Economy ministry.

The anti-reformist elements (the Salazarist bureaucracy, military and religious leaders, some industrial and commercial interests) expressed concern at the consequences for political and economic stability caused by accelerated social change and democratisation. They pinned their hopes on winning the colonial war, and their attitudes only hardened as the military situation worsened. They insisted that the *Estado Novo* retain its authoritarian character and coercive capacity while fighting a rearguard action to delay and emasculate key reformist proposals. As a result, the Industrial Reform Law was delayed until early 1972, and changes in the industrial regulations were not pushed through until shortly before the 1974 revolution.

The NIP's 'shock therapy' suited only the larger industrial interests (Nataf and Sammis 1990). The majority of SMEs, like those in the textile sector, felt threatened because they were uncompetitive in the open market and feared higher wage demands and strike activity. In their support, they could mobilise banks, who were worried at an outbreak of business failures, and commercial interests, importers in particular, who did not wish to endanger their established links with foreign suppliers. Agriculturalists also shared these concerns, particularly in relation to the scaling-down of subsidies and development policies that enticed already scarce labour to flee the land. In the end, the conservative dead-weight of traditional Portuguese industry acted as a brake on the project. The industrialists were accustomed to working closely with the state's bureaucratic apparatus, and many felt disinclined to accept the uncertainties implicit in the NIP. Other factors can be listed that undermined the possibilities of success – the overoptimistic estimates of the investment that would be forthcoming from foreign multinationals, the still-limited access to world markets and the absence of a large skilled-labour force.

Despite these limitations, the technocrats did exercise influence in three specific areas. First, they were convinced that autarky should be abandoned in favour of an export-oriented strategy based on closer links with Europe and the wider world economy. In particular, the technocrats stressed the need to engender a more competitive environment, extending even to the agricultural sector, in order to weed out the inefficient, featherbedded firms. Their imprint can be seen in the *Lei de Fomento Industrial* (Industrial Development Law, May 1972) which replaced the old industrial controls over new firm creation, adopted a more relaxed approval policy and made funds available for modernisation proposals.

Second, they promoted greater government intervention in stimulating growth through development planning. For the first time, the planning authorities focused on regional problems and prioritised industrial projects such as the refinery and port project in the western Alentejo. The Sines industrial project was Portugal's only attempt at a growth-pole strategy and exemplifies the state's new-found role as an agent for economic modernisation. Sines was chosen as the site for the new complex because of its deep-water harbour, able to handle the largest container transport, and its proximity to raw material supplies. The planners envisaged a large complex comprising a port, oil refinery, petrochemical complex, car assembly, fertiliser and metallurgical plants and an explosives factory – all capital-intensive, heavy industries. However, soon after its conception, Portugal's most ambitious ever industrial project ran into difficulties. The 1973–4 oil crisis triggered a world recession followed by a period of sluggish growth, and plunged the pivotal industries around which the whole project revolved into crisis (Lewis and Williams 1985b).

Third, they downgraded the economic importance attached to the empire. Taxes on exports to the colonies encouraged colonial industrialisation and forced metropolitan firms to relocate overseas or to seek alternative export markets. Although the economic argument might be irresistible (and there were still some who maintained that Portugal and the colonies represented a large enough market), the political battle had yet to be won. Caetano could not muster the political authority, nor did he possess the foresight to extricate Portugal from the African imbroglio: he stuck to a federalist solution and tried to shift the burden of the war to the colonies. Consequently, Portugal continued to prosecute a militarily unwinnable and economically costly conflict.

Similar obstacles were encountered by liberal elements who aspired to transform the regime from within. One particular reform group founded in 1970, the Social and Economic Development Association (SEDES), sought to elaborate a middle way between the *duros* and the communist-dominated opposition. Liberal deputies Sá Carneiro and Pinto Balsemão were prominent among the group's 147 founder members (who numbered 588 by 1972), but soon discovered that their hopes of a political opening (*abertura*) were illusory. After 1971, the hardliners ousted the technocrats, reimposed the clampdown on the trade unions and reappointed the aged Americo Tomás as President in 1973. This last move symbolised the regime's paralysis and rigidity: reform from within was no longer on the agenda. The *duros* objected to change, while the reformers were bitterly disappointed that liberalisation had been halted and reversed. The return to repression was a reflex action when confronted by unfamiliar and complex problems such as labour militancy, inflation and balance of payments deficits.

Ultimately, Caetano fell victim to accelerating pressures for change. External developments combined with internal political constraints to limit the possibilities of success. It was simply asking too much to reconcile the competing claims of a resource-devouring and politically unpopular colonial war, demands for political liberalisation, new economic policies and the need to deliver improved

*Table 2.1*:    Annual GDP Growth at Constant Market Prices (percentage annual change).

|          | 1961–70 | 1971 | 1972 | 1973 | 1974 | 1975 | 1976 | 1977 |
|----------|---------|------|------|------|------|------|------|------|
| Portugal | 6.4     | 6.6  | 8.0  | 11.2 | 1.1  | -4.3 | 6.9  | 5.5  |
| EC 12    | 4.8     | 3.3  | 4.2  | 6.3  | 1.9  | -1.1 | 4.8  | 2.4  |

|          | 1978 | 1979 | 1980 | 1981 | 1982 | 1983 | 1984 | 1985 |
|----------|------|------|------|------|------|------|------|------|
| Portugal | 3.4  | 6.1  | 4.8  | 1.3  | 2.2  | 0.0  | -1.4 | 2.8  |
| EC 12    | 3.0  | 3.2  | 1.3  | 0.2  | 0.8  | 1.6  | 2.3  | 2.5  |

*Source*: European Commission 1991b.

living standards (Cravinho 1983). The economic strategy was not unsuccessful – GDP growth averaged over 7.6 per cent during 1968–73 and industry averaged nine per cent annual growth between 1970 and 1973 – but it also generated new problems (inflation, industrial unrest) and exacerbated existing ones (regional inequalities, unemployment).

DECOLONISATION

The change of regime in 1974 set in motion a series of structural changes encapsulated in the broad, and suitably vague, three D's: decolonisation, democratisation and development. In only one area did real consensus exist among the armed forces movement (MFA) responsible for the coup – the need to terminate the unwinnable African wars and bring to a close the colonial era. Disentangling Portugal from its colonial connections proved, in the short term at least, to have economic consequences that endured throughout the 1970s.

It is interesting to note the areas of overlap among the conservatives and the radicals in the highly-charged political atmosphere during 1975–6. In his *Portugal e o Futuro* (Portugal and the future), General António de Spinola proposed a Lusitanian Commonwealth embracing Brazil. He echoed Salazarist fears that foreign domination would lead to a loss of freedom and independence. The radical perspective shared the concern that economic underdevelopment and geographical peripherality exposed the country to exploitation. Portugal was perceived as part of the Third World – a view reinforced by contacts with national liberation movements in Africa and an ignorance of their own country caused by extended service abroad. Both the conservative and the MFA perceptions took an essentially pessimistic view and were employed to justify authoritarian solutions and political experiments. Reality soon overtook the proponents of a federalist solution. Independence came swiftly to Guinea-Bissau, Mozambique, Cape Verde and São Tomé, while an orderly withdrawal from Angola became impossible as the country plunged into civil war. The sudden collapse of Portuguese authority and the precipitous exodus of hundreds of thousands of refugees crippled the Angolan economy. Similarly, the Portuguese withdrawal triggered economic disintegration in Mozambique. For the former colonial power, there were negative consequences; but, in order to assess the economic impact of decolonisation, it is necessary to distinguish between the immediate and the longer-term impacts. The thrust of the argument is that, whatever the immediate consequences, the damage to the metropolitan economy was minimised through a combination of public policy measures, external assistance and the ability to call into play a variety of 'shock-absorbers' to limit the social impact.

Short-term negative effects were registered in two broad areas. First, independence for the colonies meant the loss of favourable trading relationships along with the bulk of the overseas assets. The imperial system had enabled Portugal to sell a wide range of goods to the colonies and in return receive a limited number of imports, mainly raw materials. The traditionally large trading surplus (about Esc 20 billion) with the escudo zone disappeared as foreign competitors ousted Portugal from her former colonial markets. Unable to rely on cheap raw materials and increasingly exposed to international competition, some branches of Portuguese industry faced extinction.

Second, the rapid retreat from empire generated a concentrated influx of refugees (*retornados*). Up to 800,000 former colonial settlers and officials were repatriated during 1975–6. The refugees arrived in numbers only slightly smaller than those absorbed by France following the Algerian war, but the difference lay in the capacity to absorb such an inflow – the French population (46,000,000) was over five times larger than Portugal's (9,000,000). The suddenness of their departure meant that most of the *retornados* arrived without resources and required immediate assistance in terms of accommodation, funds etc. in the context of an economy buffeted by recession. The age structure of the repatriates (fifty per cent under sixteen years of age) required substantial immediate investment in an already underfunded education system, while further pressure was exerted on the chronically deficient housing stock and social services. Integration into the labour force was made even more difficult by the occupational structure of the *retornados* – nearly seventy per cent sought employment in the service sector and twenty per cent in industry.

The OECD (1976) regarded the assimilation problems as 'almost insuperable', yet ten years later Mark Hudson (EIU 1986) could describe as 'spectacular' the success in absorbing the refugees. Assimilation was undoubtedly a costly short-term process (an estimated fourteen billion escudos in benefits, or eleven per cent of budget expenses), but was outweighed by the benefits derived from decolonisation. In the first place, military expenditure could be reduced to a level more in keeping with Portugal's small-power status. When the revolution occurred, the armed forces totalled just under 250,000 (a quarter of all adult males). A rapid demobilisation ensued, and, by mid-1976, military strength had been reduced to approximately 46,000 (Baklanoff 1978). During thirteen years of war, Portugal lost 8,000 dead and 28,000 wounded at an economic cost estimated at £2.5 billion (*The Observer* 1977).

Additionally, once the artificial cushion provided by industrial regulation and the existence of a captive colonial market disappeared, Portugal had to rely on its own export efforts. Substitute markets had to be found following the loss of the colonies, and raw materials such as cotton fibre, vegetable oils, coffee and sugar had to be purchased at high prices on world markets. More clearly than ever, the Portuguese economy required structural reform and a more efficient use of resources. The third positive factor derived from jettisoning the myths and assumptions surrounding the empire. Portugal now had to accept a more realistic, albeit diminished role as part of the larger European economy.

The question remains of how Portugal managed to absorb a refugee influx equivalent to almost ten per cent of her population without triggering an economic collapse. It should not be forgotten that the labour market suffered a triple blow: in addition to the *retornados* must be added thousands of returned migrants *regressados* displaced from their jobs in industrialised Europe during the 1970s recession who joined the substantial number of demobilised soldiers in the search for work. It is impossible to overestimate the potential strains and pressures exerted on the social and economic fabric by such developments. Unemployment was a new phenomenon for the Portuguese authorities. Until 1974, officially the jobless total had remained between two and three per cent of the labour force as a result of emigration and the demands made by extended periods of military service.

A number of mechanisms were utilised in order to lessen the impact on the labour market. In a still largely traditional society, agriculture functioned as an absorber of labour. Many Portuguese families retained a small plot of land which they could fall back on for subsistence when times were hard. In addition, a rapid expansion occurred in the numbers working for the state. Civil servants returning from the colonies were guaranteed posts in the domestic bureaucracy, joined the payroll of newly nationalised firms or found employment in the expanded health and education services. Graham (1990) provides statistics for the explosion in public-sector employment after the revolution: state employment increased from 207,781 in 1968 to 383,308 a decade later and totalled well over 500,000 by 1983. According to the World Bank (1978), employment in public administration grew at an average annual rate of almost sixteen per cent during the five years after 1973. Political clientilism, particularly at local government level, explains some of the growth which, while alleviating the short-term employment problem, was unhealthy in the long run because the bureaucracy expanded merely 'to accommodate a new political clientele superimposed upon it, rather than being modernised by the infusion of new people and ideas' (Maxwell 1986).

Yet not even a burgeoning public sector could deflect the full impact of such a greatly expanded labour force. Unemployment became inevitable among a workforce that Krugman and Braga de Macedo (1981) estimate grew at thirteen per cent between 1974 and 1977. Official figures put the 1973 unemployment rate at 2.7 per cent of the labour force, rising to a peak of 8.1 per cent five years later (European Commission 1991b). However, official statistics are unreliable and certainly understate the true picture by failing to take into account substantial disguised unemployment. Young people in general and young women in particular were hardest hit, and the problem was made worse by the rising female participation rate. Krugman and Braga de Macedo are probably closer to the mark with their own estimates that the percentage unemployment rate rose from 3.1 in 1973 to 14.4 in 1976 before declining slightly to 12.8 in 1977. These figures are broadly in line with those reported by the Ministry of Labour, which put the number of jobless at just under 500,000 in 1976.

The *retornados* represented a political as well as an economic problem. The government fully recognised their potential for causing friction both in the political arena (they felt betrayed by a left-wing government) and socially (in some cases they turned to crime). In order to expedite reintegration into Portuguese society, a government agency, the Institute for Aid to National Refugees (IARN), doled out money for social needs and allowances and spent US$170,000,000 helping refugees set up their own businesses. Each new job cost an estimated US$4,820. The practice of housing refugees in hotel and holiday accommodation, together with the fraud associated with welfare payments (a fifth of the relief funds for 1976 were misappropriated according to Robinson (1979)), stirred up resentment but fell short of open warfare. At the end of November 1976, welfare payments were suspended and attempts began to stem the flow of refugees from the impoverished post-independence regimes and the new arrivals from Portuguese Timor (Harvey 1978).

NATIONALISATION

During 1975–6, a fundamental shift took place in Portugal's political economy. The MFA and the provisional governments dominated by the PCP (Portuguese Communist Party) dismantled the former monopolies and substantially extended the state-owned sector. As part of the commitment to the 'transition to socialism', the new rulers promised to nationalise basic industries, create jobs, raise the minimum wage, impose price controls and implement an agrarian reform.

The size of the public sector doubled during the sixteen months from March 1975 to July 1976 when 244 privately-owned companies were nationalised (Baklanoff 1978). The process advanced through a series of stages and took different forms, beginning with the nationalisations of the banks and insurance companies in September 1974 (see Table 2.2). In subsequent months, the following industries came under state control: steel, tobacco, brewing, paper paste, water, bus companies in Lisbon and Oporto and national passenger transport (Romão 1983). In many cases, the candidates for nationalisation were self-selecting. Key industries, constituting the 'commanding heights of the economy', were brought under state control in order to fulfil the government's

38                                    *The Portuguese Economy since 1974*

*Table 2.2*:    The Nationalisation Timetable 1974–5.

| | |
|---|---|
| **1974** | |
| September | Bank of Portugal, National Overseas Bank, Bank of Angola. |
| | |
| **1975** | |
| March | All credit and insurance companies (except foreign-owned). Establishment of Instituto de Participações do Estado (IPE) to oversee enterprises with state holding. |
| April | Petroleum companies, railways, national shipping and airline transport companies. |
| May | Tobacco, cement and paper pulp companies. |
| August | Petrochemicals and brewing. |
| September | Shipyards and Companhia União Fabril. |

*Source*: ILO (1979).

anti-monopoly aims. In other cases, the workforce occupied their factories and demanded state intervention to forestall further economic sabotage allegedly practised by the management. In this way, the boundaries of state intervention extended into the medium- and small-firm sector involved in textiles, metallurgy, construction, wholesale business etc. Kayman (1987) estimates that official recognition and assistance was provided to 787 self-managing cooperatives – a process that he insists 'owed much more to the self-determination of local workers ... than to any action by the government'. In addition, many 'unanticipated nationalisations' occurred when the banks were taken into the state sector, because they held shares in hundreds of SMEs (Baklanoff 1984).

Whether by direct state intervention or through independent action taken by grass-roots popular movements, the public sector took on an entirely new character and a transformed economic role. Its share in value added rose from nine per cent in 1973 to thirty per cent in 1976, the share of fixed investment increased from ten per cent to almost forty-seven per cent and the share in employment all but doubled from thirteen per cent to twenty-four per cent during the same three year period. Almost overnight, the state, which possessed no manufacturing interests prior to 25 April, acquired fourteen per cent of the value added and fifty-one per cent of the fixed investment in the secondary sector (EIU 1989). The task of administering this diverse economic empire fell to the Instituto de Participação de Estado (IPE), although in practice the key industries were managed by the ministry responsible.

A number of consequences stemmed from the transformation in the Portuguese political economy that occurred during 1974–6. First, although precise calculations and comparisons are notoriously difficult, the economy emerged from the revolution with one of the largest public sectors in western Europe. Moreover, it was the modern, large-scale and technologically advanced industries that came under state control while the more traditional, smaller scale industries remained largely untouched.

Second, the damage caused by the exodus of human capital following the anti-fascist *saneamento* (purges) campaign and the collapse of private-sector confidence weakened an already shaky economy. As Baklanoff (1986) noted, 'wittingly or unwittingly the revolutionary regime had moved against the bulk of the technocratic class' – a point underlined earlier by Makler (1979), who calculated that the haemorrhage among managerial and technical personnel in the larger firms exceeded fifty per cent. The newly expanded public sector soon began to feel the effects and suffer from a shortage of trained and experienced staff.

Third, the nationalised industries were compelled to operate in a difficult environment. It was unclear whether they should abide by the rules of the market economy or fulfil some ill-defined social criteria. This ambiguity became particularly acute in three areas: wages, jobs and prices. Public-sector enterprises seemed much less prepared to keep down labour costs when confronted with trade-union demands for higher wages. Strong political pressure was exerted to maintain and, in the case of the *retornados*, to increase already unjustifiably high staffing levels in order to absorb surplus labour. In return, companies received government subsidies. Indeed, public enterprises were kept afloat by the extensive subsidisation, which increased at an annual average rate of over fifty per cent between 1974 and 1980. Further distortions resulted from government pressure to limit price rises in areas such as public transport, which was already crippled by huge losses and burdened with obsolete stock.

Fourth, the creation of state monopolies relegated market forces to a subsidiary role. State-run industries such as paper and pulp, brewing and cement operated without competition, while those that did, like the national airline TAP, struggled to cope with the loss of African business (Baklanoff 1986). The nationalised banks, although nominally in competition with one another, found themselves subjected to considerable state interference. Apart from the compulsory absorption of over 7,000 employees from the ex-colonies, they suffered from political interference and excessive bureaucracy. The Portuguese-owned commercial banks were reduced in number from fifteen to nine (foreign banks were exempted, but the three principals owned by Crédit Lyonnais, Bank of London and South America and Banco do Brasil provided only a small degree of competition). The national banks, closely supervised by the Bank of Portugal, supplied the bulk of the available credit. As a consequence, the banking system, already weakened by capital outflows during 1974–5, lost any semblance of independence and financial discipline. Government interference ensured that interest rates bore little relation to inflation, preferential credit was extended to insolvent public enterprises well beyond the boundaries of financial prudence and the government itself became a major borrower. In practice, the administration did nothing to restrain the banks from running up considerable deficits – disguised and massaged by lax accountancy procedures – and encouraged foreign borrowing to cover the shortfall.

Fifth, the vastly increased public expenditure programmes generated by post-revolutionary commitments and the burgeoning current account deficits could not be financed from internal resources once the high levels of reserves had been run down. Foreign exchange reserves, which had stood at US$1.633 billion in 1973 dipped to US$250,000,000 by 1976, although gold reserves remained largely untouched (World Bank 1978a). In part, the policy was a conscious one – the provisional governments sought to avoid dealings with capitalist institutions – and also unavoidable as international banks and financial institutions regarded Portugal as a bad risk (EIU 1986). By the time the first constitutional government took office in 1976, the state relied on external borrowings from the international capital markets as well as bilateral and multilateral agencies to finance expenditure (Lister 1988). The revival of emigrant remittances was considered to be fundamentally important in order to compensate for the balance of payments deficit, and financial incentives were introduced to resuscitate the inflow. A decree law (February 1976) allowed emigrants to avoid the consequences of escudos devaluations by opening deposit accounts in foreign currencies at preferential rates (Leeds 1984a).

Sixth, between 1970 and 1985, Portugal recorded one of the fastest rates of growth in long-term indebtedness in the world (Lister 1988). As a result, a large proportion of government revenue (around eleven per cent) went to servicing the debt (OECD 1981). The rapid increase in the public debt is a major feature of the post 1974 economy. The direct public debt, excluding most state enterprise debts, climbed inexorably from nineteen per cent of GDP in 1973 to reach eighty per cent by 1987. The decision to run a large deficit funded by external sources certainly increased Portugal's dependency as the authorities forfeited the ability to operate the major levers of macroeconomic policy to promote nationally determined objectives. Paralysed by successive economic crises, a large nationalised sector afforded little protection in dealings with the International Monetary Fund (IMF) and international financiers. As Maxwell (1986) stresses, nationalisation did not serve to assert national independence, rather the reverse. It is at least understandable on the one hand as a natural reaction to the budget fetishism and overcaution associated with Salazarist economics. It can also be understood as a conscious decision to ensure social stability and democratic consolidation through the expansion of public expenditure. A more Machiavellian interpretation is that the more reliant the country became on western institutions and governments, the less likelihood there was of a reversion to the revolutionary politics of 1974–6. Clearly, political priorities took precedence over strictly economic considerations during the 1970s. It meant that resources, inefficiently allocated under the previous regime, were still directed largely by non-market forces often to the detriment of productive investment. Acclimatisation to the realities of the market economy had to be postponed until the late 1980s.

### AGRARIAN REFORM

The demise of the old regime precipitated a crisis followed by major reforms in the rural sector. The process was confined primarily to southern Portugal, a region dominated by large, often uncultivated, estates, devoted principally to the production of grain, olives, cork and livestock and managed by or on behalf of absentee landlords. The workforce employed on the *latifúndia* were landless, low-paid wage labourers or rural proletarians whose predicament worsened as the economy slumped in the early 1970s and the landlords required fewer workers.

The workforce responded by forming unions to demand secure employment, higher wages and better working conditions. Land seizures began early in 1975 amid bureaucratic indecision and a crisis in state authority. As Bermeo (1986) makes clear, the government did not initiate rural change, rather it responded to events. During a period of 'genuine popular collectivisation' (Kayman 1987), over 1,000,000 hectares or a fifth of all agricultural land owned by 1,300 large landowners was transformed into cooperatives. In the process, the *latifúndia* of the Alentejo disappeared and upwards of 150,000 peasants benefited (World Bank 1978b). What had been a predominantly grass-roots phenomenon quickly became communist-dominated as the PCP established its control over the agricultural unions and the supply of support services. The agrarian reform introduced a destabilising element into the rural political economy, as a sector crucial to the country's well-being fell under the control of a party at odds with the authorities in Lisbon throughout the 1970s and early 1980s. Given the growing propensity to import foodstuffs as consumption rose because of increased demand, political disagreements over agriculture inevitably aggravated an already dire situation. The tragedy for the agrarian sector was that once again, for political reasons, it had been excluded from the modernisation process. In turn, the failure to pursue a balanced development strategy exerted greater pressures on other sectors that were incapable of absorbing the surplus rural workforce in the short or medium term. Political rivalry between the socialists and the communists ensured that technical assistance, fertilisers etc. were denied to the reformed sector.

The problems generated by a politically contentious and economically disrupting agrarian reform can be summarised as follows. First, the change in ownership did little to improve efficiency in the rural economy because an often aging and illiterate workforce lacked the requisite management skills and administrative experience. Consequently, the cooperatives, starved of funds and support from the extension services, failed to find a niche in the post-revolutionary economy. It would have been difficult in any case to overcome the resistance put up by landowners and tenants, the slump in agricultural investment and the slaughter of breeding stock for food without considerable state support. Second, the uncertainty about landownership persisted long after belated attempts were made to establish a legal framework. Until the agrarian reform law (September 1977) introduced by the Socialist agriculture minister Antonio Barreto, legislation had been piecemeal and focused on land distribution. The so-called *lei Barreto* allowed compensation for owners of expropriated land and the return of 'illegally' seized property to its previous owners. According to Bermeo (1986), some 569,000 hectares had reverted to private ownership and over 100 cooperatives dissolved by January 1981. Third, and finally, the focus on the Alentejo distracted attention from the equally urgent need to tackle the problem common to the north and centre regions – excessive land fragmentation. Although not directly involved in the upheavals, the smallholders felt threatened by the attack on private ownership and the drop in their income caused by price controls. Whether through the lack of political will or the low priority accorded to agriculture, the rural sector continued to perform indifferently prior to entry into the European Community. Only when externally-driven pressures and assistance were applied did Portuguese agriculture begin to respond and adopt a new agenda.

THE POST REVOLUTIONARY ECONOMY

It is impossible to find an exact correlation between political stability and economic performance. Nevertheless, it is unquestionable that instability in Portugal's post-revolutionary political system was not conducive to sound management and economic progress. Although there were expansionary spurts, notably in 1976–7 and 1980–2, growth was uncontrolled, electorally-motivated and subsequently unsustainable. Indeed, economic policy had to be formulated in the context of severe internal (political and constitutional problems) and external (international economic crises) blockages and constraints throughout the 1970s and early 1980s.

Political instability characterised Portuguese democracy during the thirteen years between 1974 and 1987. This is indicated by the high government turnover – seventeen (six provisional and ten constitutional). No prime minister completed a full four-year term, and no parliament lasted more than two-and-a-half years. Prior to 1987, no single party was able to secure an outright majority because the distribution of votes among the four major parties (PS, PSD, CDS and PCP) remained more or less unchanged. Portugal experimented with the limited number of political options available to overcome the deadlock: a minority administration, a coalition government, and a non-party, technocratic cabinet (see Table 2.3). Whatever the form of government, democratic consolidation proved elusive as both politicians and political parties earned the not unjustified reputation as quarrelsome, factional, elitist and indecisive. Inevitably, the almost non-stop electioneering (six parliamentary and three presidential, as well as local polls) left little time for tackling urgent issues on the economic agenda. As a result, economic policy was formulated in the short-term electoral context. Significantly, political factionalism and personal rivalries precluded an all-party

*Table 2.3*:   Composition and Duration of Governments in Portugal 1976–85.

| Dates | Prime Minister | Parties represented in government | Duration |
|---|---|---|---|
| 1976–7 | M. Soares | minority PS | 17 months |
| 1978 | M. Soares | PS, CDS | 6 months |
| 1978 | Nobre da Costa | independent | 18 days |
| 1978–9 | Mota Pinto | " | 8 months |
| 1979–80 | L. Pintasilgo | " | 5 months |
| 1980 | Sá Carneiro | PSD, CDS (AD) | 11 months |
| 1981 | P. Balsemão | " | 5 months |
| 1981–2 | P. Balsemão | " | 3 months |
| 1983 | M. Soares | PS, PSD (CB) | 24 months |
| 1985 | Cavaco Silva | minority PSD | 21 months |

*Source*: Compiled by author.

economic programme like Spain's Moncloa Pact (October 1977), despite urging from President Ramalho Eanes and the existence of a policy consensus among all the major political parties bar the communists. Political stability was compromised further by friction between a directly elected president and a prime minister leading a popularly elected government. Relations between the two executive branches were particularly sour during the prime ministerships of Mario Soares and Sá Carneiro.

The 1976 constitution did not provide a firm foundation for stable democratic government. It reflected the revolutionary origins of Portuguese democracy by institutionalising a socialist, interventionist model which sat uneasily with the general consensus in favour of a mixed economy, liberal democracy and membership of western economic and military organisations. There could be no synchronisation between the political and economic systems as long as the military-dominated Council of the Revolution (CR) carried out its task of defending the radical socioeconomic model defined in the constitution. Indeed, full civilianisation did not occur until General Eanes stepped down at the end of his second term as president in 1986. A start was made on constitutional revision in 1982 when the ideological references were deleted, the CR abolished (to be replaced by an advisory council of state dominated by the political parties) and presidential powers trimmed. However, the changes were to some extent cosmetic, and structural economic reform had to wait until a second revision received the necessary two-thirds majority and came into effect in 1989.

The political transformation of 25 April 1974 occurred at an inauspicious time for the Portuguese economy. It would be harder to imagine a more damaging combination of shocks than the disintegration of a long-established regime followed by a political and social revolution at home, fused with unanticipated external developments which included a world economic crisis and deep recession. The ability to cope with these difficulties was further prejudiced by the unconsolidated political system and ill-defined economic structures. The elements in the multiple crises can for the purpose of analysis be divided into consecutive time periods: 1974–6, 1976–9, 1980–2 and 1983–5.

ECONOMIC DISLOCATION 1974–6

Because its own energy resources make only a minuscule contribution to meeting the country's energy needs, the Portuguese economy is particularly vulnerable to higher oil prices. The modern industrial sector developed during the 1960s and early 1970s relied heavily on cheap oil supplies which accounted for seventy per cent of energy requirements in 1973. Portugal became a prime target for the Arab oil embargo because its military bases were used by United States supply aircraft en route to Israel during the 1973 Middle East conflict. Portugal faced a massive increase in its import bill following the decision taken by the Organisation of Petroleum-exporting Countries (OPEC) to impose a fourfold increase in prices. Consequently, imports of petroleum and petroleum products which cost US$183,000,000 in 1973 jumped to US$621,000,000 in 1975 and rose further to US$743,000,000 in 1977 (World Bank 1978a). Following a second series of price hikes at the end of the decade, the import bill for petroleum totalled US$2.234 billion by 1982.

The government responded by raising energy prices to a level that made them the most expensive in Europe (OECD 1980). Despite measures to depress demand, it proved difficult to cut the import bill substantially, especially since Portugal had recently invested heavily in oil-refining facilities. Exports declined as demand contracted due to the global downturn, while revenue from non-merchandise sources that traditionally balanced the trade account declined markedly. The impact on the balance of trade was dramatic. The terms of trade registered a twenty-three per cent deterioration between 1973 and 1975, and the balance of payments moved from a small surplus averaging US$250,000,000 during 1970–3 into a current account deficit of around US$1.5 billion, or nine per cent of GDP, by 1977 (OECD 1981).

Non-merchandise income suffered a serious deterioration during the upheavals of the early 1970s. First, the trade surplus with the escudo area disappeared following decolonisation. The African share of exports declined from twenty-five per cent of the total in 1968 to eighteen per cent by 1973 and was down to five per cent by the end of the decade (Almeida Coutinho 1979). As the colonial markets contracted, Portuguese industry grappled with higher costs and lower output caused by disruptions in production. However, it merely gave further impetus to a growing trade dependency on the capitalist, especially European, economies. Second, the transfer of emigrant remittances and income from tourism was affected by uncertainties over political developments in Portugal and the economic recession in western Europe which reduced demand for emigrant labour. Third, sharpened competition and protectionist barriers erected throughout Europe, particularly quotas imposed on textile exports, combined with the flight of substantial amounts of capital to aggravate the problems.

*Table 2.4:* Balance of Payments 1973–84 (thousands of US dollars).

|  | Trade balance | as % of GDP | emig. rems and tourism | Current account balance |
|---|---|---|---|---|
| 1973 | -906 | -7.9 | 1,403 | 351 |
| 1974 | -1,987 | -14.9 | 1,315 | -823 |
| 1975 | -1,670 | -11.4 | 1,003 | -817 |
| 1976 | -2,175 | -14.1 | 1,089 | -1,289 |
| 1977 | -2,532 | -15.5 | 1,442 | -1,495 |
| 1978 | -2,408 | -13.4 | 1,598 | -826 |
| 1979 | -2,632 | -13.0 | 3,150 | -52 |
| 1980 | -4,206 | -17.0 | 3,790 | -1,251 |
| 1981 | -5,195 | -21.8 | 3,609 | -2,852 |
| 1982 | -4,833 | -20.8 | 3,208 | -3,245 |
| 1983 | -3,075 | -14.9 | 2,742 | -1,640 |
| 1984 | -2,131 | -11.1 | 2,883 | -623 |

*Source*: EIU 1986.

The international economic crisis assumed greater significance for Portugal because it coincided with momentous changes in the country's political economy. The 1974 revolution unleashed pent-up demands for social change and the redistribution of income. It also raised questions about the nature and direction of the new economic structures and left unresolved which had priority: the state or the market, the workers or the management, consumption or savings. In order to satisfy the expectations generated among the population, the government sanctioned a rapid expansion in domestic demand. Real wages in industry increased by twenty-five per cent and in commerce and agriculture by eleven per cent between 1973 and 1975 (Schmitt 1981). Spearheaded by pressure from newly liberated trade unions, labour's share of the national income rose sharply from 51.6 per cent in 1973 to 68.9 per cent two years later. The explanation for this shift, according to Krugman and Braga de Macedo (1981), is that Portugal became 'a politicised market economy' in which wages were politically determined. The government played a decisive part by allowing large increases in public expenditure and tilting the balance of bargaining power towards the workers by:

- pushing up the minimum wage;
- introducing employment protection legislation to restrict dismissals;
- raising subsidies on a range of imports, mainly foodstuffs, and providing subsidies to firms to cover wage bills;
- enforcing price controls;
- expanding public sector employment;
- allowing the money supply to expand to an annual rate of around thirty-five per cent and keeping interest rates low;
- maintaining a stable exchange rate to depress import costs;
- and extending social welfare benefits to a wider constituency.

*Table 2.5:*     Inflation (consumer prices) 1969–84 (percentage annual change).

| 1969 | 1970 | 1971 | 1972 | 1973 | 1974 | 1975 | 1976 |
|------|------|------|------|------|------|------|------|
| 7.0  | 6.3  | 8.3  | 8.9  | 11.5 | 29.2 | 20.4 | 19.3 |

| 1977 | 1978 | 1979 | 1980 | 1981 | 1982 | 1983 | 1984 |
|------|------|------|------|------|------|------|------|
| 27.2 | 22.1 | 24.2 | 16.6 | 20.0 | 22.4 | 25.5 | 29.3 |

*Source*: OECD; EIU 1986.

To fund the massive increases in public expenditure, the government turned to the Bank of Portugal and quickly ran up debts totalling just under US$2 billion by the end of 1976 (Morrison 1981). This quickly forced up the public-sector deficit to ten per cent of GDP, and, despite falling back to seven per cent in 1977, it remained at an unacceptably high level. In the context of an unreformed productive structure and the rising import propensity, buoyant domestic demand only served to fuel inflation (see Table 2.5), caused acute balance of payments difficulties and triggered an eighteen per cent fall in private and foreign investment as business confidence slumped (EIU 1986).

Once the political balance of power began to shift within the provisional governments, the emphasis moved away from expansionary policies aimed at maintaining domestic demand, keeping down unemployment and raising productivity to justify large real - wage increases (Stuart 1981). The National Reconstruction Plan (December 1975) focused on introducing expenditure controls, stimulating production, reducing the powers of the workers' commissions, raising taxes and implementing a new Foreign Investment Code to attract foreign capital (Williams 1989). This trend was consolidated by successive governments between 1976 and 1979, but sound economic management was still encumbered by the legacy of both the corporatist and the revolutionary periods. All the major political parties, apart from the PCP, mistrusted the reforms spawned by the revolutionary period. Therefore the future of the nationalised sector and the agricultural reforms continued to be contentious issues throughout the 1970s and, as a consequence, deflected attention away from structural reforms.

### THE SOCIALIST ASCENDANCY 1976–9

The first Soares administration found itself constrained by its inability to command a parliamentary majority: unpopular measures might have provoked a no-confidence motion and exacted a high electoral price. Soares's insistence on governing alone meant that he could only pass bills through the National Assembly after forging tactical alliances with the PSD, CDS or PCP, depending upon the legislation in question. Parliamentary tactics became all-important, to the detriment of strong, efficient government. Nevertheless, this does not absolve the Socialist minority government from criticism for its lack of a clear direction in economic matters. Not for the first time in Europe, the Socialists faced a dilemma common to their sister parties: the choice between long-held ideals (income redistribution, economic expansion, job creation etc.) and economic orthodoxy (wage controls, higher prices, import restrictions etc.).

The principal elements in the Socialist minority government's economic strategy comprised two austerity packages – neither had much impact on inflation; devaluations – always delayed and late; and securing large overseas loans. Soares accepted that, in order to revive the economy, he needed first to enlist the cooperation of the private sector, which remained the chief source of employment and foreign exchange earnings, and second to cut private consumption sharply and limit public spending on social programmes. The prime minister tried to reconcile business interests to the new order with talk of a 'competitive coexistence' between the private and public sectors. Stabilisation measures included wage curbs, price deregulation, limits on strike action and two measures designed to lessen Communist influence – an end to Intersindical's labour monopoly by allowing other federations to compete for members, and the restoration with compensation to their former owners of illegally-seized lands in the Alentejo in an effort to dispel any uncertainty over property rights. To its proponents, austerity was necessary to inject a note of economic realism following the spendthrift months after the overthrow of the old regime. To its critics on the left, the measures made concessions to the former regime's supporters and pro-capitalist interests while neglecting the pressing problems generated by steadily rising unemployment.

Austerity was necessary to correct the chronic balance of payments deficit. Initially, the deficit could be offset by running down foreign reserves and by overseas borrowing. The World Bank (1978a) estimated that the reserves covered twenty-seven per cent of the deficit in the course of 1976–7, while the remainder had to be borrowed from European sources in the shape of loans with gold reserves as collateral and as IMF credit on strict terms. Several factors explain the deterioration in the external account. In the first place, the trade gap widened progressively prior to 1974 but was more than compensated for by a healthy inflow of 'invisibles'. Also, exports, the growth motor during the 1960s and early 1970s, fell back sharply, and recovery was made more difficult by the slow upturn in international trade. Exporters lost market shares and experienced difficulties in adapting to new markets such as those in the Middle East, in part because their products were too narrowly specialised.

When the first dose of austerity failed to rectify the balance of payments problem, the government felt obliged to turn to the IMF. Such a move inevitably brought the issues of national independence and foreign interference to the foreground. The IMF dictated economic policy during 1977–9 through the April 1977 agreement, the austerity package (August 1977) and the stand-by arrangement (May 1978). An alternative strategy had been outlined in the planning ministry's medium-term economic plan which proposed to use state planning and economic growth to overcome structural deficiencies and to satisfy basic needs. However, the expansionists had lost the argument by August 1977, when the second crisis package was adopted. The IMF insisted as a precondition for its assistance that a consensus be forged among the political parties, the employers and the trade unions and that pro-private-sector measures be introduced. The IMF's familiar economic prescription – export stimulation through devaluation, lower wages and austerity – was hard enough to swallow, but the furore surrounding charges of external interference in domestic affairs exacted a political price. The Socialist minority administration came to grief in the parliamentary vote on the 1978 budget.

To implement the stabilisation programme, two prerequisites were required: a new government and a satisfactory outcome to talks with the IMF. The first condition was fulfilled when the right-wing CDS agreed to support a second PS administration. The second came with the acceptance by both parties of a stabilisation package designed 'to create a solid basis for long-term development'. The IMF pinpointed three causes of the crisis: wage inflation, an overvalued currency and a lax monetary policy (Korner 1986). The prescribed medicine took the form of higher interest rates, strict credit controls, cuts in public spending on social provision, subsidies on basic commodities and capital transfers to state-sector companies. Income tax and welfare contributions rose by ten per cent, sales tax by thirty per cent and public-service charges (gas, electricity, water, transport) by up to fifty per cent. Other measures included a wage ceiling (twenty per cent for 1978) and a larger monthly crawling peg devaluation (1.25 per cent) to assist exports and encourage tourism. In return, Portugal received a US$750,000,000 loan – the first step on the road to restoring international confidence.

The turnaround in Portugal's economic fortunes came surprisingly swiftly. A 1977 balance of payments deficit of US$1.5 billion was transformed into near-equilibrium within two years. Exports performed strongly (up fifteen and twenty-eight per cent in 1978 and 1979 respectively), while accumulated funds from emigrant workers withheld during 1974–6 combined with a doubling of tourism income to swell the government's coffers. GDP growth slackened somewhat but still managed 2.8 per cent and 5.6 per cent in 1978 and 1979. Industrial production grew at between six and seven per cent – twice the rate achieved by Portugal's trading partners – and real wages dropped by seventeen per cent against the 1976 figure.

Stuart (1981), an IMF economist, explained the positive outcome in the following way: the devaluations restored exchange-rate competitiveness to its pre-1973 level, and higher interest rates both boosted confidence in the escudo and slowed domestic credit growth. The measures helped to cut imports and released credit for productive investment. In fact, the external position improved so rapidly that any need to draw further on the stand-by arrangement was avoided. To what extent were the IMF measures responsible for the success of the stabilisation programme? Certainly, the IMF's intervention does not appear to be so beneficial when assessed over a longer timescale. A major factor in the improvement appears to have been the upturn in the US and European economies which constituted the principal markets for Portuguese exports. Nor can the IMF take credit for the jump in remittances and tourism revenues, which responded positively to the more settled political climate. The IMF might have congratulated itself that the prescribed deflationary policies did not eliminate growth completely, but nevertheless growth was cut by half at a stage when Portugal desperately needed sustained high growth in order to narrow the gap with the European Community which it hoped to join within a few years (Morrison 1981). Meanwhile, domestic inflation remained stubbornly high, in substantial part because the IMF-prescribed devaluations pushed up import prices.

It can be argued that the export-promotion, low-wage model advocated by the IMF differed little in its essentials from the Salazarist growth model pursued in the 1960s. Exporters, both foreign multinationals and Portuguese, benefited from IMF policies while domestic industry bore the brunt of the crisis. Bankruptcies became common among small and medium-sized firms when demand was squeezed as consumers found their purchasing power eroded (real wages fell 14.3 per cent between 1977 and 1979). However, Portuguese industrialists did not oppose the IMF because they expected private enterprise to benefit at the expense of the state sector. Meanwhile, wage- and salary-earners were bludgeoned further by a battery of price increases on basic foodstuffs and public services allied to cuts in spending on the social, health, housing and education budgets.

The Socialists paid a heavy political price for their association with the IMF. Their traditional political constituency felt the full impact of the austerity measures. The PS–CDS coalition fell apart, and defeat in the December 1979 elections was a formality. Through its acceptance of the IMF conditions, the Socialist government presided over a marked shift to the right and buttressed the position of those seeking to reverse the changes associated with 1975–6. Korner (1986) criticises Soares for sanctioning such a draconian programme and argues that Portugal required a longer period of adjustment if it was to achieve lasting stability and solve its structural problems. In contrast, Morrison (1981) believes that Soares was in a weak bargaining position but still managed to apply the maximum leverage by linking the loans to the survival of democracy. He maintains that Portugal's terms marked a watershed in the transformation in the IMF's policy from an insistence on devaluation to more emphasis on a tight monetary approach.

The Socialists, albeit hampered by minority or coalition constraints, turned out to be poor economic managers. Soares himself claimed no expertise and professed little interest in economic matters. Perhaps the party's 'polyglot' composition and mixed social base made it harder to reach a consensus on economic policy (Porto 1984). Ultimately, the achievements of the Socialist-dominated governments (1976–9) lay outside the economic sphere – reintegrating the *retornados*, consolidating democratic institutions, avoiding social conflict and setting a course for the future by lodging an application to join the European Economic Community.

THE AD GOVERNMENTS 1979–83: POPULIST EXPANSIONISM?

The first Aliança Democrática (AD) government (a centre-right coalition of the PSD, CDS and PPM) that assumed office in January 1980 enjoyed a number of distinct advantages over its predecessors. Not only was it the first majority administration since 1976, but it also inherited an improving economic situation characterised by falling inflation and a balance of payments surplus. In fact, Morrison (1981) argues that AD benefited greatly from Soares's policies and was able to focus its attention on the domestic economy rather than, as in the past, on the external sector. Under Sá Carneiro's forceful leadership, the coalition adopted a programme that called for constitutional reform and measures to stimulate the private sector.

Despite enjoying these considerable advantages, political and constitutional considerations eventually conspired to negate them. Under the Portuguese constitution, a further round of parliamentary elections had to be held in October. This forced electoral considerations to the fore and encouraged finance minister Cavaco Silva to engineer a mini-boom to boost AD's prospects of retaining their overall majority. This was successfully accomplished with the help of a more relaxed monetary policy (the money supply rose thirty per cent in 1980) which allowed higher consumer spending, reflected in a five per cent increase in private consumption during 1980 and an additional 3.5 per cent increase the following year (OECD 1982). Price increases for public services and energy consumption were postponed and food price controls strictly enforced. A six per cent escudo revaluation and a reduction in the rate of the crawling peg monthly devaluations cut import costs and helped bring inflation down to twenty per cent. The government sanctioned large wage-rises in the region of twenty per cent that allowed the workforce to benefit from the first gain (four per cent) in the purchasing power of wages since 1976.

Although he secured a parliamentary majority, Sá Carneiro did not enjoy harmonious relations with the other executive branch – the presidency. The AD's free-market programme consistently fell foul of the opposition mounted by President Eanes and the CR. Constitutional reform was considered essential if progress was to be made in areas such as labour law reform, agrarian reform and the deregulation of the private sector. Frustration mounted as the CR used its veto to block legislation on no less than twenty-three occasions during 1980. Eanes's re-election and Sá Carneiro's death ensured that constitutional revision would not be as radical as originally planned. The new PSD prime minister Francisco Balsemão was obliged to reach a compromise with the PS which ensured that, although the CR was abolished and presidential powers reduced, revisions to the economic clauses in the constitution were cosmetic. The commitment to 'the transition to socialism' and 'the construction of a socialist economy' were deleted, but interventionism remained a cardinal principle (Kayman 1987).

Under AD management, the economy once again began to exhibit its structural weaknesses. The government planned to finance expansion through foreign borrowing. As a result, imports were sucked in while exports failed to keep pace. The balance of payments deficit all but tripled from US$1.251 billion in 1980 to US$3.245 billion in 1982. The public debt/GDP ratio rose alarmingly to almost fifty per cent, and the debt-service ratio stood at a worrying twenty-three per cent. To make matters worse, the most severe drought for over 100 years badly affected agricultural output and forced up the food import bill. The combination of a deteriorating external account (the 1982 balance of payments deficit was the third-largest in history) and slower economic growth forced Portugal back into the arms of the IMF.

### THE BLOC CENTRAL 1983–5

When the CDS's Freitas do Amaral withdrew his support from the AD coalition, he revealed the fragility of Balsemão's political position. A leadership change (Mota Pinto for Balsemão) could not prevent the Socialists from gaining a clear victory but without an overall majority once again. However, the economic and financial crisis did persuade the two large centre parties to form an alliance known as the central block in June 1983. Both internal and external factors converged to produce the 1982–3 crisis. The main causes were:

- the injudicious expansionist policies pursued since 1980;
- the failure to deal with the causes because political energies were absorbed by constitutional issues; and
- the impact of the international recession caused by higher oil prices and declining world demand. In addition to falling emigrant remittances and tourism earnings, there was a sharp rise in interest rates to which Portugal had become acutely vulnerable given its growing debt.

The short-term priority became to obtain an IMF loan in order to pay the debt interest and re-establish the country's creditworthiness. The adjustment programme outlined in the letter of intent contained the familiar ingredients: a devaluation accompanied by a credit squeeze. Devaluation came in tranches – an effective 9.4 per cent devaluation in mid-1982, followed by a further two per cent in 1983 and a larger twelve per cent in June. The aim outlined in the Financial and Economic Recovery Programme was to slash the balance of payments and budget deficits through cuts in public-sector funds and subsidies on basic items, higher interest rates and taxes and strict wage restraint. Neo-corporatist mechanisms helped to lessen the possibility of conflict between management and the trade unions. Both the predominantly white-collar UGT and the largely blue-collar CGTP participated, with varying degrees of enthusiasm, in a Permanent Council for Social Concertation – a forum in which employers' representatives, trade unionists and the government hammered out agreements on wage levels, working conditions and labour laws. In addition, some industries in the nationalised sector (banking, insurance, cement and fertiliser production) were to be opened to private capital.

Even after such a brief overview, few would disagree with the conclusion that the 1970s and early 1980s were 'exceptional years in Portuguese economic history' (Cravinho 1984). Simultaneous shocks, both internal and external in origin, deflected attention away from the real priorities in economic policymaking. Following half a century of dictatorship when adjustment policies were ignored or postponed, the overwhelming priorities were to modernise the economic structures and to raise the social and welfare levels to bring them more into line with European standards. Caetano's project failed because it proved impossible to reconcile massive expenditure on the colonial wars with the pressing need for structural reforms and faster economic growth. It came to grief on the contradiction between preparing to join Europe while maintaining the colonial connection. The post-revolutionary regime introduced further complications which included uncertainties over the precise role of the public and private sectors, the difficulties in forging a consensus over the exact shape and orientation of a reordered political system and disagreements over how to tackle the country's mounting economic problems amid an unfavourable international trading environment. They merely highlighted the essential contradiction that dominated this period between a reliance on IMF-prescribed remedies and the structural nature of Portugal's economic problems. As Nataf and Sammis (1990) point out, externally-imposed shock treatment was inappropriate and short-term:

> The governments were singularly ineffectual in reversing the deficiencies in Portugal's productive capacity, but they were successful in convincing austerity-oriented international lenders, budget-minded tourists, and high interest-seeking, stability-minded emigrants that the Portuguese economy was being corrected of its excesses.

As a result, Portugal became a member of the European Community with an open economy in dire need of reconversion and restructuring, still vulnerable to the vagaries of external developments and separated by a wide gap from the more advanced industrial economies of northern and southern Europe.

# CHAPTER 3

# *The Structure of the Portuguese Economy*

At the beginning of the new decade, the Portuguese population amounted to 10,350,000 – a 0.5 per cent net average increase over the previous ten years – according to provisional estimates derived from the thirteenth census (Censo-91, the largest national operation of its kind ever carried out). The proportion of the total population living in the two principal urban centres has accelerated in recent decades. Lisbon and Oporto, which contained only six per cent of the total population in 1864, slightly more than doubled over the next 100 years to stand at thirteen per cent in 1960. Rapid urbanisation since then means that the proportion will have reached over a third by the turn of the century. The figures for the most populated districts are given in Table 3.1. In addition, some 250,000 live in the autonomous regions of the Azores and Madeira, along with an estimated 3.5–4 million (equivalent to a third of the domestic population) living abroad as emigrants.

Average life expectancy has risen in the last three decades from sixty-three to seventy-four years. For women it is 77.6 years (against a European average of 78.6), while the average lifespan for men is 70.7 years (*Expresso* 1991a). Some unusual factors had been at work during the 1970s, when the population increased by 1.3 per cent annually, thus reversing the negative (0.3 per cent annual decline) trend registered in the 1960s. This is accounted for not by an increase in the birth rate but by the influx of refugees repatriated from the colonies, coupled with a substantial reduction in the country's traditional emigration flows. In addition, the mortality rate has declined and the share of the elderly in the population has grown as a result of health-care improvements

*Table 3.1*:    Population by District 1985.

| Lisbon | 2,120,000 | Santarém | 742,000 |
|---|---|---|---|
| Oporto | 1,644,000 | Coimbra | 446,000 |
| Braga | 756,000 | Leiria | 434,000 |
| Setúbal | 742,000 | Viseu | 427,000 |
| Aveiro | 655,000 | Faro | 337,000 |

*Source*: EIU 1990e.

and the return of migrants from abroad. The consequences of these demographic changes are that Portugal will have greater numbers of aged and non-productive people among its population. Moreover, the aging of the Portuguese population is accelerating in line with continental trends (by 2040, one in five Europeans will be a pensioner).

Birth rates have fallen more steeply than in any other European country, down from 3.1 children per couple in 1960 to 2.2 twenty years later and only 1.5 in 1989. Portugal, along with Spain, Germany and Italy, has one of the lowest levels of fecundity in the world. This is reflected in the fact that the majority of births are no longer to women in the 20–24 age group, but to those aged 25–29. A series of social changes explain the declining birth rate: the postponement of the decision to start a family allied to a preference for smaller families and the career opportunities open to women. In 1960, only thirteen per cent of women in Portugal went out to work; now they constitute almost fifty per cent of the workforce. A further contributing factor is the steady erosion of traditional values as the Church's influence wanes and the youth culture places more emphasis on individual self-fulfilment. However, infant mortality was the highest in the EC12 at 12.2 per 1,000 live births compared to the European average of 8.2 in 1989. This improved to 10.9 per 1,000 live births in the following year due to a decline in infant deaths in the north, attributable apparently to the declining rural population and accelerating social change. However, there are regional variations which run counter to the recent downward trend in infant deaths. The worsening situation in the Lisbon-Tagus Valley region during 1991 can be explained by the growing number of African immigrants resident in the area with their different cultural traditions, the high proportion of home births and their low living standards.

## EMPLOYMENT

Until 1973, the twin pressures on the labour market exerted by population growth and the shift of the labour force from the agricultural sector towards industry and services were relieved by emigration. Both the total population and the workforce age group (fifteen- to sixty-four-year-olds) actually fell. Nevertheless, it did not prevent the continuation of the process that has produced a remarkable shift in sectoral employment shares over the past half-century. Estimates based on the 1930 census put the active rural population at 62.5 per cent of the total employed. By 1950, the share had fallen to just under fifty per cent, but the most dramatic fall occurred during the 1950s when the rural population contracted by almost a third, with some districts losing forty per cent of their rural workers due to emigration and internal migration to urban centres. During the early 1970s, the farming population declined by a further fourteen per cent from 918,000 to 790,088 (ILO 1979), and, on the eve of the revolution, employment in the agricultural sector had fallen to less than thirty per cent of the total (see Table 3.2). The downward trend continued during throughout the

*Table 3.2:*    Sectoral Share of GDP and Employment (percentage) 1970–90.

| | GDP | | | Employment | | |
|---|---|---|---|---|---|---|
| | 1970 | 1980 | 1988 | 1970 | 1980 | 1990(e) |
| Agriculture | 16 | 10 | 6 | 33 | 28 | 13 |
| Industry | 45 | 38 | 38 | 36 | 36 | 35 |
| Services | 39 | 52 | 56 | 31 | 36 | 47 |

(e): estimate
*Source*: Bank of Portugal cited in EIU 1991d.

1980s and, according to European Commission estimates, had fallen below twenty per cent by 1989, although it still remains well above the EC average of 7.1 per cent. An important aspect of the declining agricultural labour force in Portugal is that, unlike elsewhere in the EC, there has been no corresponding positive impact on productivity and total output. As a consequence, the contribution made by the primary sector (agriculture, forestry and fishing) to GDP continued its decline from 11.9 per cent of the total in 1977 to 6.2 per cent in 1989 (OECD 1992).

The percentage share of the labour force employed in industry grew only modestly from around thirty per cent of the total in 1960 to a fraction over thirty-five per cent in 1990. According to ILO estimates covering paid manufacturing employment, there were 626,000 industrial employees in 1985. Although this represented a two per cent decrease over 1979, it was a much smaller fall over the same period than elsewhere in the EC, where the manufacturing sector contracted substantially as a result of the recession, global competition and restructuring. In fact, industrial employment, which grew at two per cent annually during the 1960s and 1970s, stagnated for most of the 1980s. The only exceptions were the clothing, footwear and paper industries, where expansion took place in response to foreign demand. A similar pattern emerges when the role of manufacturing in the structure of production is analysed: the contribution to GDP of twenty-eight per cent in 1977 is little changed twelve years later.

In common with its EC neighbours, Portugal's service sector has expanded rapidly since the 1960s. The sector's share of total employment jumped from twenty-eight per cent in 1960 to thirty-six per cent two decades later and by 1990 accounted for forty-seven per cent. This compares with figures of just under sixty per cent of total employment (59.8 per cent) in the EC12. Obviously, Portugal has been catching up fast with its EC partners, and growth rates in service employment are among the highest in the EC in relative terms. A distinguishing feature of service employment in Portugal is its concentration in the Lisbon area. This is particularly the case for financial and business services, which made a major contribution to job-generation after 1986, public administration and transport. Tourism predominates in the Algarve and Madeira, where above-average growth occurred, while retail and repair services are more evenly distributed. Below-average growth in service employment is noticeable in the Alentejo, the Azores and Oporto (Illeris 1989). The position of services, which already made a major contribution to GDP in the mid-1970s (50.6 per cent), was consolidated during the following decade and stood at 55.7 per cent in 1989.

A number of distinctive structural features shape the Portuguese labour market. The first is the restrictive legislation governing dismissals. In making collective dismissals extremely difficult, the post-1974 labour laws denied employers the opportunity to adjust to economic shocks by reducing the numbers on the payroll. Hemmed in by legal constraints, they therefore reacted by reducing wages and, in some cases, delaying payment instead of cutting the size of the workforce. Wage arrears, caused by the failure of companies to pay their employees regularly, tend to rise during periods of economic difficulty. The number of workers involved reached a peak at just under 65,000 in 1985 before falling steadily to a low point of 7,000 in 1990 as economic activity picked up. The trend was reversed in 1991 when, according to IGT statistics, more than 16,000 workers were affected by wage arrears. The impact was felt most severely in the north, where the crisis in the textile industry began to bite deeply.

Another response to the rigidities in the labour market has been to make increased use of the fixed-term contract. This enables employers to avoid taking on labour they cannot shed later. The following figures give an indication of the trend: in the early 1980s, thirteen per cent of employment contracts were fixed-term, but by 1988, when just under three-quarters of all new contracts were temporary, the proportion had jumped to nineteen per cent – one of the highest in the EC (OECD 1989).

A further practice in common use to circumvent the inflexible labour laws is the use of child labour, particularly in the garments and footwear industry. The employment of post-primary-school children has a long history but intensifies during periods of rising demand and external competition because employers are not obliged to pay the full minimum wage to workers under the age of eighteen. Before 1987, when the compulsory age for primary education was raised from twelve to fourteen, adolescents who did not wish to continue their education and were under the legal minimum working age of fourteen often sought clandestine work. The incidence of working minors is greatest in three sectors: agriculture, particularly small family farms, small businesses and labour-intensive manufacturing industry, where many are underpaid and work a twelve-hour day in sweat-shop conditions (Miguélez Lobo 1990). A recent IGT report uncovered two cases of nine-year-olds working in Braga. Not surprisingly, the exact extent of the use of child labour is unknown, but trade unions and religious groups estimate that 200,000 children are affected, much higher than the official estimates which put the figure at between 40,000 and 70,000. Whatever the true state of affairs, there are a number of common features associated with the exploitation of child labour. First, it is clear that the legislation is widely ignored and that the authorities have, in the past, turned a blind eye to the abuses. Second, it is most prevalent in the north, particularly in the districts of Braga, Oporto and Aveiro, where the textiles, clothing and footwear industry is concentrated. It is estimated that around 10,000 pairs of shoes are produced daily in Felgueiras by illegal workers, many of them children. Child labour is also to be found in the stone, cork and building industries. Third, the employment of youths under fourteen years of age is predominant among small firms comprising up to thirty workers. While child labour may help to depress costs, the practice is probably counter-productive because it damages Portugal's image abroad (prompting condemnation from Anti-Slavery International among others) and is an indicator of backwardness. Concerned at the impact that employment of children of school age might have on exports, the minister responsible for foreign trade claimed in September 1991 that, despite all the evidence to the contrary, the reports were propaganda disseminated by groups interested in preventing Portuguese products from entering the European market.

An additional source of cheap labour for industry is the employment of illegal immigrant workers, mostly from Portuguese-speaking Africa. It is estimated that forty per cent of the 200,000 foreigners resident in Portugal do not have legal status. Large numbers began to arrive from Africa after 25 April 1974 in order to escape war, hunger and political instability, and the inflow increased after Portugal joined the EC in 1986. Most African immigrants work in the construction industry, cleaning and domestic work and other low-status and poorly-paid jobs. The principal source countries are Cape Verde, where emigrant remittances are one of the country's major earners, Angola and Guinea-Bissau. Because of their status, the illegals work as virtual slaves, able to be bought and sold between factories.

In common with many of Portugal's southern European neighbours, informal outworking is on the increase. Like child labour, it is highly concentrated in the textiles, footwear and leather goods sectors and involves a high proportion of women. Homeworking is particularly appropriate to the needs of workers who wish to fit agricultural work in with at-home industrial activities. It enables employers to avoid capital investment on factory premises and, because it is almost totally untouched by employment legislation, eliminates the social costs of employing labour (European Commission 1989). As Table 3.3 demonstrates,

*Table 3.3*:   Homeworking in Southern Europe.

|  | Year | Nos | Proportion of women |
|---|---|---|---|
| Italy | 1985 | 700,000 | over 90% |
| France | 1985 | 59,600 | 82% |
| Portugal | 1983 | 50,000 | over 90% |
| Spain | 1986 | 490,000 | 75% |

*Source*: European Commission 1989.

Portugal lags behind Italy and Spain with respect to informal work, but the phenomenon has been on the increase during the late 1980s as employers sought means to reduce their labour costs.

The growth and modernisation of the Portuguese economy has exposed serious flaws in education and training provision. Portugal occupies an unenviable position in EC tables of comparative achievement by combining the lowest levels of general education with the highest rate of illiteracy among its adult population. Education is now compulsory to the age of fourteen, but more than forty per cent of children fail to complete their schooling – four times the EC average. Just under half the Portuguese workforce have no more than six years of schooling. Only ten per cent of school-leavers enter higher education, compared to a third on average throughout the EC. The scramble for university places means that around 100,000 applicants are chasing 40,000 available places (Kaplan 1991).

An illiteracy rate of forty-four per cent of the over-fourteen age group in 1950 was reduced to twenty-nine per cent by 1974 but still remains at Third World levels. At twenty-one per cent of the over-fifteens, Portugal's illiteracy rate is three times higher than in Spain, double the Greek level and on a par with Brazil (22.3 per cent). A regional breakdown of the Portuguese figures reveals that, on average, a third of the population cannot read or write in Portalegre, Castelo Branco, Evora and Bragança, whereas in the coastal region, which includes Lisbon and Oporto, the level is 16.4 per cent. The problem is greatest among the older generation but still afflicts thousands of youngsters. The situation is worse among the poor: just over sixty per cent of youngsters belonging to low-income families in the urban conurbations around Lisbon, Oporto and Setúbal do not attend primary school, and the percentage is even higher in rural areas. Little wonder that despite programmes to tackle the deficiency it is calculated that 2,000,000 Portuguese will still be illiterate in the year 2000.

In higher education, the growing demand has been partly met by university expansion, particularly the private institutions that have been established in recent years, but critics from the old-established state universities claim that student numbers have increased at the cost of lower standards. The expansion of student numbers (fourteen per cent of the eighteen to twenty-one-year-olds according to official estimates) has not been accompanied by increased funding, despite government claims that education has the largest budget of any ministry. More encouragingly, regionally-based polytechnics, offering largely vocational education, are filling the gap. They offer degree courses for twenty per cent of students, and there are plans for the numbers to double by the year 2000 to around 50,000 (Griffiths 1990). The shortcomings of the present system in vocational training provision are apparent from the following statistics: thirty per cent of the workforce receive no vocational training whatsoever, and only some six per cent of managers, senior executives and professional people can be defined as highly qualified (European Commission 1990b). Fortunately, training and employment programmes aimed at increasing the supply of qualified workers, especially in the civil construction sector where one study indicated a shortfall of 40,000 new trainees, are now financed from EC funds. Certainly, the lack of skilled trainees is becoming ever more apparent as new technologies are introduced across a range of industries that are vital to the country's future prosperity. In general, the higher education system may be struggling to catch up, but, more encouragingly, in its female participation (53.8 per cent of students are women) Portugal leads Europe.

### THE REGIONS

There are no significant linguistic or cultural minorities, and regionalism is not as potent a force as in neighbouring Spain or other parts of Europe. Although the country is becoming more homogeneous, substantial economic imbalances remain between different parts of the country. The population is unevenly distributed and highly concentrated in the littoral or coastal areas, where three-fifths of the population live. In contrast, the interior and frontier regions have suffered for decades from depopulation, and the proportion of elderly people who remain is rising. The signs are that the drift to the coast continues despite the application of EC funds to provide access roads and establish industrial parks. The littoral registered a population gain of 1.5 per cent between 1981 and 1988 which is partly accounted for by incoming migrants but also reflects the natural increase, between two and four times the national average, in cities such as Braga, Oporto and Aveiro, where forty per cent of the population is under the age of twenty. In fact, the north is Europe's youngest region – almost thirty per cent of the 3,500,000 population is less than fifteen years old, compared to a quarter of the population as a whole.

For the purposes of this analysis, the country will be divided into the following regions: north, centre, Lisbon-Tagus Valley (centre-south) and the Alentejo-Algarve (south). Economic indicators expose as outdated the myths encapsulated in the popular saying that 'Lisboa diverte-se, Porto trabalho, Coimbra estudia e Braga reza' (Lisbon plays, Oporto works, Coimbra studies and Braga prays). As Table 3.4 demonstrates, almost half the national wealth is generated in the Lisbon-Tagus Valley area. An indication of the distribution of wealth can be obtained from figures of GDP per capita (by purchasing-power parities). Against

*Table 3.4*:   GDP Share by Region (percentage).

| | |
|---|---|
| North | 31 |
| Centre | 15 |
| Lisbon-Segtúb al | 46 |
| Alentejo-Algarve | 8 |

*Source: Publico* 30 August 1990.

an EC average of 12,168 contos, the breakdown by regions is as follows: Lisbon-Setúbal 8,778 contos, Alentejo-Algarve 5,746 contos, the north 5,432 contos and the centre 5,432 contos.

## THE NORTHERN REGION

This region comprises the Minho (Braga and Viana do Castelo), Trás-os-Montes (Vila Real and Bragança), the Douro Litoral (Oporto and Aveiro) and Beira Alta. The north displays a number of key features: first, the region is unevenly developed and there are marked differences between the coast and the interior. Many areas lag behind the national average with regard to health and social indicators. The northern interior sub-region suffers from inadequate communications exacerbated by the difficult terrain, a population drain, a heavy dependence on agriculture and low levels of industrialisation and urbanisation. There, the economy is geared overwhelmingly towards the regional market.

Second, over a quarter of the workforce is still employed in the primary sector, but the majority of farms are small-scale and productivity is low. Despite the pronounced dependence on agriculture, especially dairy products, it accounts for as little as six per cent of the regional product.

Third, manufacturing activities are concentrated in the coastal areas clustered around the industrial hub located in Oporto. Over forty per cent of the workforce is employed in the secondary sector, which accounts for forty-six per cent of the regional product. The region is vital to the Portuguese economy because a substantial proportion of northern output is exported. It accounts for thirty per cent of the country's textile exports. During the 1970s, northerners complained that their interests were neglected by central government. Since 1985, this has no longer been the case – there are more northern politicians in the government than ever before in the country's history, including figures such as Eurico de Melo, a textile magnate, and Miguel Cadilhe, former chief economist at the Banco Português do Atlântico's northern headquarters. The PSD's economic strategy was drawn up in Oporto, and the region has received its fair share of incoming EC funds to tackle its infrastructure and industrial problems.

Fourth, apart from the metropolitan area of Oporto, where the manufacturing base tends to be more diversified than elsewhere, the region relies heavily on traditional industries, principally textiles, clothing, metallurgy and machinery, wood and cork products. An example of the dangerously high degree of dependence on vulnerable industries is illustrated by the Vale de Ave, where textiles and clothing account for as much as eighty per cent of employment and output in the area. Unfortunately fierce external competition has sparked a crisis in a region where business has been slow to modernise and introduce new technologies. In part, this deficiency is explained by the preponderance of small and medium-sized firms employing less than fifty workers. Consequently, while many of the large industries concentrated around Lisbon were brought under state control, the private-sector stronghold in the north remained largely unaffected. This did permit the survival of a thriving business culture practised in the ways of circumventing Lisbon-imposed bureaucracy and controls. For instance, when the costs of exporting through Leixões became prohibitive, the northern industrialists simply rerouted their exports over the border to the Galician port of Vigo (Chislett 1991). It is no coincidence that two of the country's largest private groups, Amorim and Sonae, are northern-based and that the reprivatisation programme commenced in 1989 with one of the few northern firms to be nationalised – the brewer Unicer.

## THE CENTRAL REGION

This region comprises the Beira Litoral (Coimbra and Leiria), Beira Alta (Viseu and Guarda) and Beira Baixa (Castelo Branco). The regional economy displays a number of characteristics: first, there is still a high dependence on agriculture (forty per cent of the population works in the primary sector, which accounts for fourteen per cent of the regional GDP). Apart from the cultivation of cereal crops, livestock and wine, the region's forestry industry supplies material for the furniture, construction and paper pulp industries, and fishing is a traditional activity on the coast. The region's mining industry produces clay, sand, limestone and ores for use in the ceramics and glass manufacturing and as building materials.

Second, just under thirty per cent of the labour force is employed in the service sector in activities such as tourism (Costa da Prata and the spa towns) and in the university towns (Coimbra, Aveiro, Covilhã and Viseu).

Third, the area is reliant upon traditional industries, such as textiles and clothing, which are dispersed throughout the region. Textile firms are less aggressively export-oriented than those further north and are experiencing a series of major problems which include outdated technology, a shortage of skilled workers, low labour productivity, poor transport links and neglect by government agencies and the banks.

## THE LISBON-TAGUS VALLEY REGION

This region consists of Estremadura (Lisbon metropolitan area) and the Ribatejo (Santarém) as well as the western Alentejo (Setúbal). It contains more than a third of the population and generates almost half the national wealth – forty-six per cent of the nation's GDP. The key aspects of the regional economy are, first, that fifty-six per cent of the economically active population finds employment in the service sector. Tertiary activities are highly concentrated in the Lisbon area, which serves as the political and administrative centre. Recent moves to liberalise the financial system have enhanced Lisbon's economic weight at the expense of the north. In Setúbal, economic activity is more evenly divided between manufacturing and services.

Second, industry is highly concentrated, and basic heavy industries such as steel, shipbuilding and repairs, engineering, chemicals, car assembly and oil-refining are located in the region. The establishment of a modern sector since the 1950s is reflected in the region's growing share of national industrial production, which increased from thirty-one per cent in 1953 to over fifty per cent by the mid-1970s (Lewis and Williams 1981).

Third, agriculture plays a much smaller part in the regional economy than elsewhere, but commercial farming is well established, and productivity levels are relatively high. The region is responsible for a quarter of the total national agricultural output.

Fourth, in contrast to most other regions, there is a well-developed infrastructure consisting of road, rail and air links and educational institutions. Indeed, the expansion of the modern sectors in the Lisbon region during the last thirty years and the subsequent high levels of immigration have exacerbated existing regional disparities within Portugal.

THE SOUTHERN REGION

The country's southern region is made up of the Alentejo (Evora, Beja, Portalegre and part of Setúbal) and the Algarve (Faro). It accounts for only eight per cent of GDP and six per cent of the total population of 560,351 (1981). Among the main features of the regional economy are, first, a heavy dependence on agriculture, with the highest proportion of labour employed in the primary sector of any region – forty-six per cent. The primary sector generates twenty-seven per cent of the regional GDP. The principal products are olives, wine, oil seeds and forestry products (cork, holm-oaks and eucalyptus). Agriculture in the region is dominated by large farms with low levels of mechanisation and irrigation.

Second, the region has traditionally suffered from high unemployment, low wages and emigration, principally to the Lisbon-Tagus Valley region. The result is an increasingly unbalanced age structure: twenty per cent of the population are under fifteen years old, and those over sixty-five constitute seventeen per cent of the total.

Third, while manufacturing industry is underdeveloped, mining does make a significant contribution to the regional economy, mostly marble, granite and, more recently, tin.

Fourth, the Algarve presents a contrasting picture to the Alentejo. It has a buoyant economy as a result of its role as the country's major tourist region. The structure of employment reflects the role played by tourism: forty-eight per cent of the workforce is employed in the tertiary sector, twenty-seven per cent in the secondary sector (canned fish, cork etc.) and only twenty-five per cent in agriculture. However, unlike the rest of southern agriculture, much of the farming is highly productive. Intensive farming methods exploit the advantages accruing from over 3,000 hours of sunshine to cultivate early-ripening citrus fruit, vegetables and flowers.

## AGRICULTURE

The diminishing contribution made by agriculture to the country's GDP in no way reflects its importance to Portuguese life and society. About seventeen per cent of all families still draw all or part of their income from agriculture, and in many regions farming is a significant complementary employment activity. In 1990, agriculture still employed an estimated eighteen per cent of the workforce – still a high share compared to the EC average – although it only accounted for six per cent of GDP. In 1988, agricultural output by value was headed by cereals (wheat, maize etc.), rice, vegetables (tomatoes and potatoes), wines and fruits. In terms of animal livestock, cows and pigs were the most important. Almost half of Portugal's territory is under cultivation, but both labour productivity and yields are less than a third of the European average. As a result, Portugal is heavily dependent on imports for around fifty per cent of its food and animal feedstuff requirements.

The reasons for the sector's backwardness are fourfold, starting with ill-suited and inefficient land use. In many cases, soil conditions are inappropriate for the crops grown, and other potential uses, such as forestry, are often ignored. Two factors explain this: first, protectionism and subsidies encourage farming, especially cereal-growing, on marginal land; and second the persistence of subsistence agriculture on small family farms stands in the way of better land use.

The second reason for agricultural backwardness is the climatic conditions, such as irregular rainfall and a damaging drought during the early 1990s.

Third, the small size of farm holdings in the north and centre region means that ninety per cent of the farms occupy less than four hectares of land each, and nowhere does farm size exceed ten hectares. Indeed, the fragmentation is at its most extreme in Viana do Castelo, Aveiro and Oporto, where the average farm size is 1.53, 1.92 and 1.94 hectares respectively. The polarisation has tended to increase, and efficient medium-sized farms which underpin more successful European agricultural structures are the exception.

Finally, historic underinvestment in both infrastructure and farming means that levels of technology, mechanisation and commercialisation are notoriously low in the small-farm sector. Irrigation is particularly deficient and benefits no more than thirty per cent of the small-sized units, fifteen per cent of medium-sized units and only five per cent of the large estates. Another indicator is that Portugal has only 2.8 tractors per 100 hectares cultivated, compared to a European average of 10.9 (Spain 3.2, Greece 4.6). It does not help that the state has a record of underinvestment in rural infrastructure (roads, extension services, commercialisation) and that the upheavals following the land reforms in the mid-1970s and uncertainties since have discouraged investment in the larger farms.

The prospects for the future of Portuguese agriculture are that the severe contraction in employment will continue – EC estimates put the number of jobs that must disappear at 200,000. Inevitably, the necessary restructuring will be painful, as the upsurge in farmers' protests against the CAP during 1991 demonstrated. Farming communities throughout Portugal are caught in a pincer between lower guaranteed prices for their produce and rising costs for the factors of production (interest rates, petroleum, pesticides, machinery etc.). The paradox is that, without improvements in productivity, a contracting workforce will be unable to improve the domestically-grown food supplies to satisfy the home market, and many young farmers, who have benefited from government incentives since 1985, will be forced to quit the industry.

## INDUSTRIAL POLICY

The history and structure of Portuguese industry during the past thirty years has been shaped by macroeconomic policies pursued by successive governments and the uncertainties caused by extended periods of political instability. Consequently, the pattern of industrial development has been inconsistent, with periods of rapid growth followed by slow or negative growth and recession. Under Salazar, industrial policy was dominated by protectionism and state regulation which induced some growth but imposed a straitjacket on the development of the sector. Until the 1950s, the portfolio of industries remained limited to textiles, cork, beverages, metallurgy, mining and chemicals. When growth and diversification accelerated during the 1960s, the pace of industrial change was slow and lagged behind that achieved elsewhere in the booming European economies.

Initially, the thrust of industrial policy focused on the easier options provided by import-substitution and selling to the captive colonial markets. Moreover, only a limited number of families associated with the regime were permitted to develop new industries. As a result, many sectors still remained uncompetitive in world terms, the only exceptions being some textile and clothing firms which began to respond to the opportunities available in the European markets.

Eventually, a new industrial policy was devised in the late 1960s which aimed to enlarge Portugal's international specialisation and boost exports, particularly of durable goods. It was based on Portugal's perceived comparative advantages by exploiting its geographical location (oil-refining, shipbuilding and repair), natural resources (pyrites and other minerals) and proximity to European markets (assembly plants, manufactured goods). Initially the results were impressive: manufacturing and mining output grew at an average annual rate of just under fifteen per cent in the decade after 1963 (EIU 1989). To provide energy and intermediate goods for the expanding industrial sector, the government created a number of large-scale complexes such as the steel plants at Seixal and Maia, the Lisnave and Setenave shipyards and, most ambitious of all, the Sines deep-water port and industrial complex (petrochemicals, steel, pyrite mining and processing).

Unfortunately for the planners, by the time many of the projects were due to come on stream, the international economic crisis had rendered them obsolete or in need of radical reconsideration. However, just when hard-headed economic decisions, such as the cancellation or severe pruning of some projects, needed to be taken, changing political circumstances made any such rethinking impossible. Industrial policy became largely defensive and driven by social, rather than economic, goals. It prioritised job protection, which required ever-increasing subsidies, and generated a serious problem of low profitability in industry (Martins 1987). As a result, the industrial structure suffered serious distortions for over a decade following the 1974 revolution.

Huge public-sector losses and constitutional restrictions on denationalisation made it impossible to pursue a consistent and realistic industrial strategy until the second half of the 1980s. Then the coincidence of a reforming, pro-private-enterprise government and access to substantial EC funds made some progress on structural changes possible. The stated aim since 1985 has been to foster 'an integrated, logical, coherent and versatile industrial system' and to put manufacturing industry on a competitive footing. According to the prime minister, Cavaco Silva, private enterprise, not the state, is the 'true, irreplaceable source of economic and social development' (Financial Times Survey 1985). To meet the demands of post-1992 Europe and a more competitive international environment, attempts began to modernise an outmoded industrial structure and to overcome technological and managerial insufficiencies. Accordingly, the emphasis has switched to overhauling state-owned industries, introducing new technologies, modernising the legal framework in which business operates and improving education and training.

### THE SHAPE OF PORTUGUESE INDUSTRY

The evolution of industrial policy as outlined briefly above bequeathed a distorted and peculiar manufacturing structure. The main, interrelated features can be summarised as follows.

First, there is the fragmented and underdeveloped nature of many firms. There are only a handful of large companies or groups, other than public companies and the subsidiaries of foreign multinationals. The economy is highly dependent on a small number of large firms for its dynamism and growth. In 1990, the ten largest companies by turnover were: Petrogal (petroleum products and retailing), EDP (electricity), TAP (air transport), CTT-Telecom (telecommunications), Renault Portuguesa (motor car manufacturer and distributor), Shell (petroleum retailing), Tabaqueira (cigarettes), Mobil (fuel retailing), Portucel (paper and pulp) and Modelo Supermercados (supermarkets) (EIU 1991c). The fact that the majority of firms are small-scale would not matter if they operated in a large domestic market, as in Italy, and if a vanguard of multinationals could lead the way in export markets (EIU 1989). However, the majority of firms are tiny as Table 3.5 demonstrates. Fragmentation does have a further consequence – despite

*Table 3.5*:    Size of Workforce by Firm.

| Number employed | Number of firms |
| --- | --- |
| 1–9 | 73,016 |
| 10–19 | 13,584 |
| 20–49 | 8,858 |
| 50–99 | 2,912 |
| 200–499 | 746 |
| 500+ | 343 |
| Total | 105,859 |

widespread nationalisation during the mid-1970s, smaller firms escaped, and consequently more than half of industrial production is still in private hands.

In 1987, the vast majority of Portuguese firms (85.6 per cent) employed fewer than twenty workers each, and almost three-quarters of them had fewer than ten workers according to MESS survey figures. Indeed, firms with fewer than ten employees are the norm in practically all sectors with the exception of the water-supply industry and communications. The incidence of small firms is highest in retailing and commerce, personal and domestic services, hotel and catering and forestry. The largest concentrations of workers per firm are to be found in the manufacturing sector, especially textiles, clothing and leather goods.

Second, industrial activities are tightly concentrated in a limited geographical area along a coastal axis running from the Lisbon-Tagus Valley to Oporto, rather than being spread evenly around the country. Twenty-nine per cent of the total number of firms are located in the Lisbon area and employ 29.2 per cent of the economically active population. The figures for Oporto are 19.1 per cent and 27.7 per cent respectively. Apart from acting as a magnet for large, modern industries, small businesses cluster in the two principal urban centres – 41.6 per cent of firms with fewer than ten workers are located in the Lisbon-Tagus Valley region and 33.7 per cent on the northern littoral. It should be noted that, until recently, poor communications were a hindrance to business even in the littoral corridor.

Third, production is concentrated in a limited range of activities. In fact, the pattern of specialisation has changed remarkably little over the past fifteen years. The reliance on traditional industries such as textiles, footwear, leather goods, cork, wood products and ceramics has accentuated rather than diminished.

Fourth, industry is highly dependent on cheap labour to maintain its competitiveness. Low wages allowed labour-intensive industries to grow strongly during the 1960s and 1970s. While the general trend elsewhere in Europe was to shed labour, Portugal's traditional industries successfully created employment – for instance, the workforce in the textile industry expanded by fifty-five per cent between 1965 and 1977. Employment remained stable throughout the 1980s because of the stimulus provided by accession to the EC; but, by the end of the decade, wages costs were rising and Portuguese producers faced severe competition from the Far East and eastern Europe. As a result, restructuring became an urgent necessity – between fifteen and twenty per cent of the firms in the textile and clothing sector are expected to disappear, and employment will fall by thirty per cent.

Fifth, productivity levels are low. Both small and large firms suffer from overstaffing, use resources and energy inefficiently and employ outdated technologies, and management is often poorly trained. However, there is a high degree of diversity in terms of competitiveness and performance among firms manufacturing the same products. Small family firms, often disinclined or unable to invest in new technology, skills training or quality upgrading, will find it hard to survive in the post-1992 business environment. Firms that rely almost exclusively on the payment of the lowest possible wages in order to maintain their competitiveness coexist alongside a handful of firms displaying innovation and entrepreneurial drive. It is the latter that are the prime movers in the industrial investment boom – up seventy per cent in the four years between 1986 and 1990.

Sixth, industry is highly dependent on imported technology. Portugal acts as a base for assembly operations and produces goods under licence or patent. Among OECD countries, only Turkey has fewer patents per inhabitant than Portugal – 1.8 per 100,000 in 1987 compared to Spain's ten, Ireland's thirty-five and Greece's sixteen. There is a trend towards joint ventures with multinationals but also a noticeable shift towards disinvestment, particularly in the electronics sector, as foreign companies close down their operations, principally because Portugal has ceased to be a country of comparatively cheap labour. This is a worrying development in the light of a joint survey conducted by the Banco de Fomento Nacional and IPE, which indicated that only the larger companies planned to develop new products, upgrade quality, adopt new technologies and revamp their pricing policies.

Seventh, foreign ownership is most predominant in the electronics, car assembly and components, pharmaceuticals and food industries. Three-quarters of the electrical goods sector is controlled by multinationals such as IBM, Sony, Rank Xerox, Unisys and Olivetti. In 1991, there were 132 multinationals with subsidiaries in the country, of which seventy-two were based in EC countries and twenty-nine in the United States (see Table 3.6). The largest foreign firms ranked in terms of turnover were Renault Portuguesa, Shell, Mobil Oil, Renault Gest, Fiat Credit Portugal, Ford Lusitania, General Motors de Portugal, BP Portuguesa and Fiat Auto Portuguesa (Chislett 1991). Foreign-owned firms have shown the strongest growth in recent years: their sales grew by twenty-one per cent on average, compared to less than seventeen per cent for the top 500 firms.

*Table 3.6*:   Multinationals in Portugal: Distribution by Country.

| UK | 16 | USA | 29 |
|---|---|---|---|
| Germany | 13 | Switzerland | 12 |
| France | 11 | Japan | 5 |
| Spain | 9 | Finland | 4 |
| Italy | 8 | Brazil | 3 |
| Netherlands | 7 | Sweden | 3 |
| Denmark | 4 | Colombia | 1 |
| Belgium | 3 | Hong Kong | 1 |
| Luxembourg | 1 | South Korea | 1 |
| EC | 72 | Angola | 1 |

*Source*: *Exame* 1991a.

Finally, new firm creation accelerated noticeably following EC accession. Around half of all registered companies were established after 1985 – some 80,000 annually. These figures bear witness to a revolution among the Portuguese workforce, particularly since the procedures for starting a new business are so long-winded and strewn with bureaucratic hurdles. The obstacles confronting Portuguese entrepreneurs can be gauged from the average time taken to establish a new business throughout the EC, ranging from one to five days in the UK, one to four weeks in Spain, a month in France, eight to ten weeks in Germany and three to six months in Portugal. Given such a strong rate of new firm creation, it might be expected that the business failure rate would be correspondingly high. Paradoxically, Portugal has one of the lowest failure rates in Europe – not the result of any unique qualities displayed by Portuguese businessmen, but because of the complicated administrative processes associated with liquidation.

The problems that confront Portuguese industry are best examined by focusing more closely on specific sectors. Space does not permit a comprehensive survey, but the examples have been chosen to illustrate some of the strengths and weaknesses of the Portuguese economy and to indicate the challenges that lie ahead: the dominant activity in the manufacturing structure (textiles, clothing and footwear), a heavy industry (shipbuilding and repair), an important export-oriented industry (ceramics), an agro-industrial industry (paper, pulp and cork), a centuries-old agricultural activity (wine and port wine), a declining traditional primary activity (fishing), the more buoyant extractive sector (mining) and finally the expanding services sector (retailing, tourism and banking).

## TEXTILES AND CLOTHING

The textile industry produces a broad range of goods which range from clothing, knitwear, thread and cloth to leather goods and footwear. The industry can trace its ancestory back to the thirteenth century. Since the seventeenth century, it has survived behind protectionist barriers which were strengthened during the era of autarkic development from the 1930s to the 1970s. The textile industry acquired 'Third World' characteristics such as the use of child labour, the payment of extremely low wages, the avoidance of social security payments, a reliance on cheap cotton imports from the colonies and the captive, undemanding African markets in which to sell their mass-produced output. A shift to greater dependence on the European market for cheap cotton goods came when Portugal joined EFTA in 1960. Buoyant external demand led to a rapid expansion in the number of firms in the clothing sector, from 273 in 1973 to over 1,000 by the mid-1980s (EIU 1988). After 1974, the industry faced a series of upheavals – the loss of colonial suppliers and customers, a new system of industrial relations, a much enhanced state presence in the economy and curtailed demand in the principal export markets – but managed to survive thanks to a combination of low wages and protectionism.

A new challenge came with accession to the EC in 1986. As the tariff barriers against non-EC imports came down, Portugal's vulnerability to undercutting by low-cost Asian and Third World clothing exporters was exposed. Between 1985 and 1990, Portuguese firms experienced an increase of between twenty and twenty-five per cent in their costs of production above those of their Third World competitors and of between fifteen and twenty per cent above those of high-quality manufacturers in Italy, France and the UK. A further threat is posed by the failure to reach a consensus over the Multi-fibre Agreement (MFA), which expired in July 1991. Fears were expressed that half of Portugal's textile industry might disappear if the agreement was not renewed. In its own interests, Portugal wants a gradual liberalisation and a fifteen-year transition period in order to allow for extensive restructuring of its textile sector. The problems arise because textile production is one of the most globalised industries, in which competition is always chasing the cheapest production centres, determined usually by low wages, and is traditionally associated with countries in the early stages of industrial development.

During the 1980s, textiles became the largest industrial sector, and its share of manufactured value added actually increased by four per cent – very much against the trend across Europe, where contraction was the norm. It is the largest employer, with around 200,000 workers (predominantly female) or twenty-eight per cent of the industrial workforce. Figures for 1986 show employment by sub-sector as follows: spinning and weaving 73,000, clothing 47,000, knitwear 31,000, footwear 24,000 and woollen fibres 20,000 (Eaton 1991b). The industry is also the country's foremost exporter, accounting for around thirty per cent of the total, and is the biggest single foreign-currency earner. In the 1980s, the sector's exports grew at around ten per cent per annum and rose in value from 342 billion escudos in 1986 to 685 billion escudos in 1990. In fact, Portugal has the highest specialisation rate in textiles, footwear and clothing among the EC12. The industrial structure is highly dependent on this sector, which accounts for forty per cent of industrial output and twenty-seven per cent of manufacturing value added (compared to twenty-three per cent in Greece, sixteen per cent in Italy and eleven per cent in Spain).

The industry's structure is very fragmented, particularly the cloth, thread and woollen sectors, where the practice of sub-contracting is common. The majority of the 2,500 textile concerns employ fewer than fifty workers each. It is also concentrated geographically in the north and central interior, principally in the districts of Oporto, Braga, Castelo Branco, Santarém, Guarda and Coimbra. In particular zones such as the north's Vale de Ave, which comprises the districts of Santo Tirso, Guimarães, Familicão and Fafe, seventy-five per cent of employment is in manufacturing industry, overwhelmingly in textiles. Some firms located in the north-west are export-oriented, while those situated in the interior are more backward and less outward-looking. This is underlined by the fact that just five companies account for ninety per cent of textile exports: Manual Gonçalves, Riopele, Coelima (one of the largest European manufacturers of bed-linen), Somelos and José M. Almeida were the leading firms ranked by sales volume in 1990. They are large establishments using modern technology, with established overseas distribution networks. Significantly, only one Portuguese textile producer appears in the world's top 250 firms. Apart from a handful of medium-sized operations, the majority of firms are small-scale and use obsolete technology – Eaton (1991b) estimates that around fifty per cent of the industry's plant predates 1974 and that much imported machinery is second-hand.

Clothing, which has expanded noticeably in recent years to meet the strong demand from its principal customers in Western Europe, is made up of around 1,000, mostly tiny, firms and accounts for a third of textile exports and fifty-five per cent of its production value. However, the footwear sector expanded most during the 1980s, and Portugal is now the fifth-largest producer within the EC, with a nine per cent share of the market in 1989 behind Italy (37.6 per cent), Spain (seventeen per cent), France (15.7 per cent) and the UK (10.7 per cent). In contrast to cutbacks elsewhere in Europe, Portugal has doubled its output of shoes during the last five years and is second only to Italy in the list of exporting countries in intra-Community trade (European Commission 1991a). The sub-sector comprises around 1,000 firms employing 50,000 workers. On average they produce 105,000,000 pairs of shoes annually, of which eighty per cent are exported. Given the heavy concentration on exports, the shortfall in satisfying domestic demand necessitated the import of 13,700,000 pairs in 1991. In future, the footwear industry needs to reconquer its own domestic market and fight off competition from producers such as China, Morocco, Indonesia and eastern Europe – a task made more difficult by the steady appreciation of the escudo.

The mini-boom enjoyed by the textiles industry during 1986–7 in response to increased demand from western Europe only temporarily disguised the serious structural flaws that afflict many subsectors. The crisis that threatens wholesale closures and job losses has multiple causes: overstaffing – one estimate suggests by as much as forty per cent (EIU 1988) – and low productivity levels, outdated machinery, poor quality and design and a failure to open up new markets (Chislett 1991). The industry is further hampered by inadequate managerial skills and the lack of central government investment in the physical and social infrastructure of the regions in which the industry is located.

A worrying feature for production centres hit by the current crisis, such as the Vale de Ave, is that alternative sources of employment for workers made redundant are scarce. In Covilhã (Castelo Branco district), where the woollen goods industry is the largest employer, seventeen firms have closed with the loss of 2,000 jobs. One of the leading textile firms, Coelima, cited high interest rates and a downturn in demand when it requested government assistance in order to avoid bankruptcy. Restructuring is under way, and 50,000 jobs are likely to go as part of an estimated Esc 750 billion reconversion programme spread over fifteen years. This will involve mergers and acquisitions in order to forge groups capable of competing in the world market, investment in design and marketing in order to upgrade and diversify the portfolio of products and the introduction of modern production processes. However, restructuring projects could run into difficulties because up to eighty per cent of the workforce in the woollen goods industry are illiterate or barely literate. Technology can only be introduced successfully if the workforce is trained, and firms are already complaining that funds for such purposes are inadequate. In the meantime, the fear is that Portugal will be transformed into a mere production platform for foreign-owned forms and low-cost suppliers for European chain-stores, thereby severely curtailing the industry's ability to innovate and respond to changing patterns of demand.

### SHIPBUILDING AND REPAIR

Portugal's shipbuilding and repair industry has had a chequered history since the decision was taken in 1971 that its geographical position astride some of the world's major shipping routes could be exploited to cater for the expected new demands from the international shipping industry. Shipyards that rivalled anything the Norwegians, Swedish or Japanese could offer were built to repair and overhaul supertankers on their way to the Persian Gulf, and a tanker-flushing unit was installed. Modern handling facilities and a giant silo erected on the south bank of the Tagus for storing animal feeds were designed to make Lisbon a match for Rotterdam as a premier entrepot port. Setenave became an object of national pride because it appeared to open a new chapter in the country's long maritime history. Moreover, it constituted one of the few modern sectors in Portuguese industry and had an international outlook. Lisnave (Estaleiros Navais de Lisboa) boasted 2.7 kilometres of repair jetties and handled around twenty per cent of the world's supertanker fleet at its peak. However, the construction side of the business was dealt a severe blow when tankers were laid up during the 1973–4 oil crisis. After 25 April 1974, the industry's workforce was in the vanguard of labour unrest and political activity. Following nationalisation in 1976, orders were lost as the industry grappled with rising wage costs, a burgeoning workforce (swollen from 1,400 to 6,200) and a crippling strike record. Labour disputes transformed Lisbon into Europe's fifth-most expensive port, while Leixões (Oporto) ranked even higher in second place.

As both a strategic industry and a large employer of labour, decisions on the future of shipbuilding and repair were shaped by political rather than economic imperatives. Orders lost during 1975 were never recouped, and, for much of the 1970s, empty order books and large overheads could only be carried with the help of government subsidies and loans from the nationalised banking sector. The labour laws made it difficult to shed workers, which meant that often over 2,000 workers on the payroll were idle. During the early 1980s, when the second oil shock led to a contraction in world demand, the industry was racked by strikes, occupations, unpaid wages and crippling losses. Lisnave came close to bankruptcy as losses mounted from 5,000,000 contos in 1983 to 11,000,000 three years later. However, 1986 proved to be a turning point: the series of social contracts signed between the UGT and the government and renewed annually guaranteed a strike-free period. The workforce was slimmed to 3,700 and the debts rescheduled. In 1988, 132 ships were repaired, more than its nearest rivals in the world market in Singapore and South Korea. A year later, competition between Lisnave and Setenave was ended when Lisnave joined forces with a Norwegian company to establish Solisnor and a deal was sealed with Chevron to service the forty tankers in the multinational company's fleet. By 1990, the repair business was enjoying a boom because, faced with falling freight rates, shipowners chose to repair existing tonnage rather than gamble by ordering expensive new vessels. In that year, Solisnor and Lisnave repaired 236 tankers and cargo vessels – more than Germany, France, Greece and Spain combined – and accounted for fifteen per cent of the world's ship-repair market.

Within two years, the cyclical nature of demand was clearly demonstrated when the industry faced another major crisis. In part, the difficulties arose because competitiveness depended not only on labour costs and shipyard facilities but also on expensive imports. By 1991, Solisnor's Norwegian backers had departed and the yards' future depended on fresh orders or rescue by a

*Table 3.7*:    Major European Shipyards 1989.

|                              | Tonnage handled | Ships |
|------------------------------|-----------------|-------|
| Lisnave (Portugal)           | 12,381,481      | 123   |
| Setenave (Portugal)          | 4,595,363       | 45    |
| Blohm and Voss (Ger.)        | 4,376,018       | 68    |
| Arno-Dunkerque (Fr.)         | 4,343,429       | 65    |
| Hellenic Shipyards (Gr.)     | 4,115,295       | 55    |
| Astilleros Espanoles (Sp.)   | 3,417,776       | 55    |

*Source*: Financial Times Survey 1990.

foreign buyer. An even bigger crisis afflicted the builders of fishing vessels, such as Foznave (Figueira da Foz) and São Jacinto (Aveiro), as orders were won by Spanish yards because of the attractive financial incentives on offer despite Portuguese claims that they breached EC rules. The one bright spot amid the gloom was provided by Estaleiros de Viana do Castelo (ENVC), the largest industrial unit and employer (1,500 people) in the Alto Minho. A lengthy programme of modernisation and restructuring, which enabled the yards to match the productivity levels achieved in northern Europe, appeared to be in jeopardy when the former Soviet Union cancelled all its contracts following the collapse of communist rule. Fortunately for ENVC, the Ukraine promised to honour the contracts and requested the conversion of warships into vessels for civilian use.

## CERAMICS

The ceramics industry embraces tilemaking (azulejos), earthenware, china, sanitary ware, tableware and household goods. The tilemaking tradition dates back to the mid-fifteenth century, while more recently some Portuguese companies made their reputations as makers of china (Viste Alegre) and glass crystal (Atlantis). Portugal benefits from four centuries of design expertise and the availability of domestic supplies of the essential raw materials, for which there is a growing demand in overseas markets. The majority of firms in the industry are small and medium-sized and located on the coastal littoral north of Lisbon. Production methods vary across the subsectors ranging from traditional labour-intensive to high-technology forms. Manual work comprises a high proportion of production costs, as does energy (up to twenty per cent of costs) because of the high-temperature firing processes, and transport is an important additional cost because of weight.

Portugal is the sixth-biggest producer of ceramic goods in the EC12, valued at Ecu 292,000,000 in 1989 compared with Italy's Ecu 4.6 billion and Spain's Ecu 1.705 billion (European Commission 1991a). The restricted home market forced the industry to seek export outlets, which has required an adjustment from the lower end of the market to high-value-added products. By the late 1980s, thirty per cent of total production was exported – almost double the proportion recorded a decade earlier – to the major clients in Spain, the USA, Germany and Italy. In 1988, ornamental ware represented fifty-six per cent of exports (20.5 million contos), stimulated by a growing demand abroad for traditional styles.

The ceramics industry experienced strong growth in the 1980s and was one of the first sectors to recognise the need to restructure and invest in the introduction of new technologies and expand its productive capacity. A particular feature is the role played by foreign capital in the modernisation process. The Kuwait Investment Office (KIO) now controls some of the largest ceramic companies (azulejos and floor tiles), while Spanish firms acquired a foothold in the industry when the Roca group bought out a Leiria-based producer of tiles and sanitary ware in 1990. Consolidation is also taking place among national producers: companies involved in raw-material extraction have merged, and Fábrica de Porcelana da Vista Alegre (FPVA) fused with Cerexport to establish a ceramics group capable of meeting the post-1992 challenge.

Despite the willingness to modernise and adapt, the industry does face multiple problems: competition from rivals such as Spain and, more recently, Third World exporters; high and mounting energy costs; the end of protection after 1992; a slowdown in the building industry; high interest rates and difficulties in creating a high-quality image to promote sales abroad. The more traditional sectors are now experiencing labour shortages. For instance, the ceramics industry around Barcelos traditionally relies on homeworkers to carry out what is regarded as 'dirty work'. Many workers prefer employment in the textile industry, where wages are higher and working conditions better. In addition, a price war has broken out, with some firms selling at below production costs in order to stay in the market.

PAPER AND PULP

Forestry is one of the great success stories of Portuguese agriculture, proving to be a major export earner and supplying a paper pulp industry that successfully utilises domestically-grown resources. It is an example of an industry that exploits the country's natural advantages: the climate and soils are ideal for forestry, and haulage costs are minimal because, unlike Canada and Sweden, the raw materials are situated close to the mills and, of course, labour costs are substantially lower than among its competitors.

Forests cover over 3,000,000 hectares of the national territory and comprise forty-six per cent pine, four per cent cork and eight per cent eucalyptus. The industry expanded during the 1980s because more land became available for afforestation as the cultivation of other crops declined. The modern pulp industry is over sixty years old and suffered from many of the defects that afflicted industry in general, namely undercapitalisation and an excess of small firms (ninety paper mills) crying out for rationalisation. However, the industry has undergone a major transformation in recent years into a modern, efficient industry and a world leader, alongside Brazil and South Africa, in specialised sectors such as high-quality paper.

Expansion has caused a shortage of raw materials, and the EC-funded PEDAP launched a ten-year afforestation programme. However, excessive expansion led to complaints, and eventually restrictive legislation, to control the proliferation of eucalyptus plantations. By 1990, there were 500,000 hectares under eucalyptus forest. Environmentalists objected on the basis that the tree is destructive because it drains water and nutrients from the soil and underground reservoirs to the detriment of neighbouring crops. Protests at the damage caused by eucalyptus planting did provoke violent clashes between farmers and the police in the affected regions. Nevertheless, the eucalyptus is the fastest-growing and most economical source of pulp. Compared to pine, which takes forty years to reach maturity, the eucalyptus yields four or five crops in a lifespan of ten to fifteen years before uprooting is necessary.

The largest company in the sector is the state-run Portucel, established in 1976 from a fusion of five ailing companies. It is a major landowner, owning 100,000 hectares or about one per cent of the national territory, a large earner of foreign currency (about eighty per cent of Portucel's capacity is exported) and it produces about 800,000 tons of wood pulp annually. The company has two industrial complexes at Cacia and Setúbal and owns six mills producing pulp, paper and corrugated board. Prior to imminent denationalisation, Portucel has initiated a major investment programme in order to be able to match its modern, efficient competitors in the world market. As part of the rationalisation programme, the Setúbal paper-pulp mill joined with neighbouring papermaker Papéis Inapa (thirty-four per cent owned by Portucel) to integrate their production lines in order to incorporate the latest pollution controls and energy economies, which involve the burning of bark and sawdust to produce energy.

The 'four sisters' who traditionally dominate the pulp industry are Portucel, Soporcel, Celbi and Caima. Soporcel (Sociedade Portuguesa de Celulose) produces 300,000 tonnes a year from its mills that include Europe's largest pulp mill at Lavos, near Figueira da Foz, which produces high-grade eucalyptus pulp. The company has 55,000 hectares of forest planted, but shortfalls in supply oblige it to import substantial quantities from South America. There are plans to double the Lavos plant's capacity and introduce a new copy-paper production line in the near future. Celbi, a Swedish-owned company, produces 240,000 tonnes annually, and Caima, which has a majority British shareholding, takes only a small share of the market (120,000 tonnes in 1988). The four largest firms have been joined by a new arrival, Renova, which specialises in tissue-paper production, of which sixty per cent is exported to the Spanish market.

Portugal is the world leader in cork production, with around sixty per cent of the market (Spain is in second place with just under twenty per cent). Although Portugal produces cork for insulation and floor tiling, there is a marked dependence on bottle corks (Chislett 1991). Ninety per cent of production is destined for the world market. The principal customers are France, Germany and the USA, where cork is used by the wine trade, the building industry, motor manufacturers and the footwear industry. Cork exports have boomed in recent years, rising in value from 37,800,000 contos in 1986 to 81,500,000 contos in 1990. Nevertheless, its share in forestry export composition has declined steadily during the same period, and in 1990 it contributed approximately twenty-seven per cent of the total.

There is one dominant company in the cork industry (Amorin), but, in general, production is carried out by small firms (around 900 employ 16,000 workers), and only five per cent of them have more than 100 on the payroll. While the raw material originates in the Alentejo and Trás-os-Montes, production is mainly located in the Aveiro region, where about seventy per cent of the labour force is to be found. However, a threat to the industry's future is posed by the spread of disease among the cork oaks caused by a bark weevil. It is believed that the disease affects about twelve per cent of the trees in some areas because intensive farming has reduced the amount of potassium in the soil on which the oak thrives. The true extent of the problem will not be known for some time, because cork cannot legally be stripped from the oak until it is between twenty and twenty-five years old, and many trees are productive for up to 120 years.

WINE AND PORT WINE

For centuries, Portugal has been a major wine-exporter, and at the time of writing she is seventh in the world table of wine-producers, with 363,500 hectares devoted to viniculture. Exports have grown steadily from 410,000 hectolitres in 1974 to 702,738 hectolitres in 1989, following aggressive and imaginative marketing of the successful Mateus Rosé brand and the vinho verde wines orchestrated by Sogrape. In fact, until recently, little attention was paid to the promotion of domestically-produced wines. The Portuguese are the world's fourth-biggest wine-drinkers, with over fifty litres per head in 1990, and strong internal demand meant that wine-growers felt little incentive to raise their quality to export standards.

In order to overcome the image as a producer of low-quality wines, quality controls were introduced and nine demarcated regions (*regiões demarcadas*) identified: Algarve, Bairrada, Bucelas, Carcavelos, Colares, Dão, Madeira, Setúbal and the vinho verde region, which together account for fifteen per cent of total wine production. Five demarcated regions in the Alentejo have recently been added, and a further twenty-one situated in the north and east of the country hope for similar recognition. However, the answer to overproduction is not to be found in exports, because there is already excessive supply on world markets. In an effort to tackle the problem, approximately 4,000,000 hectares devoted to vine growing have been abandoned since Portugal joined the EC.

Port wine comes from Europe's oldest demarcated region but accounts for less than six per cent of the country's wine production. In 1990, exports totalled 661,698 hectolitres (down 3.6 per cent on 1990), valued at 40,000,000 contos. EC entry gave a stimulus to sales as duties were eased. The EC absorbs ninety per cent of port wine sales, with France still the leading market despite its share falling from forty-two per cent in 1989 to 25.8 per cent in 1991. It is followed by Belgium and Luxembourg, with the UK somewhat surprisingly, since vinho do porto has long been known as 'the Englishman's wine', only the third-most important market.

Traditional labour-intensive methods are still practised in the port wine industry, and many of the grapes are cultivated on steep terraces in the Douro valley where the use of agricultural machinery is inappropriate. However, wage costs and a growing shortage of skilled labour are gradually forcing a tradition-bound industry to employ more capital-intensive methods, especially with regard to its bottling operations. Foreign investors play a prominent role, with major names like Delaforce and Croft owned by the UK Grand Metropolitan group, Sandemans by Seagrams, Cockburns and Martinez by Allied-Lyons and Offley by Martini Rossi. Real Companhia Velha, Niepoort, Borges Barros, Noval and Ferriera are the leading national companies.

The structure of the industry makes it vulnerable during the world recession and militates against modernisation. The commercial side is dominated by twelve major companies, which sell ninety-five per cent of the port wine produced and exert control through the Instituto do Vinho do Porto (IVP – Port Wine Institute) which regulates the trade. In 1991, conflicts arose between the shippers and the producers over the large quantities of poor-quality wine entering the market. The shippers, who market high-quality port, want the government to end overproduction and bring supply into line with demand. They also want the areas allowed to produce port to be redefined and, following the example of Spain's hard-pressed sherry industry, the grubbing-up of surplus vineyards.

The predominance of small producers cultivating their vines on tiny plots also obstructs change. The majority are now grouped in over 300 cooperatives set up to ensure economies of scale, improve distribution and facilitate the use of more capital-intensive methods. Two further problems hinder the transformation of the industry: the rosé wines on which the industry prospered are declining in popularity, while cheap labour and old skills are no longer available in abundance as they once were. Additional pressures are being exerted on Madeira another traditional, fortified wine. The four different varieties of wine (Malmsey, Bual, Verdelho and Sercial) account for about a fifth of Madeira's exports. Competition from alternative sources of income, such as banana production, is progressively taking over land once used to grow grapes. In response to falling demand, the producers have set about improving production techniques and upgrading the image (*Financial Times* 1992).

In continental Portugal, some regions are starting to benefit from foreign investment. Alcantara SA (sixty per cent owned by Tate and Lyle) acquired the 135 hectare Quinta Romeira estate in the Bucelas region and employ the latest production techniques to market high-quality wines for the European market. In addition, grants from the EC Guidance Fund and other sources have encouraged the grubbing-up of old vines and replanting with new ones to produce high-quality wines and dried and table grapes.

### FISHING

Although Portugal boasts the oldest fishing fleet in Europe, the majority of vessels are outdated and of small tonnage, productivity is low, port facilities require to be updated and the canning industry is antiquated. Fishing only represents one per cent of GDP but is a prime source of employment for people living in coastal and island communities. There are high-seas fishing ports at Lisbon, Aveiro and Matosinhos, while coastal and trawler fisheries are based in Portimão and Setúbal. The numbers employed in the industry declined from 36,000 in the 1950s to 26,000 in 1974. However, the government promoted the fishing industry as a source of employment and economic growth during the 1980s, and between 1982 and 1987 there was a fifteen per cent rise (5,740) in the numbers employed in fishing (Wise 1984).

From running a trade surplus in fisheries, Portugal has become a net importer. This is partly explained by high domestic consumption levels: on average, each Portuguese eats between forty-five and fifty kilos of fish annually – the highest in Europe. However, cod (*bacalhau*), once a staple dish for every Portuguese family, is now extremely expensive. Fish catches are still declining (361,000 tons in 1988) for a variety of reasons: overfishing by Spanish factory ships, increased competition for dwindling stocks and the access to Portuguese territorial waters given to foreign fishing fleets. The traditional sardine-canning industry is hampered by overcapacity, aged machinery and declining fish stocks, and its prospects in regions such as the Algarve have been further undermined by the existence of alternative sources of employment in tourism.

The fish-canning industry comprises around fifty firms employing 8,000 workers and is mainly concentrated in the north and the Algarve. Canned sardines represent a third of total Portuguese fish exports, although the tonnage is declining, down from 34,439 tons in 1984 to 23,658 in 1990 (see Table 3.8). Strong competition from Morocco in the principal markets in Germany and the UK has led to a search for alternatives as far afield as the former Soviet Union. In the Azores, thirty per cent of employment is still dependent on farming and fishing, and the latter accounts for two per cent of regional product. Some modernisation is taking place: EC funds are easing the reduction in the size of the EC's fishing fleet, and foreign investment is helping to improve efficiency and create jobs. Heinz acquired Peniche-based Marie Elisabeth in 1988, and within three years annual production increased from 18,000,000 to 43,000,000

*Table 3.8*:    Canned Fish Exports (in tons).

|      | Sardine | Mackerel | Tuna  | Anchovies | Total  |
|------|---------|----------|-------|-----------|--------|
| 1984 | 34,439  | 2,514    | 2,637 | 1,226     | 40,874 |
| 1985 | 30,962  | 4,577    | 3,051 | 1,137     | 39,845 |
| 1986 | 26,909  | 3,531    | 3,252 | 1,248     | 35,025 |
| 1987 | 22,329  | 3,005    | 2,711 | 1,106     | 29,249 |
| 1988 | 22,034  | 3,502    | 2,598 | 982       | 29,322 |
| 1989 | 26,372  | 3,746    | 4,159 | 990       | 35,335 |
| 1990 | 23,658  | 4,378    | 4,866 | 960       | 33,923 |

*Source*: *Expresso* 9 November 1991.

cans (ninety-five per cent destined for export). New developments, including aquaculture projects, are promoting diversification into the production of canned squid, octopus, anchovies, mackerel, mussels, tuna and salmon.

## MINING

Mining has registered spectacular growth during the past few years. Although in existence since the nineteenth century, when coal, iron ore and pyrites were extracted, the industry was constrained because the reserves were scattered geographically and not commercially exploitable. Nevertheless, rising demand and the application of modern technologies transformed the country into Europe's leading producer of copper, tin and tungsten (wolfram) and the world's second-largest exporter of marble and ornamental stones. The spectacular growth recorded in the late 1980s ensured that Portugal became a net non-energy minerals exporter for the first time in its history, producing almost a quarter of the EC's metallic mineral output in 1991.

The key to the boom is the Neves Corvo mine near Beja in the southern Alentejo, which is owned by Somincor and Rio Tinto Zinc. Its copper and tin reserves are considered to be one of the world's most significant mineral discoveries in recent years. The Panasqueira mine is also the only source of tungsten in the western world, and Portugal also boasts significant iron ore, uranium and gold deposits. The Jales mine in northern Portugal produces 250 kilos of gold and silver each year. As is the case with other industries, foreign investment plays a major role in developing the industry. Finland's Outukumpu-Oy is involved in a joint venture to run a copper-smelting plant at Sines, and EC finance helped to open the tungsten and tin mines in Trás-os-Montes. By the early 1990s, the mining boom threatened to be short-lived. The collapse in the world market price for tin (in part caused by Brazilian overproduction) and wolfram (exacerbated by Chinese dumping) forced many mines to suspend production or close altogether.

Portugal is the second-largest exporter of marble in the world. Ninety per cent of production comes from Borba, Estremoz and Vila Vicosa in the Alentejo, where over 130 companies extract some 500,000 tons annually. At present, most marble is exported in blocks, but in future it is hoped to develop the value-added content before it leaves the country.

## SERVICES

In common with other EC countries, services is the dominant sector in terms of employment and income. It is also the most diverse and divides into subsectors that include public administration, wholesale and retailing, banking, insurance and commercial services (accountancy, law etc.), education, health, transport and communications, construction and property development and tourism. The tertiary sector grew faster than any other sector in the 1980s and early 1990s but was not immune from the restructuring and rationalisation that agriculture and industry have been undergoing. By 1990, almost half the civilian working population (over 2,000,000) worked in the sector – double the number employed in the early 1970s. Significantly, the self-employed emerge as the largest single group.

The motor of growth in service-sector employment between 1968 and 1986 was public administration, but the dynamism was provided by private services in the second half of the 1980s. Total employment in public administration rose by 136 per cent over an eighteen-year period. However, the most spectacular increases occurred between 1968 and 1978, after which the rate of growth slowed considerably. Public administration personnel now represent 10.3 per cent of the total economically active and twenty-six per cent of the labour force in the tertiary sector. Employment figures for education and health are 183,028 and 92,853 respectively. Considerable reductions in the size of the public administration workforce are likely if the government succeeds in obtaining a change in the law to permit dismissals. The intention is to make savings by removing unqualified and superfluous staff. However, contrary to popular perceptions, the public administration is not overstaffed in European terms. At 5.5 per 100, Portugal has one of the lowest proportions of public employees per head of population – compared to Denmark's fifteen and an EC average of 7.4. When public-sector employment stagnated during the 1980s, expansion took place in banking and newer areas such as information technology, marketing and leisure-related activities.

The wholesale and retail sector had, until recently, barely entered the twentieth century. It is characterised by a large number of small outlets and low sales per establishment, low productivity and poor management, and by the uneven modernisation of the sector, with the large urban centres in the throes of a retail revolution while the interior (districts such as Castelo Branco, Portalegre, Bragança and Evora) remains hardly touched by the new developments. There are a number of reasons for the backwardness exhibited by the retail sector. The Portuguese have a much lower level of earnings and disposable income than the rest of Europe. In 1988, West German consumer expenditure was almost twenty-five times larger than Portugal's. In addition, the Portuguese have traditionally saved a large proportion (around twenty-five per cent) of their income. This is attributable to high interest rates, an unfamiliarity with modern shopping patterns and the dearth of consumer goods.

In contrast to general European trends, the number of retail outlets actually increased between 1976 and 1988 from 78,125 to 97,458 (Corporate Intelligence 1990). This surprising development is explained by the restricted geographical spread of supermarkets, the predilection among *retornados* for setting up in business and the stimulus to small outlets provided by tourism growth (souvenirs, bars etc.). As a consequence, the number of food and drink establishments (52,000 in 1988) is proportionally higher than in Spain, Italy and Greece. In terms of employment, just over fifty per cent of outlets in the sector are run by a single individual, while just under forty per cent employ between two and four people. Only slightly in excess of 1,000 had more than twenty employees each in 1988. The large urban centres dominate in the distribution of outlets, Lisbon having 23,400 and Oporto 14,000.

Modern retailing arrived when the first supermarket opened in Saldana, Lisbon, in 1961, but not until twenty years later did a retail boom begin. The first hypermarket opened in 1985, followed closely by the first shopping centres. By the end of the decade, there were 474 supermarkets and nine hypermarkets, with rapid future expansion in the pipeline. The shopping-centre revolution is epitomised by the Amoreiras centre in Lisbon which incorporates 300 outlets, and the concept is now spreading to other parts of the capital (Benfica) as well as Oporto (Gaia) and Cascais (Cascaishopping), where they pose a challenge to the independent sector of family-owned businesses in the locality. Foreign influence is strong, and retailing has proved a magnet for inward foreign investment. Only one of the leading retail companies – Ino – is wholly Portuguese-owned. The others, Sonae, Pão de Açucar and Pingo Doce, are either controlled by foreign groups or have significant foreign participation. The northern-based Sonae group is Portugal's largest retail company in terms of sales, employs over 6,000 staff and owns subsidiaries involved in property, tourism, agribusiness and information technology. Its retailing interests have taken the form of joint ventures with French groups to develop the Modelo-Continente supermarkets chain, Printemps department stores and Conforama furniture stores.

## TOURISM

Tourism makes an important contribution to the Portuguese economy and in some regions has totally transformed the local economy. Revenue from tourist spending helps to reduce the balance of payments deficit (receipts were equivalent to thirty-seven per cent of the total deficit in 1988), it is the second-largest foreign-currency earner after the clothing and footwear sector, and it contributes sixty-seven per cent of service-sector receipts. Tourism represents between six and seven per cent of GDP, placing the industry alongside agriculture and banking in its contribution to output. The sector, which still possesses further growth potential, is a major employer, generating employment for 150,000 workers. It has been instrumental in stimulating infrastructure development.

Tourism development went through a series of stages. For the first half of the twentieth century, the chief attraction for visitors and the local middle classes was the spa resorts at Luso, Geres, Curia and Vizela. During the 1950s, foreign tourist numbers began to grow, reaching 353,000 by 1960 (Williams and Shaw 1991). During the next decade, the nature of the industry began to change as beach tourism grew more popular. Madeira pioneered the boom, following the opening of the island's airport in 1964. Numbers expanded rapidly on the mainland during the 1960s as package tourism was seen as the formula for the future of regions such as the Algarve. By 1974, the number of tourists and day-trippers reached 4,000,000. However, twin blows reversed the upward trend during the 1970s. The 1973 oil-price shock pushed up transport costs and caused a recession in the source countries which led to a reduction in tourist flows. This combined with internal political instability following the 1974 regime change to engineer a crisis throughout the industry. The number of visitors plummeted by more than half to less than 2,000,000, per capita spending fell and investment dried up. A gradual recovery followed, although it took until the end of the decade before foreign visitor numbers again reached pre-1974 levels. By the mid-1980s, tourism was in the throes of a boom involving not only the Algarve and the Atlantic islands but also Lisbon's Costa do Sol and the previously neglected central and northern regions. From just under 7,000,000 in 1980, the number of visitors leapt to over 13,000,000 in 1986, and four years later the total reached 18.4 million. Portugal's market share of the world total of tourists rose from 1.6 per cent in 1986 to 1.9 per cent in 1990 and its share of total world tourism revenue from 1.1 per cent to 1.6 per cent. The recovery in international demand sparked a revival in investment as domestic and foreign capital developed new hotels, apartments, restaurants, golf courses and other facilities. Current projects and plans include luxury marinas, sports and hotel complexes and even an Esc 9.7 billion 'Chinese garden' leisure facility to be built at Carcavelos near Lisbon by Chinese and Hong Kong companies.

Whatever its beneficial impact, tourism growth has brought problems in its wake. First, investment in infrastructure has not been commensurate with the rapid growth in numbers. Second, there is a heavy reliance on a single point of origin. Around seventy per cent of the tourists who visit the Algarve are British. Unfortunately, the British are traditionally low spenders and in this respect contrast with the relatively high-spending Germans, Swiss and French who frequent Madeira (Lewis and Williams 1989). Third, the low-spending tourist is notoriously fickle and likely to switch to alternative cheap destinations that provide sun-and-sand holidays. This problem arose because tour operators such as Thomson and Intasun exert downward pressure on prices (the so-called

*Table 3.9*:    Tourist Bednights by Country of Origin 1988 (thousands).

|                     | Country | Percentage |
|---------------------|---------|------------|
| UK                  | 5,073   | 34.9       |
| Germany             | 2,006   | 13.8       |
| Spain               | 1,233   | 8.4        |
| Netherlands         | 1,162   | 8.0        |
| France              | 725     | 5.0        |
| USA                 | 630     | 4.3        |
| Sweden              | 549     | 3.8        |
| Total (incl. others)| 14,527  | 100.0      |

*Source*: Direcção Geral do Turismo. Quoted in EIU 1991e.

*turismo de garrafão*, or demijohn tourism) in order to maintain Portugal's advantage as a cheap destination. Fourth, large areas of the Algarve have reached saturation point. The coastline suffers from unplanned development which spawned overbuilding and exerts severe strains on the infrastructure. President Mario Soares, a regular visitor to the Algarve, pointed out that unplanned development had become a major disincentive for prospective visitors when commenting that 'people don't want to live on a permanent building-site'. Efforts are now being made to control building, improve the roads, water supplies and sanitation and strike a balance in regional development between farming (especially fruit, flower and vegetable cultivation) and tourism, which for so long has prioritised the coastal strip to the detriment of the interior and western zones.

Environmental concerns are now high on the agenda and helped to mould a new tourism policy for the 1990s. In a survey conducted in 1991, Portugal was among the four European countries with the greatest percentage of beaches that failed to comply with EC standards. Beaches at Vilamoura, Portimão and Albufeira on the Algarve and the resorts on the Estoril coast outside Lisbon fell outside the legal limits set for industrial waste and sewerage. Belatedly, the authorities have started to take action and the government has launched a programme to clean up the environment. Mindful of past mistakes, future developments prioritise quality rather than quantity. The National Tourism Plan for 1989–92 aimed to reduce the current dependence for tourism receipts on three areas: British visitors, the Algarve and peak-season tourism. This placed greater emphasis on more rigorous tourism management, improved services and imaginative marketing overseas. Three tourism schools are to be opened in order to ensure a more professional approach in the future. The focus is on diversity in terms of the geographical spread, seasonality and the promotion of rural, religious and cultural tourism and sporting facilities. This is based on the realisation that tourism choice is increasingly determined by image, diversity and niche specialisation. The quality end of the market is now catered for by a network of pousadas (refurbished palaces, monasteries and manor houses). In addition to the thirty pousadas on the mainland and a handful on the islands, eight more are to be opened at Braga, Beja, Crato, Ilha da Berlengas, Guimarães (two), Queluz and an entirely new building in the village of Piodão. It is hoped that this will help to reverse the worrying trend that has seen average daily tourist expenditure fall from Esc 2,043 in 1980 to Esc 1,530 in 1991.

BANKING

Prior to 1974, the banking system suffered from a number of deficiencies. A limited number of large banks were owned by a small number of economic groups linked to the leading families. They were tightly regulated and protected by legislation that placed almost insurmountable obstacles in the way of any attempt to set up new banks. The Salazar regime used prohibitive interest rates to deter new entrants into the cosy world of the capitalist oligarchy. As a consequence, there was little competition and the banking system was, in the main, bloated, inefficient and inflexible.

During the revolution, seventeen private commercial banks were nationalised and consolidated into eight state-owned commercial operations, three foreign-owned banks (Bank of London and South America (later Lloyds), Crédit Lyonnais and Barclays Bank), a development bank (Banco Fomento Nacional), the Caixa Geral do Depósitos and Crédito Predial Português. The transfer of such large financial resources from private hands to the state compounded some old problems and generated new ones. First, the Central Bank dominated the financial system and played a pivotal role in the management of the economy. State control was exerted through rigidly-imposed interest and exchange rates, and market forces were excluded from a heavily bureaucratic system that imposed lending ceilings and persistently delayed investment decisions (Financial Times Survey 1982). Second, decisions were politically, rather than commercially, motivated. Overheads were artificially high because of overstaffing caused by the compulsory hiring of banking personnel returning from the former colonies and by overtly political appointments. The quality of management was further prejudiced by the practice of rotating the board of directors regularly, which ensured that there would be little management continuity. The banks were also obliged to accept statutory salary levels and burdensome pension obligations. They were further crippled by the obligation to lend at negative rates of interest to often inefficiently-run and indebted nationalised industries and collective farms. For political reasons, the banks were compelled to absorb bad debts estimated at 200 billion escudos (Chislett 1991). Often the true state of affairs did not come before the public eye, as accounts were either unavailable or massaged to disguise the losses.

Since 1984, it has been possible to authorise new private banks backed by national and foreign capital. By 1990, the banking system comprised ten commercial banks, six private commercial banks, thirteen foreign commercial banks and four other public and private credit institutions. These thirty-three institutions totalled 1,991 branches, with 1,103 (fifty-five per cent) located in the Lisbon area. Together the commercial banks had 47,667 employees (eighty-one per cent of the total), the private Portuguese banks 9,760 (sixteen per cent) and the foreign-owned banks 1,735 (three per cent). It should be noted, however, that staffing levels were among the first items to come under scrutiny once the privatisation process got under way and the reduction of overheads became a priority.

By the early 1990s, the outlines of the newly-emerging banking sector could be discerned. The banks had taken advantage of the high rates of economic growth and the measures taken to liberalise the economy. A system previously dominated by a clutch of large institutions was evolving into a group with a more diversified and specialised profile. Portuguese banks are beginning to

*Table 3.10*:   Portuguese Banks 1991.

| Name | Branches | Specialism |
|------|----------|------------|
| Banco Português do Atlântico (BPA) | 170 | retail |
| Banco Espírito Santo e Comercial de Lisboa (BESCL) | 190 | retail |
| Banco Pinto e Sotto Mayor (BPSM) | 188 | retail |
| Banco Nacional Ultramarino (BNU) | 160 | general |
| Banco Borges e Irmão (BBI) | 100 | retail |
| União de Bancos Portuguesas (UBP) | 152 | retail |
| Banco Fonsecas e Burnay (BFB ) | 115 | retail |
| Caixa Geraldo Depósitos (CGD) | 419 | retail/savings |
| Banco Totta e Açores (BTA) | 180 | retail |
| Banco Comercial Português (BCP) | 35 | finance |
| Banco de Comércio e Indústria (BCI) | 100 | general |
| Crédito Predial Português (CPP) | 100 | savings |
| Banco Internacional de Funchal (BANIF) | 30 | business |
| Bank of Lisbon International (BLI) | 27 | savings |
| Banco Internacional de Crédito (BIC) | 11 | finance |
| Banco Português de Investimento (BPI) | 3 | business |
| Crédit Lyonnais Portugal (CLP) | 19 | savings |
| Banco de Fomento e Exterior (BFE) | 35 | commercial |
| Banco Comercial de Macau (BCM) | 10 | general |

*Source*: *O Emigrante*, 8 November 1991.

operate at different levels: a clutch of 'superbanks' (BESCL, BPA, CGD and BCP) with European and international as well as national interests; regional banks with a predominantly national focus (BNU, UDP, BPI, BFB and BPSM); and a small group of niche banks catering for a specialist market, such as the Banco Mello, formerly Sociedade de Financiera Portuguesa.

The heavy hand of state control is gradually relaxing. The Bank of Portugal's ability to impose lending limits was restricted in 1990 and eased further the following year when all limits were lifted as long as the banks did not exceed capital ratio requirements (Chislett 1991). The days of the overstaffed bank are numbered. Portuguese banks have the highest number of employees per branch in the whole of Europe (36.3 against a European average of 25.6). Shedding staff is a priority if the national commercial banks are to compete with their new, aggressive, privately-owned competitors such as the enormously successful BCP, which had the highest net income of any Portuguese bank in 1990. As the newer banks move into retailing, their lower overheads and younger, better-qualified staff give them a marked competitive edge. With 5,000 customers per branch (two-and-a-half times as many as in Spain), Portugal is clearly un-derbanked. There is still plenty of room for growth, and new branches are opening regularly as the networks expand.

As competition and pressures from the single market in financial services take their toll, some rationalisation is inevitable and the number of banks is likely to reduce. Already, competition is squeezing the traditionally very high margins and making cost-cutting imperative. The prospect is for mergers, acquisitions and strategic alliances as the battle for market share intensifies. Foreign banks, especially Spanish, have established a foothold through the Cavaco Silva government's privatisation programme (discussed in chapter 5) and are likely to consolidate their position once the limits on foreign holdings are relaxed.

ENERGY

Portugal possesses very limited domestic energy sources and consequently is the EC country most dependent on oil imports to fulfil its energy requirements. A sudden increase in oil imports can have a dramatic impact on the prospects for the national economy, as occurred in 1973–4 and repeated in the early 1980s. Before 1974, energy did not play a major role in the trade balance (around four per cent of total imports). However, the share rose steadily to peak at 30.7 per cent of the import bill in 1984. By the end of the 1980s, energy imports were estimated at 7.4 per cent of imports, or 3.5 per cent of GDP (see Table 3.11).

It has not proved easy to restrain the demand for energy. Consumption moved strongly upwards after 1986 as living standards improved and demand from industrial users grew apace. Demand for energy was 6.6 per cent higher in 1990 than the previous year and is expected to remain at an annual rate of five per cent over the next decade. For some time, governments have invested heavily in hydroelectric capacity in order to reduce the reliance on imported energy. Electricity is the second-largest energy source, of which about a third is generated locally. Supplies are almost entirely controlled by Electricidade de Portugal (EDP), the state-owned company which enjoys a production and distribution monopoly. It is also the country's largest employer and industrial investor and, together with Petrogal, the state-owned oil monopoly, heads the list of Portugal's largest companies. The government's energy strategy can be summarised as follows:

- Petrogal now faces competition after private producers, like Esso and Cepsa, were allowed to enter the market alongside existing multinationals.

*Table 3.11*: Net Oil Import Bill 1989 (percentage of GDP).

| Belgium | 1.9 | Luxembourg | 2.8 |
|---------|-----|------------|-----|
| Denmark | 0.5 | Netherlands | 1.7 |
| France | 1.1 | Portugal | 3.5 |
| Germany | 1.1 | Spain | 1.7 |
| Greece | 2.9 | UK | -0.1 |
| Ireland | 1.5 | EC12 | 1.1 |
| Italy | 1.3 | | |

*Source*: European Commission 1991c.

Likewise, EDP now has private competitors. The government signalled its intentions when it authorised a consortium led by the German multinational Siemens and the UK's PowerGen to run a new gas-fired plant near Oporto which is expected to start production in 1996.

- Petrogal is to be privatised in a series of stages, beginning in 1992 with a twenty-five per cent stake (which appears likely to be sold to a Franco-Spanish consortium).

- Ways have been sought to restructure consumption. Encouragement has been given to the cement industry to switch from oil to coal for its power-generation, and natural gas is being developed as an alternative energy source. To this end, the government awarded a contract to a mixed consortium (with the state holding a ten per cent stake) to supply the country's natural gas principally from fields in Algeria, and a new liquefied natural gas conversion plant terminal is to be constructed at Setúbal. It is anticipated that natural gas will fulfil six per cent of energy requirements by the turn of the century.

- Alternative energy supplies will be exploited, including organic and natural sources such as wood, biomass, solar and wind power.

# CHAPTER 4

# *Portugal and Europe*

Portugal's initial application for membership of the European Economic Community made in March 1977 by Mario Soares's Socialist government was principally motivated by political considerations. European support was regarded as essential for the consolidation of the fledgling pluralist democracy and as a bulwark against a return to dictatorship. Only later did integration into the EC come to be regarded as a prerequisite for further economic growth and prosperity as well as a guarantee of political stability. The gestation period was protracted: after the first formal approaches were made to Brussels in March 1977, nine years of negotiations over entry terms followed before the accession treaty was signed in June 1985. Portugal finally became a full member of the EC on 1 January 1986.

It is far too simplistic to regard 1974 as the turning point when Portugal abandoned her colonial empire and turned towards Europe. Forces were already at work during the dictatorship that forged closer links between Portugal and her continental neighbours. Indeed, one of the principal reasons for the failure of Caetano's liberalisation strategy was his attempt to 'reconcile the irreconcilable': to integrate more closely with Europe while attempting to maintain the imperial connection and Atlanticist tradition (Sammis 1988). It is interesting to note that many industrial groups, which might be expected to be among the most enthusiastic proponents of Europeanisation, proved reluctant to abandon their substantial African interests. So the advocacy of European integration was often hedged around with qualifications, and it was only when military intervention overturned the old order and foreclosed the colonial option that Europe emerged the best, and perhaps only, hope for stability and prosperity. Nevertheless, a strong anti western current, rooted as much in the Salazarist era as in the revolutionary period, continued to generate political divisions throughout the 1970s. The 'Africa versus Europe' debate was kept alive by, among others, President Ramalho Eanes (1976–86), who favoured closer links with the former colonies despite the much-reduced economic logic.

The decolonisation process, together with the marked shifts in the patterns of trade that had occurred over the past decades, left Portugal with little choice but to opt for European vocation if economic isolation was to be avoided. The EC had played a major part in consolidating democracy in Portugal by furnishing emergency aid and loans channelled through the European Investment Bank. The extended interlude between the first overtures to Brussels and eventual accession requires explanation, particularly since the EC 9, commenting on Portugal's 1977 application, stated categorically that 'The Community cannot leave Portugal out of the process of European integrations.' Portugal had satisfied even the most searching examination of its democratic credentials by 1980. Indeed, according to every opinion poll and survey, the Portuguese had fewer doubts and stronger pro-European leanings than the public in many existing member states. Consequently, fewer problems were anticipated than during the Greek accession, when the nationalist and anti-capitalist PASOK government used the transition as a lever to extract additional assistance from Brussels and made more of the loss of sovereignty than the Iberians. In any case, the southern enlargement paled into insignificance beside the major issue facing the EC: the functioning and reform of its structures.

The intention had been for Spain and Portugal to join the EC in tandem with Greece in 1981. However, it soon became clear that the southern enlargement would have to be staggered, with the Iberians joining later in the decade once the Greek economy had been digested. The postponement is attributable to a mixture of factors. Existing members expressed concern at the problems generated by the integration of additional semi-industrialised Mediterranean economies into structures already crying out for reform. Unfortunately for the Iberians, their applications coincided with a global economic recession and a period of introspection and internal squabbling within the EC 9. An often acrimonious internal debate was under way over controversial issues such as the reform of the Common Agricultural Policy (CAP), the EC budget and the decision-making mechanism. Powerful voices argued that these should be resolved before embarking on any new admissions (Naylon 1987).

Some existing members expressed anxieties based on economic self-interest and the general functioning of the EC. The French government was concerned about the impact on its domestic agriculture, particularly the competition from wine, fruit and vegetables produced in southern Europe and the cumulative strain exerted on the CAP. Others expressed anxieties about the problems of consensus-building in a Community enlarged from nine to twelve members. The northern countries obviously feared that the balance of power would tilt south-wards with the formation of a southern European lobby which would promote its own set of interests. The northern industrial member states harboured fears that the whole character of the EC would be transformed because Spain, Portugal and Greece shared a distinct political culture: 'one involving suffocating bureau-cracies, clientilism, strong attachment to a single church, and a net outward migration of labour away from structurally-weak domestic economies'

(Featherstone 1989). Inevitably, the economic retardation of the newcomers would exert additional pressure on an already overburdened budget and jeopardise the move away from agricultural priorities by reinforcing the ranks of the farming pressure group. At a time when surpluses were proving politically embarrassing, the incorporation of a major wine-producer like Spain caused some consternation. In order to assuage such fears, especially those expressed by Greece, the EC10 attempted to mitigate the impact of the Iberian accession on vulnerable members by launching the Integrated Mediterranean Programmes (IMPs) to help the modernisation and restructuring of farming in the less efficient regions of non-Iberian southern Europe (Rittlestone 1989).

Such were the disparities in levels of development between the existing members and the new admissions that substantial pre-accession assistance was made available. With per capita incomes in Spain and Portugal standing at a half and a quarter respectively of the EC average on the eve of accession in 1986 (for Portugal, US$2,055 to US$8,013), priority was given to achieving a convergence of living standards and the alleviation of regional poverty. The economic recession ensured that a southward transfer of resources in the form of increased structural assistance could not simply be paid for out of higher economic growth. The EC was determined to avoid the renegotiations that had followed the British entry a decade earlier. Hence, lengthy and detailed negotiations, reputed to have consumed 23,000,000 sheets of paper, resulted in treaties with 403 articles

*Table 4.1*:   Portugal and Europe: The Timetable.

| | |
|---|---|
| 1957 | Six countries sign the Treaty of Rome establishing the European Economic Community. |
| 1960 | Portugal is a founder member of the European Free Trade Association (EFTA). |
| 1972 | Agreement between Portugal and the EC improving trade relations and other contacts. |
| 1974 | European Regional Development Fund (FEDER) set up. |
| 1977 | Portugal formally requests entry into EEC (March). |
| 1978 | Creation of European Monetary System (EMS). Council of Ministers accepts the principle of enlargement (April). Official opening of negotiations with Portugal. |
| 1981 | European Monetary Unit (Ecu) first appears. |
| 1985 | Completion of EC enlargement negotiations (March). Treaty of Accession signed (June). |
| 1986 | Formal entry into Community of Portugal and Spain. |
| 1987 | Single European Act (SEA) signed. |
| 1988 | Structural Funds doubled (February). |
| 1991 | EEC and EFTA agree to set up a European Economic Area (EEA) in 1993. |
| 1993 | Inauguration of single market (January). |
| 1994 | Economic and Monetary Union (Stage Two); member states move to narrow band of ERM (January). |
| 1996 | Full integration of Portugal into the Community structures as 'a member with full rights and duties'. |
| 1999 | Introduction of single currency. |

*Source*: Compiled by author.

running to some 1,300 pages. The main bones of contention related to Spain rather than to Portugal: the integration of agriculture into the CAP, the dismantling of the protective barriers surrounding infant industries and the size of the fishing fleet. Portugal's much smaller economy could be digested relatively easily, and the chief concern for the Portuguese related to the rights of migrants living in the European Community and the thorny question of labour mobility (Daltrop 1987).

Within Portugal, support for the European project gathered pace during the mid-1980s. At its peak, the Euro-optimists painted some fanciful images of Portugal becoming 'a small California in Europe' with an economic profile based on light industry, semi-exotic agriculture and an expanded service sector (*The Economist* 1988). Why did this unrealistic evaluation of Portugal's prospects in Europe gain such currency? In the first place, the almost unanimous pro-European consensus among the political elite (only the Communists expressed reservations about joining western Europe's 'capitalist club' in which they claimed Portugal would be little better than a semi-colony) meant that little meaningful debate took place about the issues and consequences. The major political parties were, in varying degrees, pro-European. The largest party to emerge from the first democratic elections, the Socialists (PS), campaigned under the slogan 'Europe is with us'. Mario Soares, who launched Portugal's entry bid, developed particularly close links with European socialist parties and governments during his pre-1974 exile which were reinforced during the post-revolutionary political and economic uncertainty. To Soares fell the task of convincing the Portuguese that a European future should replace the now-defunct imperial one (Grayson 1986). The right-of-centre PSD and right-wing CDS were unequivocally pro-western and pro-capitalist. They regarded the EC as a mechanism for dragging Portugal away from communism and in the direction of liberal capitalism. In particular, they expected that the EC would object to the 'socialist constitution', the size of the state sector and the collectivised farms. This would compel changes that would rebound to the benefit the private sector. In this and other ways, the right came to regard the EC as a useful means of bolstering their demands for liberalisation and structural change.

Second, the logic of Portugal's economic relations made it difficult to mount a counterargument, particularly when a key trading partner like the UK became a full member in 1973. Portugal appeared to have little alternative but to turn to the EC if its foreign trade were not to suffer. Pro-entry arguments were bolstered by the changes taking place in trade patterns. By 1969, the EC6 absorbed fifty-seven per cent of Portuguese exports, and the second enlargement in 1973 raised tariffs and protective barriers against Portuguese exports. In addition, Portuguese industry, especially textiles, faced strong competition from the NICs as well as its southern European neighbours and the certainty that EC exporters would pose a more serious challenge than EFTA's. The economic motive grew in importance during the recession-hit 1970s and early 1980s. It was argued that a small, open economy would have difficulty in surviving alone in a fiercely competitive and protectionist-minded world trading environment. In such circumstances, ran the argument, a small country would fare better within, rather than outside, a powerful trading bloc.

Indeed, Portugal's economic integration into Europe predated the revolution and can be seen as part of a long process going back to the early postwar period. The dictatorship had been no bar to membership of the Organisation for European Economic Cooperation (OEEC) and European payments (EPU) and monetary agreements (EMA) (Tsoulakis 1981). The importance of the UK market prompted Portugal to join EFTA in 1960, which served as a halfway house on the road to progressively closer relations with Europe. Eventually, a trade agreement was signed in July 1972 on the eve of the UK's entry into the Common Market. In 1976, Portugal's journey into the European orbit was underlined when it became a member of the Council of Europe.

Third, the psychological impact felt by acceptance into the European fold cannot be overestimated. However, it did engender some dangerously complacent attitudes. For some, Europe came to be regarded as a panacea for all the country's problems. It reflected a long-standing Portuguese belief that some externally-generated miracle or intervention would offer a cure-all, rendering difficult decisions over structural change painless and uncomplicated. In contrast to the UK, where the European issue aroused debate and even a referendum, the question of Portuguese membership was rarely contentious. It never featured as an election issue, nor in parliamentary debates, and public opinion polls consistently registered both the disinterest and the ignorance prevalent among the population. In seeking to explain the widespread indifference, Tsoulakis (1981) identifies a combination of factors: isolation from the outside world, illiteracy and the paucity of foreign news coverage in the press, the political instability and the failure to tackle the economic crises that made membership 'like a luxury good which could only be purchased once other basic needs had been satisfied'. The Portuguese public, therefore, was never presented with an alternative to the 'benefits without costs' scenario. The bonanza mentality was fuelled by the apparently generous transitional arrangements and access structural funds to modernise the economy. Europe gave the impression of being all 'take' and very little 'give'. Political leaders such as Cavaco Silva spoke of the 'needed shock to the Portuguese economy' that entry would administer, but did little to dispel the euphoria which he skilfully manipulated to the PSD's political advantage during the 1987 election campaign.

When Portugal began negotiations over entry terms with Brussels, it was obvious that a broad range of problems would have to be tackled. With the modernisation and adjustment programme still in its infancy, the economy was in no shape to face full-blown external competition from the advanced industrial economies of the EC. EFTA membership might have been expected to narrow the gap but in fact made only a marginal difference because Portugal had not been compelled to dismantle its protectionist structures. As Hudson (1989) points out, in comparative terms Portugal was in a less fortunate position than the NICs, such as Brazil and South Korea, which have enjoyed protectionism for decades and still maintain barriers against open economic relations with the industrialised countries. Portugal's peripheral role in the European economy would remain unaltered. Producers still faced handicaps such as high transport and distribution costs, and educational, technological and infrastructural deficiencies. In addition, the country was still regarded as a dumping ground for cheap goods by many European companies.

Evidence of the concern among Portuguese industrialists over the consequences arising from accession is provided in a survey conducted by the Confederation of Portuguese Industry among its 40,000 members. Sixty-two per cent of those questioned opposed EC entry (*Time* 1985). Their fears were threefold. First, long-standing protectionist policies had ensured the survival of small, inefficient firms, and it was feared that the removal of insulation from competition would signal their inevitable demise. Second, the structure of national industry made it vulnerable to fierce competition in a shrinking market. Third, high-cost Portuguese producers of industrial goods face strong competition not only from efficient EC exporters but also from non-EC areas, notably the USA, Japan, the NICs and the EFTA group. The pressure on Portuguese industry to restructure and upgrade its products was intense.

The industrial sector, dominated by traditional industries such as steel and shipbuilding, required significant rationalisation if it was to survive, let alone compete in an open market. A further area of concern related to fears that the much stronger Spanish economy would flood the country with its industrial output and that imports from third countries that benefited from concessionary tariff arrangements would inflict further damage. However, some branches of manufacturing industry viewed economic integration more positively. Portugal had a strong export trade in fabrics and clothes, based on its low-wage economy, and the more efficient producers looked forward to freedom of access to a market limited in the past by quotas and voluntary restrictions. Other industrialists favoured accession on the grounds that it would impose much-needed economic disciplines and exert downward pressure on interest rates, which stood at punitively high levels and acted as a disincentive to investment. In the end, Portuguese industry settled for the dismantling of tariff barriers over a seven-year period, starting in March 1986, at annual reductions of ten or fifteen per cent. The transition period for textiles was set at three years, with free entry to EC markets, including Spain, starting in 1989. Madeira and the Azores were, with some minor exceptions, included as fully integrated members.

The Iberian economies contained large and backward rural sectors. On accession, farm acreage in the EC increased by thirty per cent, the rural labour force by twenty-five per cent and the number of farms by thirty-two per cent.

This put further pressure on the CAP (already absorbing around seventy-five per cent of the budget) and necessitated substantial assistance to transform and modernise the primary sector. It meant that the EC12 would acquire surplus mountains of citrus fruits, tomatoes, wines and olive oil. The chief problem involved meshing two contrasting agricultural systems: the EC's high-price policy and Iberia's low-price and poor-productivity farm sector. The costs of the CAP, originally designed for the EC6 and based on guaranteed, above-world-market prices and the accumulation of surplus production, were bound to escalate with three new members and strain the budget to breaking point.

The scale of the problem was not lost on the negotiators. Four out of five Portuguese farmers own fewer than ten hectares of land each, and productivity is less than a third of the EC10 average (Grayson 1986). Given that small farmers have difficulty in adjusting to new types of production, the priority was to provide inducements to some 500,000 of them to leave the land and to restructure and mechanise the sector. Clearly, the Regional and Social Funds had to be expanded, expenditure raised and generous pre-accession aid granted. The second problem area related to Iberian agricultural products (wine, olive oil, vegetables, citrus fruit), which compete directly with more expensive French and Italian output. As the Iberians import cereals and meat in substantial quantities, the former suppliers of cheap foodstuffs (USA, Brazil, Argentina) would be displaced by EC producers. Consumers faced paying higher prices for basic foodstuffs, and a possible trade war could ignite when EC duties applied to Iberian agricultural imports.

Labour migration threatened to be a major sticking point in the negotiations as they took place against the background of high unemployment in the EC's northern industrial regions. The German government in particular feared that a flood of workers from southern Europe would worsen employment prospects and burden the social security system. In the end, a compromise was reached: the Portuguese resident in EC countries on 1 January 1986 were given equal status with nationals, and the free movement of labour would be phased in over seven years (ten years for Luxembourg).

Fish quotas posed a difficult problem, given Portugal's large coastline and the superior size and modernity of the Spanish fleet. In fact, Spain and Portugal generated a major fishing crisis because the size of the EC's fishing fleet rose by eighty per cent overnight. The Common Fisheries policy had been built on a fragile consensus, and the Iberian accession threatened to undermine it. After some difficult negotiations, Portugal was granted a ten-year transition period, but access to the twelve-mile coastal zones and 'Irish Box' was delayed until after completion of the transition. The Portuguese failed to win a 15,000,000-ton duty-free quota on sardines, having to settle for 5,000,000 tons with duties to be phased out over a decade. A separate bilateral deal with Spain was agreed in May 1985 which gave local authorities powers to license fishing in coastal waters (EIU 1986). This excluded the most modern Spanish vessels from

Portuguese waters and defused fears that Spain's much more modern fishing fleet would be free to fish territorial waters, including those around Madeira and the Azores.

## COMMUNITY STRUCTURAL FUNDS

Aware that Portugal would be unable by her own efforts to narrow the development deficit with her new partners, Brussels dispensed pre-accession support amounting to some Ecu 600,000,000. In January 1986, Portugal became eligible for direct funding from the Community Structural Fund (CSF) budgets. The CSF's principal components comprise:

- the European Regional Development Fund (FEDER), which is the main financial instrument in the development policy and prioritises infrastructure and related projects;
- the Social Fund (FSE), which channels funds into employment training and job creation schemes; and
- the European Agricultural Guidance Fund (FEOGA), which finances agricultural modernisation through farming, marketing and training programmes. It also assists land-consolidation and subsidises the transfer of farm workers from the land.

The main instrument for the application of the structural funds within Portugal between 1989 and 1993 is the Community Support Framework (*Quadro Comunitário de Apoio*). The QCA provides for better coordination between the different programmes in order to ensure their effective deployment and strikes a balance between sectoral and regional development priorities (set out in the Regional Development Plan, the *Plano de Desenvolvimento Regional* or PDR) and between productive investment and infrastructure investment. The structural funds have two interrelated sets of objectives – first, to promote rapid economic growth in order to modernise the country's economic and social structures, to ameliorate the overall standard of living and to improve international competitiveness; and, second, to promote economic and social cohesion and ensure that the wealth created is evenly distributed.

## REGIONAL DEVELOPMENT

The need to tackle regional development problems was recognised when Britain became a member in 1973, and the European Regional Development Fund (FEDER) was launched three years later in order to complement existing national policies and programmes. Fears were expressed that the Single Market project would benefit primarily the core industrial regions in the so-called 'golden triangle' bounded by Milan, Frankfurt and London and lead to a widening of the development deficit on the EC's southern and western fringes. In the late 1980s, earnings per head in the four poorest countries (Portugal, Greece, Spain and Ireland) stood at less than two-thirds of the EC average, and in Portugal and Greece average incomes were only a third of those in the ten wealthiest areas.

*Table 4.2:*    Structural Funds as a Percentage of GDP.

| Member states | 1988 | 1993 |
|---|---|---|
| Belgium | 0.1 | 0.1 |
| Denmark | 0.1 | 0.1 |
| France | 0.1 | 0.1 |
| Germany | 0.0 | 0.1 |
| Greece | 1.6 | 2.9 |
| Ireland | 1.5 | 2.7 |
| Italy | 0.2 | 0.3 |
| Luxembourg | 0.2 | 0.2 |
| Netherlands | 0.1 | 0.1 |
| Portugal | 2.4 | 3.7 |
| Spain | 0.5 | 0.8 |
| United Kingdom | 0.2 | 0.2 |

*Source*: European Commission 1990a.

As the quid pro quo for acceptance of the Single European Act, approved by the heads of government in 1987, the southern Europeans extracted a commitment to strengthen 'economic and social cohesion', and in February 1988 the Commission President, Jacques Delors, announced that agreement had been reached to double the structural funds to Ecu 63 billion over the five years to 1993. Priority status meant that over fourteen per cent of the EC's regional funding was earmarked for Portugal, which was expected to amount to 3.7 per cent of the country's GDP by 1993. Portugal receives the bulk of its assistance from the funds targeted at laggard regions (almost Ecu 7 billion) and a small amount from the agricultural modernisation fund. The funds are allocated as follows: fifty per cent for the modernisation of the economic structure, thirty per cent for the development of human resources and the remaining twenty per cent to local development projects.

Major criticisms had been levelled at the EC's earlier attempts to promote regional development during the 1960s. They focused on, first, the uncoordinated way in which the money was spent, often on large infrastructure projects of dubious value and, second, the absence of evidence that disparities were in fact reducing as a result of EC funding. The convergence process came to an abrupt halt during the 1970s when Italy's underdeveloped southern region, the mezzogiorno, began to fall further behind northern Italy and, despite a considerable injection of EC funds during the 1980s, the per capita income gap between Greece and the EC average continued to widen. The conclusion to be drawn was that structural funds are much more likely to be effective when complemented by appropriate domestic economic policies.

The EC's response to past failures was to introduce changes in the administration of the structural fund budget. It was agreed to increase the EC's contribution to three-quarters (national governments make up the balance). In the past, there had been little supervision of the funds handed over to national governments but, with the injection of new money in 1988, the European Commission insisted on closer involvement in regional development and encouraged a shift away from infrastructure spending towards training and development programmes. Nevertheless, the record remains patchy despite regional development swallowing a quarter of the total budget. During the second half of the 1980s, the four poorest states recorded annual average growth rates 1.2 per cent above the rest of the EC. Yet, as Table 4.3 demonstrates, the collective GDP per head among the four poorest member states moved up only from sixty-six per cent to sixty-nine per cent of the EC average. Portugal reduced the gap by 4.6 per cent and in the process overtook Greece, which actually registered a 3.3 per cent fall. Clearly, catching up is a slow process, and long-term efforts will be required. Indeed, the EC's own studies estimate that it will take two decades for the less developed member states to achieve a GDP per head of ninety per cent of the EC average. To this end, Portugal has supported Spanish pressure for a greater commitment to narrowing the economic differences among the twelve as the price for economic and monetary union. Madrid is now calling for reform of the EC budget to benefit the poorer regions and the introduction of new instruments of economic and social cohesion.

In order to coordinate the various sources of investment aid into an integrated programme, an agreement was reached between Brussels and Lisbon in February 1988 on the creation of a special programme: PEDIP (*Programa Específico de Desenvolvimento da Indústria Portuguesa*, the Plan for the Development of Portuguese Industry), to be run by the Industry Ministry. This five-year programme has become the principal instrument of Portuguese industrial policy. It has a number of specific objectives: to modernise industry, strengthen its competitive edge through reconversion, establish and nurture new industries and reduce and eliminate comparative structural disadvantages. Grants worth 2.35 billion ecu have been provided from FEDER loans, Social Fund monies, EIB

*Table 4.3*:   The Gap between Richer and Poorer Member States:
        GDP at Current Market Prices and Purchasing Parities (EC12 = 100).

| Year | Greece | Ireland | Spain | Portugal |
|---|---|---|---|---|
| 1975 | 57.3 | 62.7 | 81.9 | 52.2 |
| 1980 | 58.1 | 64.0 | 74.2 | 55.0 |
| 1986 | 55.9 | 63.4 | 72.8 | 52.5 |
| 1987 | 54.1 | 64.4 | 74.7 | 53.7 |
| 1988 | 54.2 | 64.7 | 75.7 | 53.7 |
| 1989 | 54.0 | 67.0 | 76.9 | 54.9 |
| 1990 | 52.9 | 68.6 | 77.8 | 55.6 |
| 1991 | 52.6 | 68.7 | 79.2 | 57.1 |
| 1986–91 | -3.3 | +5.3 | +6.4 | +4.6 |

*Source*: European Commission 1990b.

*Table 4.4*:  Structural Fund Expenditure 1989–93 (percentage breakdown by main categories).

|  | Portugal | Spain | Greece | Ireland |
|---|---|---|---|---|
| Infrastructure | 27.3 | 53.1 | 31.3 | 17.1 |
| Aids to productive Investment | 17.0 | 9.9 | 7.0 | 26.5 |
| Agriculture | 11.9 | 14.0 | 13.0 | 24.5 |
| Manpower | 28.0 | 22.7 | 13.7 | 31.2 |
| Regional programmes | 15.6 | — | — | — |
| Others | 0.2 | 0.3 | 0.4 | 0.6 |
| Total | 100.0 | 100.0 | 100.0 | 100.0 |

*Source*: European Commission 1990a.

credits, the New Community Instrument (NCI) and a special budget set aside for Portugal. The Portuguese government's twenty-five per cent contribution was estimated at Ecu 350,000,000 (Hudson 1989). According to PEDIP's head, Abelino Santana, the aim is to achieve 'a deep modification of Portugal's productive structure' with an emphasis on modernising and diversifying the industrial base and establishing export-led companies (Financial Times Survey 1989b). Assistance is provided to develop infrastructures that benefit industrial growth, subsidise research and development and provide financial backing for productive investment.

The PEDIP programmes cover:
- basic infrastructure aid for transport, port and energy projects;
- occupational training for technical and managerial staff in industrial enterprises;
- investment incentives for restructuring and modernisation;
- financial support for small and medium-sized enterprises (SMEs) through the provision of investment credits to promising firms;
- productivity improvements; and
- quality and industrial design missions to improve product quality, managerial skills and consumer protection (OECD 1989).

By the end of 1989, forty per cent of the 4,000 projects submitted had been approved. Three-quarters (Esc 28 billion) of total public investment in industry went into schemes for modernisation and reconversion. Esc 6.5 billion was spent on industrial training for 57,000 workers during 1989. The manufacturing sector (textiles, clothing, machinery and vehicles) was the main beneficiary of these two support schemes (OECD 1991).

It is still rather early to assess the impact that PEDIP has made on Portugal's outdated industrial structure. Many projects have not yet come to fruition, and earlier investments have still not begun to show their full potential returns. During the early stages of operation three major problems arose: first, bureaucratic

incompetence; second, the larger companies were creaming off the lion's share
of the funds; and third, many companies were unprepared to absorb the grants.
By the end of 1990, the programmes approved involved investments totalling
455,000,000 contos which qualified for incentives worth 138,000,000 contos.
Just under three-quarters were approved under SINPEDIP (technology and equipment acquisition and environmental schemes), fourteen per cent in basic infrastructure and technology, five per cent in productivity, quality and design
missions, four per cent in training and a similar amount for restructuring in the
woollen industry. As for the regional distribution of the investment, ninety per
cent of SINPEDIP funds were concentrated in the districts of Oporto, Lisbon,
Braga, Aveiro and Leiria. While it may be premature to assert with confidence
that Portuguese industry will be able to compete on equal terms with its
European partners, important steps have been taken to improve the supply-side
profile in both quantitative and qualitative terms. The early indications are that,
as far as foreign trade and investment is concerned, the traditional sectors have
begun to figure less prominently while the modern sectors have improved their
share.

Additionally, a new incentive scheme was created to encourage the use of
telecommunications systems use under the EC's STAR programme framework.
New instruments helped to promote regional development: SIBR (*Sistema de
Incentivos de Base Regional*) provides funds for the modernisation of companies located in the poorer regions. Between 1988 and 1990, the less
developed regions received nearly sixty per cent of the incentives as part of
the shift away from traditional towards non-traditional, often high-technology, industries. In 1991, the European Commission approved Portugal's
application to participate in the STRIDE programme, which promotes the
spread of technology among Portuguese firms and supports the establishment
of science and technology parks. Portugal also benefited from the VALOREN
programme for natural resources and innovations in new and renewable
energy projects, and from SIURE, which encourages energy conservation
among private-sector companies.

## THE EFTA INDUSTRIAL FUND

Although Portugal ceased to be a member of the European Free Trade Association (EFTA) at the end of 1985, the Industrial Fund (*Fundo EFTA para o
Desenvolvimento Industrial de Portugal*, or IDF), established in 1976 to provide
funds for Portuguese industry, continues in operation until 2002. However, the
EFTA contribution is decidedly small beer when compared to the CSF. The
96,400,000 contos provided by EFTA between 1977 and 1989 must be set beside
the 200,000,000 contos invested by the EC between 1986 and 1989. Nevertheless, the IDF has assisted employment creation and job security across a broad
range of sectors including, most recently, tourism. However, as Eaton (1991a)
points out, the distribution of IDF funds has exacerbated regional disparities to

the detriment of the underresourced interior and eastern regions and done little to reverse the polarisation of economic activity.

The Social Fund (CSF) has a significant role to play in Portugal through its contribution to the improvement in 'human capital'. In a country with an illiteracy level (fifteen per cent) well above the EC average (3.6 per cent) and a moribund technical training programme, expenditure on vocational training schemes (306,000,000 contos with a CSF contribution of 230,000,000 in 1989–90) is of vital importance. Indeed, among the EC countries, only Ireland takes a bigger per capita share of the funds available. The importance attached to education and training is revealed by the planned distribution of CSF funds for 1989–93: training absorbs the largest proportional share (28.0 per cent), followed closely by infrastructure investment (27.3 per cent), while aids to productive investment, regional programmes and agriculture receive 17.0, 15.6 and 11.0 per cent respectively.

The agricultural sector was expected to experience most difficulty in adjusting to the changed circumstances because of increased competition, the structural obstacles that perennially hindered productivity and technological improvements and the need for a reduction in guaranteed prices which, in specific cases, were actually higher than EC levels. A ten-year, Ecu 700,000,000 assistance programme for Portuguese agriculture, PEDAP (*Programa Específico de Desenvolvimento da Agricultura Portuguesa*), commenced in 1986 and immediately fears were expressed that this extended period was too short for Portugal's backward agriculture to adapt. Two years later, the transition period was extended to 2001, a measure regarded as necessary in order to allow further progress towards both diversification into higher-value agricultural crops and productivity improvements in the dairy and other vulnerable sectors. Four modifications were introduced in order to increase the effectiveness of the EC's programmes to tackle deep-seated structural problems:

- EC contribution rates rose to seventy-five per cent;
- the programme was extended to embrace environmental protection;
- Brussels insisted on fewer projects but with a wider scope; and
- committees were established representing national, regional and local interests to assess project effectiveness (Eisfeld 1989).

An indication of the deficiencies suffered by the agricultural sector can be obtained from the distribution of PEDAP funds, which are targeted at development projects covering afforestation, soil improvement, irrigation, road, water supply and electric power provision in rural areas along with crop, livestock and marketing improvements. The programme's second thrust provides incentives aimed at farm consolidation, retirement schemes for older farmers and the establishment of cooperatives. A third area provides technical training which earmarks young farmers in particular. Complementing these changes, the new 1988 agrarian reform law sought to encourage larger farm units by raising the size of farms subject to reprivatisation and allowing land to be subdivided. The aim is to slim down still further the collective sector, which had seen its size cut from 500 farms in 1975 to just 130 in 1988.

A start has been made on the daunting and much-postponed task of modernising and transforming the structure of Portuguese agriculture. Total EC assistance to agriculture involved over Esc 100 billion approved between 1986–8, in addition to a further Esc 27 billion under the agricultural guarantee fund from which Portugal is the third-largest beneficiary. Farmers also received substantial ESF funds for infrastructure and training projects which totalled Esc 93 billion in 1988 alone. It is estimated that 300,000 farmers have benefited either directly or indirectly from PEDAP funds. In all, 22,033 projects were approved, involving total investment of 101,400,000 contos. Between 1989 and 1993, agriculture will have access to 210,000,000 contos from the structural funds (15.9 per cent of the total available to Portugal) together with a state contribution of 89,000,000 contos (7.4 per cent of total government investment).

External funds have combined with pressures exerted by market forces to stimulate change. Apart from improvements in irrigation and rural road links, mechanisation is beginning to spread to regions previously low on technology take-up. Government subsidies have been cut back, although they remain on fertilisers and oil, the private sector has become involved in distribution, and low-quality production, such as poor-quality vines (covered by a special improvement programme, *Programa de Melhoramento das Estructuras Vitivinícolas*, the Programme for the Improvement of Vine-growing Structures) and fruit, have been replaced by more commercial crops, such as sunflower and maize (OECD 1989).

Preliminary indications are that in some areas Portuguese agriculture has belatedly begun to respond to the challenge of market forces. Between 1986 and 1990, EC subsidies helped to raise rural incomes by eighteen per cent – three times the EC average. A start has been made on tackling the problem of an aging and uneducated workforce and the dearth of investment in the sector. EC policy is encouraging farmers over the age of fifty-five to retire and is promoting the consolidation of small rural properties, but it is a costly exercise and is limited so far to pilot zones such as Entre Douro e Minho and Caldas de Rainha.

Major changes are inevitable if agriculture is to derive the benefits to be gained from access to a European market where prices are generally higher than in Portugal. Investments in education and training must transform a largely traditional and illiterate workforce into one that embraces new techniques and blend business skills such as accountancy and marketing with agricultural knowledge. Modest progress has already been achieved in horticulture and fruit- and flower-growing. Investment in cheese-production in order to improve quality control has resulted in the creation of regions of origin such as Serra da Estrela and Serpa. Further improvements are constrained by high interest rates (twenty-eight per cent in January 1991, compared with Spain's 15.8 per cent) and the high cost of inputs such as fertilisers, animal feeds, land costs etc. The outcome is that agricultural practices that have changed little in centuries coexist alongside state-of-the-art agricultural techniques and practices. Future prospects are overshadowed by uncertainty about the long-awaited reform of the CAP and the outcome of lengthy and contentious negotiations over the GATT. The USA, which has traditionally supplied the Iberian market with wheat and corn, hopes to re-enter a market from which it has been excluded since January 1991 by tariffs that protect EC producers from third-party competition.

Portugal's fishing fleet enjoys the EC's largest exclusive economic zone, but, in common with its European partners, the overall balance of advantage since accession has been far from positive. Fish stocks within the EEZ are severely depleted of all but sardines, tuna and swordfish – a deficiency reflected in EC fish imports, which rose from 1,500,000 tons in 1986 to 2,500,000 in 1990. Some 49,000,000 contos have been invested in the fishing fleet for the purchase of new boats and reconversions, but since Portugal lost the right to conduct bilateral negotiations over fish quotas, fish catches have fallen from 401,000 tons (1986) to 346,000 tons (1988).

EC FUNDS: BLESSING OR CURSE?

While access to Community funds has been almost universally welcomed, voices have warned that the investment influx has created a 'quimera de ouro' (pot of gold) mentality, not dissimilar to the impact made by Brazilian gold in the eighteenth century. The debate on the 'EC millions' began prior to 1986 at national and local government level. Anxieties were expressed that partisan criteria might be applied in the allocation of funds and that some regions would benefit disproportionately. The debate focused on the two concepts of equity versus efficiency. Was it more important to create jobs in backward regions or to prepare the economy for the single market in 1992? Inevitably, there has been a battle between political and developmental criteria in decisions concerning the distribution of funds.

From the outset, a satisfactory application of the incoming funds has presented problems. It is recognised that the EC coffers alone cannot correct regional disequilibria, nor bring Portuguese living standards closer to the EC average. Indeed, the lesson learned during FEDER's early years was that EC-financed projects tended to reinforce existing infrastructure and the distribution of wealth rather than reduce regional imbalances. Some commentators argued that more money was not the answer and cited Portugal's poor record in utilising preaccession funds to support their case. Deficient structures meant that some EC transfers were still to be spent, and irregularities had been uncovered. In fact,

EC lawyers directed the Portuguese authorities to investigate fraudulent misuse of fiscal transfers from Brussels after several million ecus disappeared from the Social Fund (Eisfeld 1989). A German magazine identified professional training companies as the culprits. They set up 'phantom courses' in order to qualify for the funds, which then disappeared into the pockets of 'consultants'. It was soon realised that merely sending a sack of projects to Brussels without identifying priorities or planning was counterproductive. In particular, the Portuguese bureaucracy was blamed for delays and incompetence. It was to meet these complaints that the EC demanded that more rigorous auditing and controls be applied when doubling the structural funds in 1988.

Whereas most of her European partners directed a substantial portion of their efforts to meeting the challenge of 1992, Portugal faced the twin demands of, on the one hand, investment-starved regions and, on the other, enterprises requiring cash injections for modernisation in order simply to survive the anticipated competition in the single market. Among the priorities identified was the development of larger, more efficient, firms able to compete with multinationals which in many cases are world leaders in their respective fields. Initially, such developments were largely confined to the banking sector, and doubts surfaced, given the traditional resistance to change in Portugal, that industry would utilise the structural funds to paper over its deficiencies rather than for the purpose of modernisation and, as a consequence, adjustment and restructuring would be postponed rather than accelerated as Brussels intended.

FOREIGN TRADE PATTERNS

When Portugal signed the accession treaty in 1985, trade relations with the new partners were already well established. The EC10 was the destination for sixty-three per cent of Portuguese exports and supplied forty-six per cent of the country's imports. During the second half of the decade, intra-Community trade patterns were consolidated: by 1990, the EC took seventy-four per cent of Portugal's exports and supplied seventy per cent of the imports. The closer trade

*Table 4.5*: Portugal's Main Trade Partners 1985–90 (percentage share).

| | Exports | | Imports | |
|---|---|---|---|---|
| | 1985 | 1990 | 1985 | 1990 |
| UK | 14.6 | 12.1 | 7.5 | 7.6 |
| Germany | 13.8 | 16.7 | 11.4 | 14.3 |
| France | 12.7 | 15.5 | 8.0 | 11.5 |
| USA | 9.2 | 4.8 | 9.7 | 3.9 |
| Netherlands | 6.9 | 5.7 | 3.2 | 5.8 |
| Spain | 4.1 | 13.3 | 7.3 | 14.4 |
| Italy | 4.0 | 4.0 | 5.1 | 10.0 |
| Sweden | 3.7 | 4.1 | 7.3 | 14.4 |

*Source*: Freire de Sousa 1991.

ties were accompanied by changes in the direction of economic relations with Portugal's partners. These can be summarised as follows.

Exports:
- The UK, traditionally the leading market for Portuguese exports, dropped to fourth place in the list of recipient countries.
- Germany and France took over as the main markets for Portuguese exports.
- Spain improved its position dramatically, moving up from sixth to third place.
- Italy, the Netherlands and the USA lost ground in percentage terms.

Imports:
- Spain improved its position to move from fifth to first place as the main source of Portugal's imports.
- Most EC countries improved their position apart from the UK.
- The USA, the second-most important supplier in 1985, dropped to eighth place.

There has been a general worsening in Portugal's trade balance with other EC countries since accession. The trade account with the EC was transformed from a small positive balance (8,900,000 contos) in 1985 into a deficit (731,900,000 contos) five years later. Only three trade deficits with individual member states were recorded in 1985 (Germany, Italy and Spain), but this had risen to seven by 1990 (France, Belgium, Germany, Italy, Ireland, Luxembourg and Spain). A surge in industrial imports from EC partners was to be expected in the short term as Portugal acquired the machinery, equipment and raw materials in order to develop new industries as part of its modernisation programme. It is therefore too early to assess fully the impact made by EC membership on the patterns of foreign trade. The impression provided by the composition of exports is that only modest shifts have occurred. However, the apparent stability may be

*Table 4.6*:   Portugal's Trade Balances (in millions of contos).

|                          | 1985  | 1990   |
|--------------------------|-------|--------|
| Belgium and Luxembourg   | 6.4   | -74.4  |
| Denmark                  | 12.2  | 18.5   |
| France                   | 18.1  | -45.6  |
| Germany                  | -15.2 | -118.1 |
| Greece                   | 1.7   | 7.2    |
| Ireland                  | 1.1   | -3.7   |
| Italy                    | -28.5 | -258.6 |
| Netherlands              | 25.5  | -71.2  |
| Spain                    | -56.1 | -201.1 |
| UK                       | 43.6  | 15.1   |
| EC                       | 8.9   | -731.9 |

*Source*: Freire de Sousa 1991.

deceptive, particularly given the high levels of inward foreign investment since 1986 which will in future boost exports from the non-traditional sectors such as motor vehicles, machine tools and electrical goods.

The degree of openness of the economy to the outside world as measured by the weight of total exports and imports in the GDP grew by sixteen per cent (fifteen per cent in relation to EC countries) after entry into the EC. In fact, Portugal's economic profile is rapidly moving into line with other small European economies. The weight of external trade in GDP has risen steadily from thirty per cent in 1980 to approximately forty-five per cent in 1990 and is still increasing. At present, Portugal is the fourth-most open economy in the EC behind Belgium (eighty-five per cent), Ireland (eighty-two per cent) and the Netherlands (sixty-five per cent).

### THE EMERGENCE OF THE IBERIAN MARKET

Bilateral trade relations between Portugal and Spain have been described as 'possibly the most important single aspect of accession for the smaller country' (Naylon 1987). Certainly, chief among the reservations expressed at the time of accession was the impact of free trade with the much larger Spanish economy. In part, the misgivings can be traced back in history to Spain's attempts to annex or dominate Portugal. The adversarial relationship was put on ice under the twentieth-century dictatorships, as both regimes pursued protectionist policies which reduced intra-Iberian trade to a trickle. It has been calculated that Spanish goods faced protective duties higher than (in some cases double) those that applied to EC countries as a result of administrative restrictions imposed following a sharp deterioration in the trade deficit between the two countries during the early 1980s. More recently, concern has focused on the sheer size of Spain's rapidly growing productive capacity: with a GDP double that of Portugal, Spain is Europe's fifth-largest economy (tenth in global terms). In addition, the Portuguese economy is quite heavily dependent on its neighbour's transport system for the movement of goods and for its energy requirements.

However, since the 1970s, the Iberians have undergone parallel political and economic processes more or less simultaneously. Both countries emerged from autocratic rule in mid-decade, joined the EC together and enjoyed economic growth rates above the European average during the 1980s. The apparent convergence has not meant that closer relations have inevitably ensued. The two countries crossed swords over fishing rights during the negotiations over Iberian entry into the EC, and a decision taken in 1985 to allow products with only thirty per cent of their value added in Portugal to cross the border duty-free prompted protests from Spain's business community about a prospective flood of goods assembled from components imported from West Germany and other advanced member states. Nevertheless, the under-lying assumption has been that Iberian unification is part and parcel of the wider European process.

Surprisingly, it is not the area of bilateral trade that has generated most concern in Portugal. In the 1970s, imports from across the border accounted for five per cent of Portugal's total imports, and exports to Spain accounted for less than 2.5 per cent of total exports. Since joining the EC there has been a spectacular growth in bilateral trade. Between 1985 and 1990, Portuguese exports to Spain grew at an annual average rate of 10.8 per cent (4.5 per cent for all exports), while imports from Spain increased at an annual average rate of 8.7 per cent (5.1 per cent for all imports). As Table 4.5 shows, in 1985, Spain was Portugal's second-largest supplier with 7.3 per cent of the total, while Portuguese cross-border exports constituted a mere 4.1 per cent of total exports – the sixth-most important market. Five years later, Spain had become Portugal's second main supplier with 14.4 per cent of total imports. Despite warnings that the trade imbalance would become heavily weighted in Spain's favour, Portuguese exports to her neighbour have expanded and the gap has closed, with textiles and leather goods registering particularly strong growth.

In 1985, exports covered forty-five per cent of imports; in 1989, they covered sixty per cent, leaving a trade deficit in excess of US$1 billion (*The Economist* 1990). A further improvement was recorded in 1990 when Portugal exported products worth 312,000,000 contos to its neighbour (a thirteen per cent increase over the previous year) and the rate of coverage rose to over sixty-five per cent. This performance reduced the unfavourable trade deficit by ten per cent from 183,300,000 contos to 166,500,000 contos. However, the deficit worsened again in 1991 to 206,000,000 contos (19.2 per cent up on the previous year) as Spanish exports expanded at a faster rate than the imports of Portugal's products.

It had been expected that Portugal would find it hard to compete in the neighbouring market, but this has not been the case. The Spanish market absorbed 12.5 per cent of Portuguese exports in 1989, as compared to only 4.1 per cent in 1985. Spain moved from sixth to third place among the most important markets for Portuguese goods following four years when average yearly export growth exceeded ten per cent (against 4.5 per cent for all exports). In 1990, the increase in Spain's cross-border exports was much more modest at 4.3 per cent, representing just over six per cent of Spain's total exports.

Although a cause for concern, the trade imbalance has not deteriorated as sharply as in most pessimistic predictions. Why, then, has there been so much talk about an 'invasion' from across the border and accusations that the Spanish were acquiring with money what their ancestors failed to do by force of arms? First, the Portuguese are wary that integration into an Iberian Common Market, which already exists in practice, is the first stage in an absorption process that could lead to the dilution or extinction of Portugal's economic, cultural and even political identity. There is ample evidence that, for multinational capital, Portugal is regarded an Iberian province that can be served from headquarters in Spain. In the process, Portugal could become more and more peripheral. The inferiority complex was fed by the attention that Spain has received as 1992 – *o ano espanhol* (Spain's year) – approached. Both Spain's international prestige and a further boost to her economy are expected to come from the Barcelona Olympics, the Seville World Fair and Madrid's designation as European City of Culture (Lisbon has to wait until 1994 for the honour). Harmony was not improved when an article appeared in the Madrid daily newspaper *El País*, which contained derogatory comments such as 'Portugal is a Third World country' where 'everyone travels by donkey'. Despite official disclaimers from Madrid, the suspicion remained that many Spaniards endorsed this caricature of their neighbours.

Second, the Spanish have been prime movers in the foreign investment boom. With the peseta appreciating strongly against the escudo, Portuguese assets have become attractively cheap. Spanish direct investment in Portugal totalled 8,300,000 contos in 1986 and rose to 77,800,000 contos in 1989 before falling over forty per cent to 55,300,000 contos in 1990. Portugal was the second-most important recipient of Spanish foreign investment in 1990, but slipped back to fourth place in the following year as the pace of cross-border investment slackened. The principal destination for Spanish investment in Portugal was the finance and insurance sector, followed by commerce, mining and chemicals. However, despite the welcome given to cross-border investment by the Portuguese authorities, Spanish investment exhibited three disappointing features as far as they were concerned. There was very little inter-firm cooperation and few joint venture projects, investment in the manufacturing sector was very low, and investment capital was directed in the main to the purchase of existing companies rather than to the creation of new ones.

In 1986, the Spanish held social capital in 285 companies. Two years later, the figure had risen to 660, and by 1989 it totalled over 1,000. In over two-thirds of the cases, the Spanish held more than fifty per cent of the social capital in these companies. By contrast, Portuguese capital figured in only sixty-five Spanish companies in 1988, rising to a little under 100 by 1990. The disparity is usually explained by a combination of factors: the high cost of gaining a foothold in the large Spanish market; the lack of entrepreneurial initiative compounded by the belief that it is difficult to sell in Spain; the low quality of Portuguese products and a persistently poor image abroad. Indeed, few products are sold abroad with a Portuguese trademark. Cortefiel, which manufactures many of its clothes across the border for sale in Spain, does not market under a Portuguese label. However, the company, which has a network of seventy stores in Spain, opened its first Portuguese branch in December 1991. There are exceptions: Viste Alegre porcelain, Mateus Rosé wines and some clothing companies are examples of brand names with a strong international image. Cenoura, the children's wear manufacturer, has a good reputation for design and has opened shops on a franchise basis in Spain and Ireland. Generally speaking, however, Portuguese products are regarded as 'third-rate' and typified by cheap, low-quality towels. In contrast, Spanish exporters are recognised as more aggressive and supported by a much stronger business structure. Among the factors encouraging cross-border investment are geographical proximity, similar market profiles in terms of tastes and culture, Portugal's small but expanding market, and, not least, a platform to penetrate third markets in the Portuguese-speaking world.

It is in Portugal's financial sector that Spanish companies have made most impact and caused the most alarm, leading to calls for tighter restrictions on foreign incursions. In fact, Spanish investors laid the groundwork for their assault in the early 1980s. Usually the first step was to open a small representative office with the job of monitoring market conditions. Once both countries were inside the EC the Spanish began to take a small stake in established Portuguese banks during privatisation. However, Banesto's five per cent stake in the Banco Totta e Açores (BTA) was deceptive. They also hold a forty-nine per cent partnership share in Valores Ibéricos, which owns over twenty per cent of BTA, and, according to the most recent estimates, Banesto has amassed a forty per cent stake in the Portuguese bank. In other cases, Spanish banks have gained a foothold by buying out existing foreign operators, as when the Banco Bilbao Vizcaya (BBV) acquired the British-owned Lloyds network for 25,000,000 contos in June 1990. In another move, the Banco Santander gained control of the Banco Comércio e Indústria and thereby acquired stakes in a range of Portuguese businesses.

Spain's assault on the neighbouring market has been felt particularly keenly in the ceramics industry. Although Spanish ceramics exports are not high-quality, Portuguese companies are not price-competitive largely because energy costs are very much lower for their Spanish competitors. Overproduction has led to accusations of dumping in order to off load surplus stocks. The external pressures on the Portuguese ceramics industry have made restructuring imperative and compelled companies to merge to form larger groups, such as Cinca and Grupo Apolo, specialising in a particular sector of the market. The move into the quality end of the market has proved costly and forced Portuguese companies to seek out foreign investors, such as the British multinational Ibstock Johnson, at the cost of surrendering overall control.

As integration becomes a reality, the existence of common interests is acknowledged at governmental level. The two heads of government meet every year to discuss matters of mutual interest. Evidence that an 'Iberian lobby' was emerging came at the sixth annual summit held in Seville in February 1990, when Cavaco Silva and Felipe González agreed to argue in unison for the continuation of structural funds after 1992. Both leaders warned that the diversion of funds to eastern Europe would endanger social cohesion within the EC and urged that democratic institutions and the market economy should be firmly rooted before significant sums are channelled to the east. Leaders of the southern and peripheral countries argued at the Maastricht summit in December 1991 that, unless there was a southward transfer of wealth before a single European currency was in place, they would find themselves permanently trapped at the foot of the EC development table. The demands for more money by the poorer southern states bore fruit when the EC agreed to greater fiscal transfers in the run-up to currency union.

The two leaders also agreed to promote cross-frontier development and, in the context of 1992, pointed to an extra frontier for those countries on the EC's periphery: the frontier of distance. In fact, improvements in communications are under way. Nine bridges have been built on the Luso-Spanish border with financial co-participation from the EC. There are also funds for a high-speed rail network. Disappointingly, only the Madrid-Seville stretch will be ready in time for 1992. Opposition to the high-speed link has come from the Oporto business community on the grounds that it primarily benefits Spanish interests and would leave isolated Portugal's northern 'industrial pole'. Meanwhile, EC funds for cross-border regions are encouraging cooperation in regional development among four frontier regions: northern and central Portugal and Galicia and Castilla-León in Spain. Using the European Regional Frontier Association as a forum, they have discussed common issues such as transport and communication, tourism, natural resources and regional development. So far, cooperation has been limited to areas such as tourism projects and trade fairs, but, given the strong cultural and linguistic links between Galicia and northern Portugal and their shared economic problems, there is potential for further developments in this area. However, closer collaboration may be undermined by concern over the glut of milk products (cartoned milk, cheese, butter and yoghurt) currently being vigorously promoted for sale in Portugal.

### THE IMPACT OF CHANGE IN EASTERN EUROPE

The eighteen-nation European Economic Space that emerged from the convulsions in Eastern Europe and the former Soviet Union during 1989–91 differs markedly from the Europe that Portugal joined in 1986. Falling trade barriers, a bigger market and greater competition seemed certain to benefit low-wage economies such as Portugal, Greece and Spain. However, German reunification and political and economic developments elsewhere in Eastern Europe threaten this scenario. Eastern Europe, and in particular eastern Germany, is an alternative attraction to southern Europe because of its low wage costs, skilled labour force and the projected investment boom as German capital moves east.

For the southern Europeans, the concern is that the European axis will tilt eastwards. This will distance Portugal from the decision-making centres and reduce her ability to influence events. A more practical worry concerns the diversion of funds and resources to eastern Europe. The prospect is that Portugal might suffer a significant reduction in economic aid after 1993. It has become increasingly urgent to take swift advantage of the EC funds on offer and to promote trade links with the emerging eastern European economies. One of the first indicators that the region is a rival attraction came with the decision by

Suzuki Motors to suspend studies into the establishment of a car assembly plant in Portugal in favour of a site in Hungary. For the Portuguese, the hope is that interest among foreign investors in the former Comecon bloc will subside, much as occurred with China a decade ago.

INTEGRATION: THE BALANCE-SHEET

It is still too early to pass more than an interim judgement on the impact that EC membership has made on the Portuguese economy. Nonetheless, it is possible to review the first six years of integration in the light of pre-1986 assessments of the likely impact of integration. In general, the analyses tended to be cautious, occasionally pessimistic and, in some quarters, defeatist. It was asked how a country with such a weak industrial base, backward agriculture, poor infrastructure and dependence on external energy sources could expect to compete with the advanced industrial economies of northern Europe.

Cravinho (1984) pointed out the threat posed to the domestic market by aggressive EC exporters, and especially the Spanish, as well as low-labour-cost Third World exporters who are exempted from customs duties under various arrangements. Portuguese exporters were expected to find themselves confined to the low-technology, cheap-labour end of the market, where their competitive position could only be maintained by regular devaluations and sustained downward pressure on real wage levels. Ashoff (1980) argued that EC entry was unlikely to provide much of a boost to export opportunities because Portugal already enjoyed free access to the Common Market for industrial products. He predicted that the development differential between the new and the old EC members would widen rather than narrow. This view was supported by Marques Mendes and Thirlwall (1989), who foresaw very bleak growth prospects for Portugal's economy because EC integration would tend to enhance rather than reverse 'the perverse trend in export specialisation'. They concluded that it was very unlikely that Portugal could achieve the rates of growth necessary to close the gap with the richer member states.

Braga de Macedo (1984) warned that there was no certainty that integration would actually bring benefits given the EC's 'irrational' existing structures, especially the CAP, and doubted Portugal's capacity to respond to the post-1986 challenges because of the restraints imposed by the contradictory constitutional system. He encapsulated the equivocal attitude in the title of a book published to mark the accession: 'undoubted costs, uncertain benefits'. Pitta e Cunha (1983) stressed the need for an urgent redefinition of the relationship between the public and private sectors and, in particular, the extent of government control over the economy. While conceding that the EC had the potential to act as 'a catalyst for the sorely needed rationalisation and modernisation of crippled industrial and agricultural structures', he nevertheless doubted whether Portugal's economic and administrative structures would be capable of absorbing such a large transfer of EC resources. The short-term adjustment costs were expected to produce a substantial increase in unemployment, bankruptcies and a worsening balance of payments situation.

Most of the pre-accession analyses either ignored or were unaware of a series of short-term factors that have conditioned the way in which the Portuguese economy has responded to the challenges posed. In the first place, the full impact has been cushioned by transition periods and extensions granted to Portugal in the application of EC directives. For instance, the removal of controls on the movement of capital was applied to the more advanced EC countries in 1990, while Portugal, along with Spain, Greece and Ireland, was allowed to delay lifting them until 1995. Appeals have already been made to extend the transition period for agriculture and the textile industry from ten years to fifteen. So the consequences of full integration have been postponed until 1996, but even so the question is still being asked whether this is long enough to modernise an underdeveloped and protected economy so that it can compete with some of the most advanced industrial states in the world.

The second factor was the speed of change within the EC at the time of accession. A mood of optimism prevailed that the integration process could be accelerated towards economic and even political union. The third factor was global economic conditions: strong demand in the European and world markets and favourable terms of trade created a environment that encouraged Portuguese exports, assisted growth in output and employment and permitted domestic consumption to rise without aggravating the balance of payments. This underlined the benefits to be derived from membership and helped to dispel, perhaps prematurely, some of the earlier gloomy prognostications about the cost of adjustment. Fourth, the psychological impact of joining the EC transformed attitudes and generated new opportunities. Diana Smith (1990) described it as 'the most positive politico-economic force to have touched Portugal since the country made its first transatlantic discoveries'. Certainly, joining the EC 12 did give a short-term boost to national confidence and acted as a catalyst and dynamic force across industry, finance and even agriculture.

### THE SINGLE EUROPEAN MARKET (SEM)

Portugal's industrial structure was expected to face the most difficult adjustment problems in the run-up to the *mercado único* (single market). Not only are tariff barriers coming down as a result of joining the EC, but the end of the transitional phase also coincides with the completion of the 1992 project. Both Portugal and Greece appended separate declarations to the Single European Act (SEA) to the effect that progress towards a single market should not damage sensitive and vital sectors of their economies. Industry has therefore been engaged in a race against time. The challenge has been to utilise incoming EC resources to modernise the productive structures in order to compete on equal terms with Portugal's European partners.

The European Commission (1990a) published an evaluation of the consequences that could ensue for Portuguese industry in the single market. Some 120 industries were analysed and divided into three categories: above average, average and low competitiveness. Nine strong points (comprising twenty-two per cent of total employment and fourteen per cent of the value added in industry) were identified: ceramics, household textiles, wines, footwear, knitwear and ready-made clothing, fish and seafood, and insulated wires and cables. However, the study warned that, as competitiveness in these areas is dependent upon prices, low wage costs and flexible working conditions (including homeworking), they are highly dependent on export markets and therefore extremely vulnerable to growing competition from Europe and the NIEs. The middle-ranking sectors deemed to have average competitiveness include confectionery, shipbuilding, metal products, carpets and car bodies. The weak points (representing twelve per cent of total employment and sixteen per cent of value added) are identified as electrical goods, wool and cotton textiles, agrochemicals, glass and glassware, motor vehicles and textile machinery. These sectors are particularly vulnerable to import penetration, and accession may well have a negative impact.

The report concluded that, although the internal market presented opportunities, 'Portuguese industry still shows major structural imbalances in particular as regards technological dependency, low specialisation of human resources and the low rationalisation of management, above all in the SMEs'. It also highlighted the reticence displayed by businessmen over collaboration with their European partners in fields such as distribution and research and development. Portugal was advised to transform its industrial specialisation pattern by upgrading product quality in traditional sectors and moving into high-technology industries. This process requires the modernisation of the industrial base and substantial investment in professional training.

In a survey on the social effects of 1992, the Ministry of Employment and Social Security (MESS) examined over forty sectors regarded as sensitive to the arrival of the SEM. They represent 57.1 per cent of employment and 47.3 per cent of gross value added in manufacturing industry. Two major conclusions were drawn: first, important manufacturing sectors, such as textiles and footwear,

*Table 4.7*:   Sectors of Portuguese Industry under Threat Post-1992 (by country/group of countries).

| | |
|---|---|
| Italy: | ornamental stone, ceramics, footwear, ready-made clothing, tanning, industrial machinery |
| Spain: | ceramics, wines, footwear, wires and cables, woollen textiles, chemicals, vehicle assembly, white technology goods |
| Greece: | clothing, footwear, wires and cables |
| Eastern Europe: | agricultural foodstuffs, forestry products, paper paste |
| Other OECD: | clothing, textiles and yarns, pharmeceuticals, electronics, white technology, chemicals |
| NICS and Third World: | electronics and microelectronics, footwear, clothing |

*Source*: *Exame* 1991a.

expected to reduce their workforce as part of the rationalisation measures imposed by international competition, and second, the distribution of the layoffs is likely to be concentrated principally in the districts of Braga, Castelo Branco and Guarda, where firms specialise in the production of clothing, knitwear and woollen goods. Some early indications that the repercussions will not all be positive came from data provided by the Companhia de Seguros de Crédito (COSEC), which calculated that in excess of 760 firms have closed since 1986. The sectors most seriously affected were textiles, clothing, food and drink and civil construction. Among the most often-cited causes for the business failures were poor management and current market conditions. Obviously, more detailed work has to be carried out covering a longer time-span before the true extent of the impact can be evaluated.

One of the few detailed studies so far undertaken on the regional effects of EC entry was published by the University of Coimbra. It concluded that, during the three-year period between 1985 and 1987, intra-Community exports tripled and imports (measured in dollars at current prices) increased eighteen-fold. The sectors in Portugal's central region that benefited most from the surge in exports were wood products, cement and minerals. Clearly, the costs of consolidating interdependence were eased considerably by the growth in the European and global economies and the favourable terms of trade during the transition period. Because of the external environment, unemployment was not aggravated, bankruptcies were kept to a minimum and the stop-go policies of the 1970s and early 1980s were not repeated.

### PORTUGAL AND MONETARY UNION

Portugal became the eleventh EC country (the exception is Greece) to join the Exchange Rate Mechanism (ERM) in April 1992. The surprise decision came after a debate about the timing of such a move. The arguments for delay centred on the requirement to bring inflation more firmly under control (the 1992 rate was twice the German level) and reduce the differential between Portugal and its EC partners. It was also pointed out that Portugal faced twin shocks because the restructuring process was occurring simultaneously with the removal of subsidies and other policy instruments as part of the preparations for 1992. Echoing these concerns, Gibson and Tsakalotos (1992), in their comparative study of southern European economies, recommended a gradualist approach to avoid financial instability and minimise the impact that financial liberalisation might have on the real economy. In particular, they saw the retention of capital controls for a specified period as essential in order to allow some policy independence. Moreover, a gradual strategy would allow the EC time to develop further mechanisms to ensure the smooth integration of the southern European member states. In the same study, Cassola e Barata (1992) warned that ERM entry accompanied by the rapid removal of capital controls could have adverse consequences, particularly given the size of the public deficit and the current-account deficit. He concluded with a warning that the timescale may be dangerously truncated: 'Portugal would probably be better off if "1992" were in the year 2002'.

Rejecting the 'economist' school of integration, Portugal's finance minister, Jorge Braga de Macedo, opted for a 'monetarist' strategy in order to achieve what government policy had so far singularly failed to do: to impose greater financial discipline and encourage price stability. He expected that his decision would administer 'shock treatment' to the Portuguese economy and necessitate a sharp reduction in the budget deficit along with modifications in monetary and exchange-rate policies. Like the Spanish peseta, the escudo began trading in the wide band which allows it to fluctuate by six per cent either side of its central rate.

In fact, one of the overriding motives behind Portugal's ERM decision was political. By announcing the move before Portugal's presidency of the EC terminated in June, Lisbon underscored its political commitment to membership and signalled its determination to join economic and monetary union (EMU) at its launch in 1997. Domestically, its value was also symbolic: to reinforce the anti-inflation strategy and lend credibility to monetary policy. Any advantages must be weighed against the recognition that the government has opted for a high-risk strategy. Cavaco Silva has to explain why austerity is required when the economy has apparently been performing so well over the past few years. It can legitimately be asked whether such austerity and discipline is appropriate for an economy in the process of catching up with its European partners, and almost inevitably there will be a price to pay in terms of higher unemployment and lower output. In addition, it is salutary to note that Spanish inflation did not fall automatically following Madrid's decision to join the ERM in June 1989.

Portugal will not find it easy to meet the convergence terms for joining EMU, as Table 4.8 demonstrates. The criteria laid down include a sustainable inflation rate not more than 1.5 per cent above the average for the three lowest states; a budget deficit of not more than three per cent of GDP; a national debt at sixty per cent of GDP or lower, and interest rates not more than two per cent above the average for the three best-performing states. In late 1991, the government's *Plano de Convergência* (Convergence Plan) set an inflation target of between seven and nine per cent for 1992 and between four and six per cent for 1993–5. The intention is to reduce the inflation differential between Portugal and the EC average while maintaining the above-average growth rate.

Portugal considers that economic and social cohesion (CES) is a central objective of the EC. In concert with other less-developed member states, Lisbon wants to see a reform of the structural funds and a reduction in national co-participation obligations. Matching Brussels's contribution has exerted a strain on government finances and placed obstacles in the way of reducing the budget deficit. In this context, public investment cuts of around 70,000,000 contos were announced in November 1991 which affected spending on vocational

*Table 4.8*:   Convergence: Economic Criteria.

|  | Inflation %| Budget deficit % GDP | Total public debt % GDP | Long-term interest rates % |
|---|---|---|---|---|
| Belgium | 3.2 | 6.3 | 129.4 | 9.3 |
| Denmark | 2.4 | 1.7 | 66.7 | 10.1 |
| France | 3.0 | 1.5 | 47.2 | 9.0 |
| Germany | 4.6 | 3.6 | 45.4 | 8.7 |
| Greece | 18.3 | 17.9 | 96.4 | 19.5 |
| Ireland | 3.0 | 4.1 | 102.8 | 9.2 |
| Italy | 6.4 | 9.9 | 101.2 | 12.9 |
| Luxembourg | 3.4 | -2.0 | 6.9 | 8.2 |
| Netherlands | 3.2 | 4.4 | 78.4 | 8.9 |
| Portugal | 11.7 | 5.4 | 64.7 | 17.1 |
| Spain | 5.8 | 3.9 | 45.6 | 12.4 |
| UK | 6.5 | 1.9 | 43.8 | 9.9 |

*Source*: European Commission 1991b.

training, infrastructure (including tourism) projects and science and technology. Clearly, a tension has arisen between the requirement to catch up with the rest of Portugal's partners and the exigencies of ever-closer economic integration. It is sobering to note that according to one calculation, assuming that current growth rates are sustained, it will not be until 2040 that Portugal reaches the average EC level of development (*Exame* 1991a).

The possibility does exist that Portugal, along with Greece, will be left behind in a two-speed EMU at the end of 1993. Both countries continue to maintain autonomous exchange-rate policies in order to maintain their competitive positions and allow adjustment to domestic and external shocks. EMU would mean abandoning this policy mechanism, which has led to fears that monetary unification will amplify the impact on the EC's poorer regions of the shocks stemming from the single market. For this reason, Portugal has joined other southern European members in calling for the continuation of structural funds after the time-table ends in 1993.

Small local businesses, which abound in Portugal, may well suffer from the impact of EMU on the credit market. In its report on the single market, the Commission (1990a) cites the hypothetical case of a small enterprise in northern Portugal which at present obtains credit through its local bank and asks whether it will be any better off when it has access to the larger banks elsewhere in the EC. In fact, it may find that it is crowded out along with other local borrowers for failing to meet the eligibility criteria of the larger banks, whereas the local bank would eventually extend some credit.

PORTUGAL AND THE EC PRESIDENCY

Portugal's occupancy of the EC presidency in the first half of 1992 was expected both to raise the consciousness of Europe within the country and to dispel its image abroad as a marginal country on the continental periphery (Brassloff 1991). Certainly, within the country the EC remains popular. An opinion poll conducted for the *Express* (1991b) newspaper shortly before Portugal assumed the presidency revealed that seventy-nine per cent felt that the country was better off since joining the EC, fifty-nine per cent favoured greater economic integration, seventy-two per cent wanted a wider Europe embracing the former eastern bloc countries, and sixty-nine per cent supported political union and a federal state. The pro-European mood may not be misplaced. According to a recent EFTA study on the effects of 1992, Portugal emerges as one of the beneficiaries from a future European Economic Space (EES).

Portugal opted for a non-controversial presidency with the emphasis placed on consolidation and the avoidance of a two-speed Europe. Nevertheless, the economic problems on the agenda for the first half of 1992 were formidable. They included:

- the aftermath of negotiations over EMU and closer political union;
- completion of the single market programme;
- reform of the CAP;
- reform of EC finances and the structural funds; and
- the debate on EC enlargement.

Such tasks may deflect Portugal from developing closer European ties with southern Africa, where investment opportunities exist following the end of the civil wars in Angola and Mozambique, and Latin America, especially Brazil. It is expected that the country's profile and prestige will be raised, and, as long as there is progress towards convergence and living standards continue to rise, the loss of economic sovereignty implied in EMU and even moves towards a federal Europe will be regarded as positive steps.

Six years on from accession, Portugal has taken its place as a natural member of the European Community. Atlanticism no longer competes as an alternative scenario. This represents one of the most remarkable transformations in post-Salazarist Portugal, although perhaps it can be attributed to the absence of viable alternatives rather than unalloyed enthusiasm for federalism. Nor is it clear whether attitudes will change once the 'long honeymoon' provided by the transition period comes to an end. However, a broad consensus exists on the desirability of closer integration, even though the motives may differ: some see Europe as an anchor for Portuguese democracy, others as the inevitable consequence of growing interdependence, while others regard it as a way of forcing through reforms of the country's economic structures. Whatever the reasons, it is clear that Portugal is prepared to play a constructive role in future developments and that EC issues are firmly at the centre of the national political agenda.

CHAPTER 5

# Economic Boom and Modernisation
## The Economy under Cavaco Silva, 1985–91

In the mid-1980s, Portugal was presented with the opportunity to confront many of the problems inherited from the dictatorship and compounded during the revolution of 1974–5. In essence, two major structural weaknesses can be identified: one political, the other economic. Politically, Portugal was plagued by unstable, short-lived administrations and frequent elections. Economically Portugal was hamstrung by an overprotected, stagnant economy struggling to recover from the internal and external shocks inflicted during the 1970s. Relief came in the form of assistance from the IMF, but proved to be only short-term and exacerbated, rather than reduced, external dependency. Despite this unpromising background, Portuguese democracy began its second decade with the international and domestic conjunctures in rare symmetry. A favourable set of circumstances generated optimism that sustained growth might be achieved without a return to the familiar stop–go pattern of the 1970s and early 1980s. This chapter will attempt to account for and analyse the boom in the late 1980s during which Portugal enjoyed five consecutive years of economic growth for the first time since the Second World War.

### POLITICAL STABILITY

A vital ingredient in providing a firm foundation for economic growth and lifting hopes about future prospects was the achievement of medium-term political stability. The process came in three discernible stages:

1985–87 PSD minority government (eighty-eight seats in 250-seat parliament)
1987–91 PSD absolute majority (153 seats)
1991 to date PSD second consecutive absolute majority (130 seats in 230-seat parliament).

The October 1985 general election brought to power a minority Social Democrat government under the leadership of Aníbal Cavaco Silva, a Bank of Portugal economist and former finance minister. He took office at a time that proved to be politically and economically propitious. The main opposition party, the PS, had lost its founder and leader and was plagued by internal divisions. In contrast, Cavaco was able to present himself as untainted by past failures and having a firm grip on his own (previously divided) party. His technocratic and managerial, if somewhat aloof, approach tuned in well with the mood of a country weary of political intrigue and on the brink of entry into the EC.

With thirty months of its term still to run, the minority government fell to a parliamentary censure motion and Cavaco was able to go back to the electorate to ask for a majority in the July 1987 election. The emphasis on growth in order to bridge the gap between living standards in Portugal and the rest of Europe went down well with a public tired of austerity and the country's unenviable position at the foot of most European tables of socioeconomic indicators. Cavaco's campaign, launched under the slogan '*Portugal no pode parar*' (Portugal cannot slow down), tuned into the agenda of the European right associated with Thatcherism which seemed to be accepted by governments, including socialist ones, throughout Europe: rolling back the state, support for the private sector, reliance on market forces etc. In contrast, the opposition parties had little to offer either ideologically or programmatically.

The PSD's outright majority in 1987 guaranteed that Portugal would enjoy an extended period of political stability for the first time since 1974 and enabled the government to think of longer-term planning. It marked the end, for a few years at least, of minority governments, unstable coalitions and almost constant electioneering. Portugal now had its first-ever single-party majority government – a remarkable achievement in a multi-party proportional system and a landmark, ranking alongside the 1974 revolution, in the country's political development (Gallagher 1988; Corkill 1988). By the end of August 1990, Cavaco became only the second head of government under a democratic system to remain in office for five consecutive years and the first since 25 April 1974 to complete a full four-year term. When he went to the country again in October 1991, the prime minister secured a second overall majority with a slightly increased percentage vote, thereby ensuring a further four years of political stability and continuity.

*Table 5.1*:   Election Results 1987–91 (percentage of vote).

|  |  | 1985 General | 1987 General | 1989 European | 1989 Local | 1991 General |
|---|---|---|---|---|---|---|
| PSD | (Social Democrats) | 29.8 | 50.1 | 32.7 | 31.0 | 50.4 |
| PS | (Socialists) | 20.7 | 22.2 | 28.5 | 32.0 | 29.3 |
| CDU | (Communists and allies) | 15.5 | 12.1 | 14.4 | 13.0 | 8.8 |
| CDS | (Centre Democrats) | 9.9 | 4.4 | 14.2 | 9.0 | 4.4 |
|  | Others | 24.1 | 11.2 | 10.2 | 15.0 | 7.1 |

*Source*: Corkill (1988).

Apart from majority government, a second important element in the extended period of political stability was the prime minister's acceptance of 'cohabitation' with a socialist president. In the 1986 presidential election, Cavaco's favoured candidate Diogo Freitas do Amaral was narrowly defeated (51.3 per cent to 48.7 per cent) by Mario Soares. It raised the uncomfortable prospect that a socialist president (the first civilian to hold the office since 1926) might be at loggerheads with a reformist, centre-right prime minister, particularly in such contentious areas as constitutional reform and the privatisation of state enterprises. When Soares stood for re-election in January 1990, Cavaco decided not to run a candidate against the incumbent president – an indication that the two men had established a working relationship based on mutual respect (Corkill 1991).

ECONOMIC RECOVERY AND 'CONTROLLED PROGRESS'

The origins of the economic boom can be traced to the 1983–5 Soares-Mota Pinto administration's austerity package which provided the platform for a strong, sustainable medium-term recovery. While it is generally conceded that the deflation was too severe – investment declined by 7.5 per cent and eighteen per cent during 1983 and 1984, domestic demand slumped by almost seven per cent and real wages fell by seventeen per cent over the two years – nevertheless the measures did guarantee that the upturn would be quite marked. Faced with lower domestic demand, industry responded by switching output towards exports (OECD 1986). The current account had shown enough improvement by 1985 to register a positive balance amounting to US$300,000,000 – the first surplus since 1973, whereupon foreign investment began to flow in at record levels.

The Cavaco government's first programme, unveiled in November 1985 under the title 'controlled progress', emphasised economic expansion, reduced state intervention and the stimulation of productive investment. The improvement in the trade balance meant that the government could reflate the economy and even allow the external deficit to deteriorate in order to stimulate change and encourage the private sector. Despite containing some contradictions, the programme represented a marked advance in terms of signposting the future direction that the economy should take. The specific fiscal and monetary measures implemented included interest-rate reductions on borrowing and lending and the suspension for four months of the crawling peg currency devaluations which had been operating at a one per cent monthly average. Lower interest rates quickly had the desired effect, and the 1986 budget launched a major investment drive in areas such as infrastructure, agriculture and education.

During 1986–7, Portugal began to reap the economic harvest from an exceptionally favourable set of exogenous factors. Lower oil prices and declining interest rates revived the world economy and combined with the onset of pre-accession aid from Brussels to administer a much-needed boost to the Portuguese economy. Cavaco's rejection of past policies aimed at dampening down demand along with the emphasis on encouraging investment apparently signalled a policy shift away from the externally-prescribed recipes of the past. As a first step, the government presented an expansionary budget to the Assembly in December 1986 and predicted growth at between three and four per cent and a continued decline in the inflation rate to below 8.5 per cent.

In summary, the government's main objectives were:
- to achieve high and sustainable rates of GDP growth;
- to lower the unemployment rate;
- to bring inflation under control;
- to correct the disequilibrium in the balance of payments; and
- to stimulate investment and reduce the public-sector deficit.

Structural constraints on growth were to be progressively removed by means of a policy agenda that included:
- the liberalisation of the financial system;
- an overhaul of the tax system;
- the reform of the labour laws; and
- a privatisation programme aimed at substantially reducing the weight of the public sector and cutting the public debt.

In order to assess the progress made in achieving these targets, each of the specific policy areas will be analysed in turn.

### GROWTH AND EMPLOYMENT

Two aspects of economic policy for which the government could claim success were GDP growth and the fall in unemployment. As Table 5.2 indicates, Portugal achieved what Williams (1991) calls 'one of the most remarkable economic performances in recent years'. Not only were GDP increases superior to the EC average, but Portugal's per capita GDP also rose off the bottom of the EC league table to overtake Greece. Even when growth slowed in 1990, the Portuguese rate was still above the EC average. Of course, it is hardly surprising that the economy did so well, given such a positive set of circumstances which are unlikely to be repeated in the future.

Unemployment has fallen steadily since 1985 to reach the lowest levels since

*Table 5.2*:   Economic Growth and Unemployment in Portugal 1985–91 (percentage change).

|                    | 1985 | 1986 | 1987 | 1988 | 1989 | 1990 | 1991 |
|--------------------|------|------|------|------|------|------|------|
| GDP growth         | 3.0  | 4.1  | 5.0  | 4.0  | 5.4  | 4.2  | 2.7  |
| EC average         | 2.5  | 2.7  | 2.9  | 4.0  | 3.3  | 2.8  | 1.3  |
| Unemployment (%)   | 8.7  | 8.6  | 7.1  | 5.8  | 5.1  | 4.6  | 4.5  |

*Source*: OECD 1991b.

the 1970s. In 1990, Portugal recorded the second-lowest average annual rate of unemployment in the EC (Table 5.2), at 4.6 per cent – half the EC average. A particular feature of the impressive performance in job-creation has been the greater use of female labour. However, it is not possible to attribute the fall in unemployment exclusively to the creation of new jobs. First, the number of people on specially-designed, EC-funded training programmes disguises the true state of affairs. Second, the statistics do not take into account the number of poorly-paid workers who are employed clandestinely with little job security. Long-term unemployment has remained fairly high at around forty per cent of total unemployed and among young workers (over eleven per cent in 1989). Furthermore, the rate is set to rise after 1992 in line with the rest of the EC as the cushion provided by the transition arrangements is removed. A recent study carried out by the Gulbenkian Foundation predicted that unemployment could reach between ten and fourteen per cent by the year 2005. The four main areas where job losses are expected to be quite extensive in the coming years are agriculture, textiles, state banking and the bureaucracy. So far, the government has shied away from making difficult decisions, particularly with regard to cuts in the state payroll, but it cannot delay beyond the end of 1992, by which time unemployment could re-emerge as a potent political issue.

### INFLATION

Since the revolution, Portugal has become accustomed to a high inflation rate, fluctuating at rates between sixteen and twenty-nine per cent for the ten-year period 1975–85. Although Portugal's inflation remained high and well above the EC average for 1983–5, there were encouraging signs that the underlying trend was downwards. The increases during 1983–4 are attributable to the stabilisation programme which involved the dismantling of price controls, subsidy cuts, particularly on food, and higher charges for rent, transport and other services. The large escudo devaluation also contributed to the upward pressure on prices by making imports more expensive, as also did the imposition of VAT, which, according to OECD estimates, added two per cent to consumer prices in 1986 (OECD 1989). The decision to raise petroleum taxes substantially and to deny the consumer the benefits of tumbling world oil prices and cheaper agricultural imports would almost certainly have stoked up inflation had not external developments cushioned their impact.

The negative effects of these measures were more than compensated for by

*Table 5.3*: Inflation in Portugal and the EC 1985–91 (percentage increase).

|            | 1985 | 1986 | 1987 | 1988 | 1989 | 1990 | 1991 |
|------------|------|------|------|------|------|------|------|
| Portugal   | 19.3 | 11.7 | 9.4  | 9.7  | 12.6 | 13.4 | 11.4 |
| EC average | 6.2  | 3.8  | 3.4  | 3.7  | 5.3  | 5.7  | 5.0  |

*Source*: OECD 1991b.

the exceptional set of exogenous factors that came to Portugal's assistance from 1985 onwards. The improving international economic climate, which saw renewed expansion in world trade and strong growth throughout the European economy, provided a breathing space and a unique opportunity to close the gap separating Portugal from its European partners through sustained economic growth and a programme of rapid modernisation and structural change. At this juncture, the economy's openness and dependence on external fluctuations worked to Portugal's advantage. The precipitous slide in the dollar's international value provided an unexpected windfall, and Portugal shared the benefits accruing from the halving of world petroleum prices – net oil imports stood at a globally high estimated equivalent eight per cent of GDP in 1985 (EIU 1989) – and from the weakening dollar, the currency in which agro-food imports, mostly of US origin, are priced. The upshot was that consumer prices fell substantially, reducing from an annual increase of just under thirty per cent to a low of 11.7 per cent in 1986 – a major improvement, but still above the EC average. The ability to deliver both growth and lower inflation was greatly assisted by the drop in international and domestic interest rates. The authorities progressively reduced the interest rate between mid-1985 and mid-1986, thereby providing a boost to business activity, consumer confidence and investment plans (OECD 1988/9).

The downward trend in inflation halted in 1988 when the government considerably overshot its six per cent inflation target. Indeed, while inflation was a largely imported phenomenon during the early 1980s, it was largely internally generated by the late 1980s as a result of the growth in consumption, real wage increases and the persistent budget deficit. The reversal in the inflationary trend during 1989–90 owed much to high and rising demand pressures. Total domestic demand grew at a rate of more than eight per cent per year between 1986 and 1988, while private consumption averaged 6.5 per cent over the same period (OECD 1990/1). Upward pressures were exerted by wage rises above the agreed levels, which employers were able to afford from their profits, increases in the minimum wage rates which formed part of the catching-up process for the lower-paid, and record low unemployment combined with buoyant labour demand. Instead of achieving a rate closer to the EC12 average, inflation peaked at 13.4 per cent in 1990 (the second-highest in the EC). Clearly, the causes of inflation had not been eliminated, and it owed something to the government's commitment to growth rather than to tackling the root causes of inflation. The failure to apply strict budgetary controls inevitably led to high expenditure increases which could not be reversed for political reasons until after the 1991 elections. Apart from internal factors, the resurgence could be attributed to exogenous causes: higher prices for food imports, rising international interest rates and higher oil prices.

The government's anti-inflation strategy did not rely exclusively on neo-liberal remedies. An incomes policy was added to the budgetary, monetary and

*Table 5.4*: Incidence of Strikes and Evolution of Wages/Minimum Wage 1986–91.

|  | 1986 | 1987 | 1988 | 1989 | 1990 | 1991 |
|---|---|---|---|---|---|---|
| Strikes | 363 | 213 | 181 | 362 | n.a. | n.a. |
| Wages (% change) | 18.9 | 14.5 | 12.0 | 13.2 | n.a. | n.a. |
| Real wages (% change) | 7.2 | 5.1 | 2.4 | 0.6 | n.a. | n.a. |
| Minimum wage (industry and services, in contos) | 22.5 | 25.2 | 27.2 | 31.5 | 35.0 | 40.1 |

*Source*: *Expresso*; MESS.

fiscal mechanisms employed to contain inflationary pressures. In October 1990, the Confederations of Industry and Trade joined the second-largest confederation, the General Workers' Union (UGT), in signing the government's social pact (*Acordo Económico e Social* (AES), the Economic and Social Agreement). In return for a commitment to industrial harmony and a voluntary wage ceiling, the union won improvements in welfare benefits, shorter hours (a reduction in the working week from forty-eight to forty hours by 1995) and an increase in the minimum wage to 40,100 Esc. While the AES constituted an additional plank in efforts to bring down inflation, the suspicion existed that, with an election in the offing, Cavaco accepted terms which might well have been rejected in other circumstances. The agreement was undoubtedly generous and threatened to undermine Portugal's competitiveness as a low-wage economy. Nevertheless, the social pact did begin to move Portugal more into line with the rest of the EC in terms of its non-labour costs such as pensions, social security provisions, holidays etc.

The government favoured conciliation in order to prevent further disruption to growth and output. Table 5.4 provides MESS figures which reveal that strike activity tailed off after 1985 to reach a low point in 1988 but revived strongly in 1989, when there were twice as many disputes as in the previous year. There were special features to the new wave of labour discontent, namely the involvement of professional groups which had seen their earnings eroded by inflation, such as doctors, teachers, lawyers, air traffic controllers, customs officers and the police, which the PSD government could ill afford to alienate permanently. In addition, profound changes were under way within the labour movement which predisposed the trade unions to corporatist-style solutions. First, union membership had fallen by over ten per cent in the four-year period 1986–90 to forty-two per cent of the economically active population – a significant drop, but still a high proportion in comparison with the more advanced industrial countries, where the average is twenty-eight per cent. Second, a readjustment has occurred in the relative strength of the two major confederations, the CGTP and UGT. The former's share of the unionised workforce plummeted from three-quarters to fifty-seven per cent, while the UGT saw its share grow from a fifth to a third of the total. A significant feature is the progress made by the independent, professionally-based unions which comprise the *Organizacões Sindicais Independentes* (Independent Union Organisations), which represented ten per cent of the total unionised workforce by 1990. Of the seventeen new unions established in 1989, the majority represented professional groups. Third, adversity is bringing the two largest confederations closer together. They began to submit joint demands to the government and the employers amid talks about a possible merger.

THE BALANCE OF PAYMENTS

A particular feature of the Portuguese economy in this period was the strong export performance. The expansion was impressive: up in volume by 23.5 per cent in 1989 and 21.7 per cent in 1990 before slowing to 11.8 per cent in 1991 (OECD 1991). However, export growth was soon threatened by a cluster of factors: persistently high inflation, an overvalued currency, a recession in the main export markets and strong competition from competitors in the developing world. Crucially, the growth in exports failed to compensate for the high volume of imports pouring into the country. Inevitably, the trade account deteriorated, and the trade gap widened alarmingly from US $1.7 billion in 1986 to US $7.3 billion in 1991. Expansionary policies had carried fewer risks when external factors were so favourable. However, the external deflationary climate could not be sustained indefinitely.

After a temporary dip, import growth restarted in 1990 and exports were threatened by adverse factors such as an exchange-rate policy based on permitting a real, effective appreciation, worsening terms of trade and an economic recession in important markets such as the UK and France. However, these developments were compensated for by improvements in terms of output and export growth resulting from recent investment in the modernisation of Portuguese industry, expressed in growth rates of over thirty per cent for motor vehicle and machinery exports in 1989 (OECD 1991). As a result, the current-account deficit was cut by half in 1989 (from 2.4 per cent of GDP to 1.2 per cent) due to an amelioration in the trading position and an improvement in receipts from invisibles.

*Table 5.5:*   Balance of Trade and Current Account 1986–90 (millions of US dollars).

|  | 1986 | 1987 | 1988 | 1989 | 1990 |
|---|---|---|---|---|---|
| Exports | 7.202 | 9.268 | 10.875 | 12.716 | 16.301 |
| Imports | 8.874 | 12.849 | 16.393 | 17.594 | 23.129 |
| Trade balance | -1.762 | -3.581 | -5.518 | -5.152 | -6.828 |
| Current balance (as percentage of GDP) | 4.0 | 1.2 | -2.4 | -1.2 | -0.3 |

*Source*: OECD 1991.

*Table 5.6*:   Tourism and Tourist Receipts 1985–9.

|  | 1985 | 1986 | 1987 | 1988 | 1989 | 1990 |
|---|---|---|---|---|---|---|
| Foreign Visitors (millions) | 11.6 | 13.0 | 16.2 | 16.1 | 16.5 | 18.4 |
| Tourists (millions) | 4.9 | 5.4 | 6.1 | 6.6 | 7.1 | 8.0 |
| Receipts (million contos) | 191.8 | 228.4 | 302.6 | 349.1 | 424.8 | 506.0 |
| Receipts per tourist (dollars) | 229.0 | 281.0 | 355.0 | 368.0 | 381.0 | n.a. |
| Receipts as % of GNP | 5.4 | 5.1 | 5.8 | 5.8 | 5.9 | n.a. |

*Source*: Bank of Portugal and INE statistics.

The surplus on invisibles such as tourism, investment income, emigrant remittances and other transfers contributed to the upturn after 1985 and was equivalent to ten per cent of GDP in 1988–9. In the mid-1980s, tourism experienced a boom, not only on the Algarve and the Atlantic islands but also on Lisbon's 'Costa do Sol' and even in the previously neglected central and northern regions. The volume of tourists visiting the country had grown steadily even during the recession years in the early 1980s, and, as Table 5.6 demonstrates, the numbers surged impressively from 1985–90 and tourism receipts more than doubled from just under 200,000,000 contos to over 500,000,000 contos. Receipts from tourism provided twelve per cent of the government's current income and six per cent of GDP (compared to an EC average of 1.7 per cent and Spain's five per cent). In 1988, tourism receipts grew by 13.5 per cent in dollar terms due to an increase in the number of higher-spending tourists (OECD 1989). Moreover, the buoyant and expanding tourism sector had a far wider impact in terms of generating employment (an estimated 150,000 people and many more indirectly) and in stimulating infrastructure development (EIU 1989).

While Spain experienced a damaging drop in visitor numbers during 1990 as a result of increased competition and changing consumer tastes, Portugal's income from tourism grew steadily (up by seventeen per cent in the first six months of 1990 over the previous year). Clearly, Portugal had begun to reap the benefits from the funds injected by SIFIT (System of Financial Incentives for Tourism), which invested Esc 62 billion during 1988–91, and from the continuing high level of foreign investment attracted by the sector. The funds, allocated by the *Direccão Geral do Turismo*, were intended to encourage tourism projects in less-developed regions and are allocated using criteria such as location, employment generation and the contribution to regional development.

Remittances grew apace in the late 1980s despite a drop in the number of emigrants. In 1989, emigrant remittances were equivalent to twenty per cent of total exports of goods and services (OECD 1991). During 1990, Portuguese residents abroad sent back 684,000,000 contos – a twenty-two per cent increase over the 1989 figure. Half the total came from the estimated 1,000,000 emigrants resident in EC countries and a third from France alone (229,000,000 contos), followed by Switzerland (119,000,000 contos) and Germany (46,000,000 contos). Significantly, however, the first signs of a drop in the level of remittances were registered among emigrants living in Belgium, Denmark, France and the Netherlands, who contributed less than in 1989. Indeed, the long-term trend is for a reduction in the overall total of remittances. There are two principal reasons for this. First, the number of emigrants is diminishing; second, while the first generation of emigrants preferred to live frugally and invest their savings in the mother country in the form of a house or some other symbol of social status, the second and third generation are better integrated into the host society and are less likely to dream of returning one day to their homeland. This phenomenon is already apparent among emigrants to the USA and Canada, and the expectations are that it will be repeated among emigrants in post-1992 Europe. It means that, while emigrants' remittances currently make an important contribution to the balance of payments by covering approximately two-thirds of the external deficit, the underlying trend is for their importance to diminish (OECD 1989).

While external factors predominate in any explanation of revival in economic fortunes, the surge in private consumption owed much to government policy. A deliberate effort was made to reverse the decline in real wages which had occurred every year since 1976 with the exception of 1980. They had fallen back particularly sharply during 1982–4 as the labour market contracted and the incomes policy began to bite. During 1985–6, the government sanctioned large pay rises, and real wages recovered strongly. Public-sector pay rises exceeded twenty per cent in 1985 and fell only slightly short of that figure the following year. Initially higher labour costs were compensated for by productivity increases and by reductions made in social security contributions for both employers and employees. Public spending expanded substantially as the government not only paid for higher wages but also introduced an early retirement scheme for civil servants. In addition, it boosted welfare payments, with higher pension and unemployment benefits and extended entitlement. Portugal's 2,000,000 pensioners, among the worst-provided-for in the EC, were given added buying power through a series of annual pension increases. Finance minister Miguel Cadilhe signalled approval for a consumer boom by shifting the burden from income tax to indirect taxation. The tax base grew substantially with the introduction of VAT (which at almost Esc 234 billion yielded a figure much higher than forecast), the first stage in a long-term tax-reform strategy. The standard rate of VAT was set at seventeen per cent, but just under a third of total consumption was exempted completely, while another third was subject to a reduced rate of eight per cent and a rate of thirty per cent was imposed on luxury items (OECD 1992).

*Table 5.7*:  Growth in Real Total Domestic Demand 1985–91 (percentage change).

|          | 1985 | 1986 | 1987 | 1988 | 1989 | 1990 | 1991 |
|----------|------|------|------|------|------|------|------|
| Portugal | 0.9  | 8.3  | 10.4 | 7.4  | 4.2  | 6.1  | 4.8  |
| EC       | 2.2  | 3.9  | 3.8  | 4.7  | 3.5  | 3.0  | n.a. |

*Source*: OECD 1991.

The government, therefore, consciously adopted an expansionist strategy based on stimulating domestic demand and consumer spending following a decade of stagnation. In continental Portugal, the purchasing power grew by twenty-one per cent between 1980–1 and 1989–90, with the bulk of the growth concentrated in the late 1980s. Private consumption leapt forward, registering seven per cent growth in 1986 and continuing the high rate of expansion in 1987 (6.8 per cent) and 1988 (6.5 per cent). The 'consumer society' had arrived in Portugal in tandem with entry into the EC, leading many Portuguese, prompted by advertising and retailers, to equate 'Europeanism' with a consumer spree. The boom certainly sucked in luxury goods as car import quotas were relaxed and tariffs on luxury durable goods fell. Motor car sales, measured in units sold, rocketed to 22.6 per cent in 1985 and no less impressively in the following two years, with seventeen per cent and 12.9 per cent increases respectively (EIU 1989).

The government set about producing a medium-term economic programme, *Programa de Correcão Estructural do Déficie Externo e do Desemprego* (PCEDED), Programme for the Structural Adjustment of the Foreign Deficit and Unemployment, launched in March 1987. Whatever its shortcomings – and these became apparent within a year – the document marked a major step forward as it represented a serious attempt at setting a coherent policy framework and promised to banish the stop–go cycle. In the first stage (1987–90), economic growth, employment and investment in neglected areas, such as energy and agriculture, would narrow the gap between Portugal and its EC partners and reduce its vulnerability to fluctuations in the external economic environment. Based on the assumption that inflation would be under control by 1988, thus perhaps permitting an early entry into the ERM, the PCEDED envisaged a GDP growth average of 3.7 per cent in the first stage and 4.3 per cent for 1991–4. The Programme's annual revision in 1988 upgraded the growth forecast slightly but, ominously, revised upwards the prediction for imports. In general, the forecasts erred on the side of optimism, especially with regard to inflation, employment, the public debt and the balance of payments (OECD 1989). PCEDED's critics focused on the failure to address specific problems such as the unwieldy and inefficient bureaucracy and widespread tax evasion. Above all, it came under attack for its excessive optimism and reliance on paternalistic planning (EIU 1989).

By 1990, the PCEDED had been made obsolete by setbacks on the domestic scene, notably inflation and strong capital inflows and a less favourable external economic climate which included a surge in imported food prices. In addition, Brussels announced a new timetable for economic and monetary union (OECD 1991). In July, the government responded to the changed conditions with the launch of QUANTUM – *Quadro de Adjustmento Nacional para a Transicão para a União Económica e Monetaria* (National Adjustment Framework for the Transition to Economic and Monetary Union) – which outlined a convergence programme required for full participation in the EMU process. The new programme anticipated that the inflation differential would be removed by 1995 through the application of a tight monetary policy, but within months it had to be revised because of the Gulf War. A revised QUANTUM (Q2) was presented in December 1991 with lower targets for exports, public expenditure reductions and a worsening unemployment scenario.

## INVESTMENT: ENGINE OF GROWTH

Since 1985, Portugal has experienced an investment boom stimulated by a combination of revived corporate profits, lower interest rates and EC-assisted infrastructure investment. The share of investment in total GDP increased by over a third to around thirty per cent, making a major contribution to the revival in business confidence and a period of sustained high growth rates. A prominent feature of the investment expansion was the contribution made by direct foreign investment (DFI), which was given a pivotal role to play in the government's economic strategy as a mechanism for transferring technology, modernising the industrial base and diversifying the export portfolio. By 1990, the surge in foreign investment was cited as proof that Cavaco Silva's economic management had been given the seal of approval by investors abroad. Indeed, Portugal soon occupied a high ranking (twenty-sixth in a list of 129 countries, according to a 1991 survey) in the International Risk Guides, which assess individual countries according to their investment potential using financial, economic and political variables.

Portugal's attraction as a location for foreign capital has not won universal applause and has sparked a debate over the present and future part that DFI should play in Portugal's economic development. Before assessing the reasons for the boom, it is first necessary to understand why DFI had been so sluggish, averaging a mere US$140 million annually in the first half of the 1980s (EIU 1986). Such a meagre level of foreign investment is perhaps surprising, given that Portugal stood on the threshold of the EC and boasted labour costs that were well below other OECD countries and even compared favourably with some Asian NICs. The problem was rooted in a traditional suspicion of foreign capital which even Coca Cola could not overcome under the old regime. By missing out on the multinational investment boom during the 1960s and early 1970s, when investors sought sites for large projects such as motor vehicle manufacturing plants, Portugal condemned itself to be marginalised when the revival began in the 1980s.

It is possible to identify the inhibitors that restricted Portugal to a fraction of the US$3 billion that flowed into Spain, a country with unit labour costs sixty per cent higher than its Iberian neighbour. The 1977 Foreign Investment Code did little to remove the bureaucratic obstacles and delays facing any proposed investment project. Manufacturing investment in particular suffered from the limited home market, the unstable political situation in the 1970s, poor infra-structure and support industries, insufficiently attractive financial incentives and a dearth of skilled workers and managers. However, the most often-quoted impediment was presented by the time-consuming and cumbersome bureau-cratic hurdles to be negotiated before a project received official approval (Buckley and Artisien 1983). Investors preferred to await the legislation sched-uled for 1988 that promised a new incentive scheme coupled with reforms in the restrictive labour laws.

In the past, DFI had principally flowed into a limited range of natural resources (wines, cork, wood etc.). When permitted to invest in manufacturing industry, foreign companies set up assembly plants or other low-technology operations in order to take advantage of Portugal's cheap wages and favourable tax regimes. However, the situation was transformed once access to the European market was guaranteed and EC funds became available. Rather than repatriating their profits, foreign companies began to augment their Portuguese investments. Central to this new climate was the liberalising July 1986 investment code which allowed for a staged sychronisation to 1993 with the EC's rules on the free movement of capital. EC companies were put on a par with national companies with regard to profit repatriation and the export of proceeds from any invest-ments sold. In addition, foreign investors were encouraged to participate in the privatisation of state monopoly interests. The government now had a blank cheque to offer an impressive array of incentives to potential investors. Projects receive incentives according to their economic importance and, in the case of manufacturing investment, the siting of the plant, its contribution to exports and foreign currency earnings, the value added to natural resources and the technol-ogy transferred (BPCC 1989).

Foreign investors have been able to negotiate investment contracts and cut through bureaucratic red tape with the assistance of the Portuguese Institute of Foreign Trade (*Instituto de Comércio Externo de Portugal,* ICEP), which re-placed the old Foreign Investment Institute (IIE). The ICEP promotes Portugal as 'a gateway to Europe' offering competitive incentives, political and economic stability and excellent growth prospects. Low labour costs are no longer pro-moted as a major advantage. Indeed, a recent EC report demonstrated that there was little overall difference between unit wage costs in the EC12, as low wages are habitually accompanied by lower productivity.

In the late 1980s and early 1990s, foreign capital inflows exceeded all expectations. In fact, just when the balance of payments once again threatened to strangle continued growth, inward investment injected further life by covering

*Table 5.8*:    Growth of DFI 1980–90 (millions of contos).

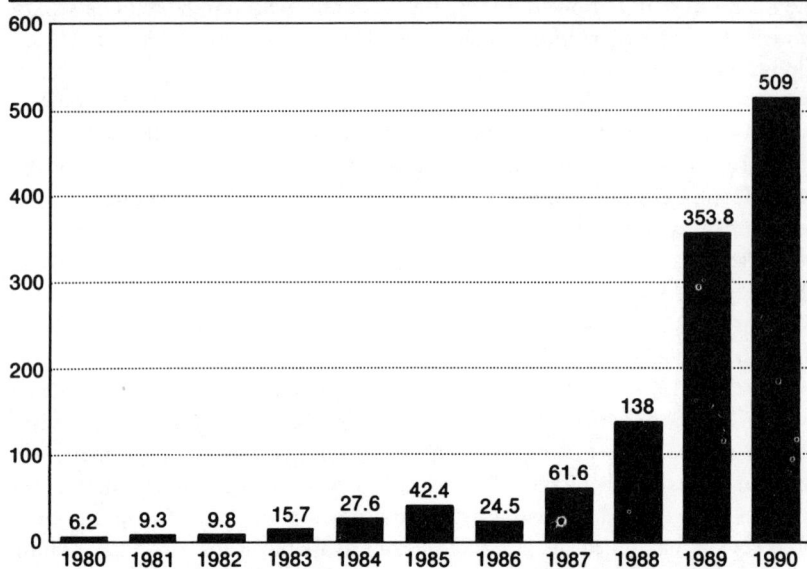

*Source*: ICEP.

*Table 5.9*:    Sectoral share of DFI 1980–90 (percentage).

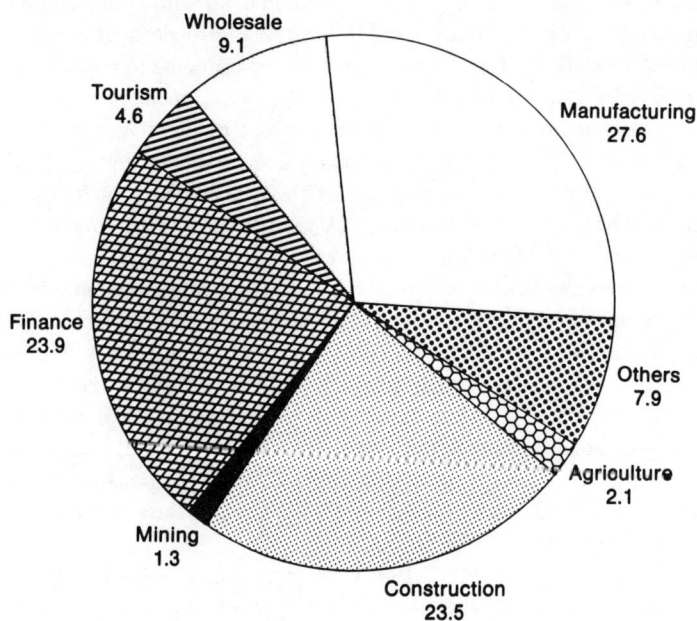

*Source*: ICEP.

the whole of the trade deficit. During the late 1980s, foreign investment doubled annually, rising from 24,500,000 contos in 1986 (US$163,000,000) to over 500,000,000 contos (US$3.5 billion) in 1990, and, despite the uncertainties caused by the Gulf War, the figures for 1991 suggest a 100 per cent increase over the previous year to around US$6 billion. As a proportion of GDP, foreign investment increased from 0.6 per cent in 1986 to 3.7 per cent in 1990. The sectors that attracted most foreign investment were property and services, banking and finance, restaurants and hotels, metal products, transport equipment, chemicals, textiles, clothing and footwear. In the period between 1980 and 1989, the service sector absorbed forty per cent of inward DFI, with manufacturing industry the second-largest recipient with just over thirty per cent. OECD estimates point to a steady decline in the proportion going into manufacturing industry, which absorbed 65.9 per cent of the total in 1978, 46.8 per cent in 1983 and 34.6 per cent in 1984. Since then, the service sector has attracted most inward investment, boosted in particular by interest in banking and financial services because of recent liberalisation and privatisation measures. Within the manufacturing sector, the main areas of activity were the chemicals (thirty-nine per cent) and electromechanical industries (thirty-four per cent), followed at some distance by textiles, non-metallurgic industry, paper and printing and food and drink, all with single-figure percentage shares of the DFI attracted into the country during 1990.

Inward investment by origin for 1980–9 indicated a heavy dependence on EC countries, which furnished two-thirds of the total, while the US share has fallen gradually. Bank of Portugal figures show the EC's percentage share rising steadily from 38.9 per cent in 1984 to 68.5 per cent in 1988. During the period 1980–9, 64.5 per cent of total DFI originated in the EC, with the UK, France, Spain and West Germany the most important source countries. The most significant development in recent years is the emergence of Spain as the major investor in Portugal. The UK has traditionally been among the leading investors, with a stock of foreign investment in 1986 amounting to Esc 22.8 billion, or about a fifth of the total (BPCC 1989). The small size of the Portuguese economy means that the DFI explosion places a high share of economic activity in the hands of foreign companies. According to the European Commission (1991a), firms with foreign involvement account for at least nine per cent of total employment, almost a quarter of total sales in manufacturing industry, twenty-one per cent of imports and twenty-five per cent of total exports, and this dependence is on the increase. In the biggest foreign investment in Portugal for twelve years, Ford, after considering alternative sites in Spain and Ireland, announced its decision to build an Esc 22.3 billion car audio equipment plant in Setúbal. General Motors selected a neighbouring location for a new US$9.4 billion plant to manufacture electronic ignitions systems, mainly for export. The Finnish firm Valmet agreed to invest Esc 4.2 billion in a joint venture with PIE to manufacture tractors at Montijo on the Setúbal peninsula, and the German company Continental announced a joint venture with Mabor, Portugal's tyre manufacturer. In addition, there were deals with Samsung for the production of colour TV and video components, and, in a significant move into hardware technology, the Korean multinational began discussions on a new investment project, initially expected to be located in Indonesia or Ireland, to manufacture semiconductors. However, there were disappointments. Fiat, after considering sites in Portugal for two new motor vehicle factories that would generate 8,500 jobs, opted for southern Italy, citing inadequate incentives and a preference for investment in the national economy.

FORD-VW: 'THE JEWEL IN THE CROWN'

In 1991, the motor manufacturers Ford and Volkswagen and the Portuguese government signed an agreement which authorised a factory to be built at Palmela on the Setúbal peninsula. The plant will produce the VX62, a new multi-purpose vehicle to rival the Renault Espace. The anticipated investment of 450,000,000 contos is expected to create directly or indirectly 15,000 jobs and to turn out 180,000 vehicles valued at 500,000,000 contos annually, which will constitute twenty per cent of Portugal's total exports. As a result of the multiplier effect, a further 50,000,000 contos will be invested in the components industry. To begin with, the value added nationally will be forty per cent, rising to fifty-five per cent by 1998.

Ford had previously shown interest in Portugal as a manufacturing site in the late 1970s, but, on that occasion, plans for a factory adjacent to the Sines complex fell through. This time, Portugal faced direct competition from two Spanish candidates – Seville (with Felipe González lobbying strongly for his home town) and Murcia, as well as a late bid from eastern Germany. The decision appears to have gone Palmela's way for a combination of reasons: the incentives on offer; cheap labour and low operating costs; the high growth and healthy investment climate; a strike-free, adaptable labour force and a strong commitment to training; and the proximity to Lisbon and access to the European markets.

The government hopes that the Ford-VW project will act as a magnet for more investment and contribute to the transformation of Portuguese industry. In fact, it presents a major challenge to components manufacturers. Concern has been expressed that, given the small and fragmented nature of Portuguese industry, Spanish firms may be in a better position to supply the new factory once internal tariff barriers disappear at the end of 1992. In order to avert such a scenario, the Industry Ministry set up the *Gabinete de Apoio á Participacão Nacional no Projecto Ford-VW* (GAPIN) to assist the components industry in achieving the levels of capacity and quality required by the multinationals. It also encourages firms to establish joint ventures with existing Ford suppliers in order to bridge the financial and technology gap between the Portuguese and their foreign counterparts.

The largest industrial project ever undertaken in Portugal is cited as proof that regional policy is working. The pro-DFI lobby expects the overseas investors not only to create jobs, transfer technology and boost exports, but also to stimulate demand for locally-manufactured components and lead to the creation of many more SMEs. It is cited as proof that the collaboration between Brussels and Lisbon is working. Setúbal became a favoured site following an EC decision to fund the first *Operação Integrada de Desenvolvimento* (OID), or Integrated Development Operation. The stated aim is to coordinate all relevant EC grants and loans in order to assist economically depressed regions. The programme for Setúbal channelled 100,000,000 contos into some 400 projects, including the Tagus Bridge extension and new motorway construction. It is claimed that the decisions to locate production operations in the region taken by Ford, General Motors and Valmet were influenced by the infrastructure investment and the availability of funds from European sources. There is ample evidence that Portugal has proved to be a magnet for foreign investment. An interesting feature of the phenomenon is that not only new projects but also relocated investment has been attracted. An example is Colgate-Palmolive's decision taken in 1991 to close its operations in Spain and transfer its toothpaste production across the border.

The massive inflow of foreign capital is not without its critics. In September 1989, Mario Soares articulated fears that the excessive internationalisation of the Portuguese economy means that important business decisions are taken abroad. Others argue that the overdependence on a small group of multinationals merely replicates the failed development model of the 1950s and 1960s and point to the example of Portugal's 'white elephant', the Sines complex, in support of their case. The Ford-VW project has intensified this debate, which was fuelled further when the French firm Matra, which manufactures the rival Espace, decided to ask the European Commission to investigate the legality of the proposed state aid. Criticism has focused on two main areas. First, foreign investors receive the lion's share of the substantial incentives on offer at the expense of domestic industry. Indeed, the success in attracting such prestige projects is attributable to the generous incentives on offer – in this case 140,000,000 contos (98,000,000 provided by the EC). In contrast, over a two-year period, 62,000,000 contos in incentives have been divided among 1,200 investment projects worth a total of 277,000,000 contos. The charge, then, is that the government has been 'buying investment', distorting market forces and diverting funds from the urgent and necessary reconversion of the textiles and footwear industries. It is argued that the project merely reinforces the gap between large industry using advanced technologies and SMEs still involved in artisan production. Second, critics warn that structural change in Portuguese industry is in the hands of foreigners. They point out that a growing proportion of national exports are conducted on an intra-company basis over which Portugal exerts no influence. Ultimately, the success of the Ford-VW project depends not on the skills of the workforce but on the ability to compete with the Japanese on the world market.

It could be argued that the structure of Portuguese industry is far better suited to the type of investment envisaged in the PepsiCo snack-food production project, where thousands of small firms have been contracted to produce high-quality potatoes for the processing plant, whose output is destined for the Iberian market. Nevertheless, Portugal has done remarkably well against fierce competition to win an impressive share of foreign investment, and the indications are that multinational companies play a vital role in the transfer of technology and the upgrading of skills which will be required in the future if Portugal is to survive the challenge from the NICs.

It may be too early to assess the full impact that the new investment wave has made on the Portuguese economy, but a study undertaken by ICEP reveals that only a quarter of the new DFI is going into the creation of new companies and that over half the total is destined for larger companies already established. A further indication that foreign capital is concentrated in low-risk operations is the growth in acquisitions by European firms of Portuguese factories, particularly in the textile and footwear industries.

Portuguese companies have proved slow to respond to the challenge of internationalisation. This may, in part, be attributable to the small domestic market, which is a poor base for ventures overseas. An analysis of Portuguese DFI reveals a number of key features.

First, the levels are extremely modest, although rising: the cumulative increase over the past five years is 600 per cent. Portuguese foreign investment, which totalled 15.4 per cent in 1989, rose to 24,000,000 contos in 1990 and is expected to almost double during 1991. However, Portugal's stock of DFI only amounts to 0.001 per cent of the total for the OECD countries.

Second, the principal outlet for Portuguese investment is the EC, which was the destination for 61.6 per cent of the total in 1989 and 78.9 per cent in 1990. The UK is the most popular destination, with 58.6 per cent of the EC total in 1989 and 47.6 per cent the following year.

Third, the strongest growth has been recorded in Spain, which was in receipt of thirty-two per cent of total Portuguese investment in the EC in 1990. Increasingly, Spain is the preferred starting point for internationalisation among Portuguese companies.

Fourth, only a small number of firms have devised DFI strategies, including the Amorim group, Ccnoura and Petrogal. In the future, strong growth is expected in the PALOP countries, where opportunities are expected to exist for investments in the manufacturing sector, especially in textiles, clothing and leather goods.

## FINANCIAL LIBERALISATION AND THE BANKING REVOLUTION

From 1984, Portugal's financial sector (banking, insurance and stock markets) underwent a process of transformation in preparation for its integration into an enlarged EC. However, in recognition of the enormous task faced in converting from a state-controlled to a market-oriented system, the European Commissioners conceded an extra three years' grace (to 1995) to allow Portuguese banks and financial institutions to prepare themselves for the challenge of the European market. To this end, the government pursued a two-pronged strategy. The first stage involved the restructuring of the antiquated banking system, to be followed later by the development of the capital markets. Even as late as 1984, Portugal fully merited its reputation as 'the backwater of European banking'. Since the revolution, ninety per cent of the banking system had been under state control and organised around one basic function: to fund the government's huge deficit by providing low (non-market) interest rates and loans to public enterprises. In return, the banks enjoyed protection from the competition of privately-owned rivals and in the process became 'monuments of inefficiency' burdened by high labour costs, overstaffing, outdated technology and poor customer services.

Progress towards a more modern operating environment commenced in 1984, when a new banking law opened the system to domestic and foreign private-sector banks. Under the new regulations, which initially limited foreign banks to one branch each, ten new private banks were authorised (six foreign: Manufacturers Hanover Trust, Barclays, Banque National de Paris, Chase Manhattan, Citibank, Générale de Banque of Belgium; and four national: Banco Português de Investimentos, Banco Comercial Português, Banco de Comércio e Indústria and Banco Internacional de Crédito). Although their share of total lending remained small, the new private banks had a galvanising effect on the nationalised sector through their introduction of competition for customers and stricter accounting procedures. However, many problems remained to be tackled: undercapitalisation, overstaffing and bad debts. As if to highlight the difficulties, the new private banks outperformed the state sector, returning balance-sheets indicating that they were more than twice as profitable as their nationalised competitors.

Faced with the uncertainties of deregulation and the uncomfortable prospect of full-blown European competition, the government chose to strengthen some state banks while privatising others. A major problem is that Portuguese banks are small by international standards. In a listing of the 1,000 largest banks in the world ranked according to capital, only nine Portuguese institutions appear: Caixa Geral do Depósitos (181st), Banco Comercial Português (392nd), Banco Espírito Santo e Comercial (514th), Banco Totta e Açores (586th), Banco Nacional Ultramarino (601st), Banco Português do Atlântico (827th), Banco de Fomento Exterior (919th), Banco Pinto e Sotto Mayor (968th) and União de Bancos Portugueses (969th). The Caixa owes its position to its role as a savings bank in a country with the highest rate of household savings in Europe: during the mid-1980s, the Portuguese were saving over a quarter of their disposable income. The aim was to create two strong financial groups – one centred on the

CGD, incorporating the BNU and the Fidelidade insurance group, and the second specialising in foreign trade finance, led by the Banco de Fomento Nacional, which will embrace the Banco Borges e Irmão and the Cosec export credit company. Whether these groups can survive what Miguel Beleza, the finance minister, described as the 'competition shock' from efficient foreign and private banks determined to gain a larger share of the domestic market remains to be seen. State banks are still hemmed in by regulations, and the government has been lethargic in removing these. However, banking regulations do eventually have to conform to EC standards, and state control over credit will be relaxed.

THE FINANCIAL MARKETS

For many years, Portugal's two *bolsas* (in Lisbon's Terreiro do Paço and Oporto's Palacio da Bolsa) deserved their reputation as 'sleepy places that played little part in their domestic economies' (*The Economist* 1988). The markets were shut down in 1974 and, despite reopening two years later, remained in a comatose state. As late as 1986, only thirty shares were quoted on the exchanges. Between 1986 and 1989, the number of companies quoted more than tripled, while the volume of transactions grew from 23,700,000 to 400,000,000 contos. Trading volumes on the stock-markets continued to rise and had reached two billion contos by the end of 1990. The modest upsurge in activity is explained by companies seeking alternatives to expensive bank loans for investment projects and a growing foreign interest in the Portuguese *bolsas*. In 1987, Portugal received a reminder that stock-markets can be volatile places. During the October crash, the gains made over the previous year were wiped out as foreign money drained away. Recovery was slow and underlined the dangers faced by such a small, marginal stock-market. When foreign investors account for more than half the turnover on the Lisbon exchange, changes in international market conditions have a disproportionate impact on the financial periphery. When the world markets are weak, Lisbon is one of the first to suffer. The recovery can be attributed to the sustained expansionary climate (which helped to neutralise the competing attractions offered by eastern Europe), the stimulus provided by the privatisation programme and the improvements emanating from the modernisation of the exchanges. These were a new stock-market law (1991), continuous computerised trading, an independent securities exchange commission and a new daily index in accordance with EC rules. This surge in activity is explained by the growth of business outside the exchanges (*fora de bolsa*), which accounted for sixty-five per cent of the business transacted.

The stock-markets suffered from one principal weakness which severely restricted their ability to play a dynamic role as suppliers of capital to the business sector. The government has long regarded them as servants of its interests, whether as a source for funding its financial requirements, absorbing the public debt, or executing the privatisation policy. In such a small market, liquidity is soon exhausted, and private-sector companies are forced to turn to the banks, where they must pay high interest rates on their borrowings. The progress still to be made before the markets play a role similar to European stock-markets is indicated by the following summary of current problems:

- the absence of a nucleus of institutional investors with market knowledge;
- an excessive dependence on foreign investors;
- the lack of clear rules and regulations (the two *bolsas* operate under different rules) and investor protection;
- high taxes are paid on profits, dividends and dealings; and
- a majority of the large companies are not quoted.

Reform of the antiquated taxation system was a key element in the government's modernisation programme. Historically, Portugal evolved a distorted tax system with a great number of exemptions, fiscal benefits and high marginal rates (a top rate of eighty-four per cent after the 1974 revolution) which encouraged widespread tax avoidance and evasion but produced only a limited tax revenue. Whereas income tax accounted for about a third of total tax revenue in the rest of Europe, in Portugal it brought in barely twenty per cent. Since 1986, when VAT was introduced, efforts have been made to bring the Portuguese tax system more into line with the rest of the EC by widening the tax base and improving both its equity and efficiency. In 1988, the complex system was simplified by introducing two taxes – one personal (IRS) and the other corporate (IRC) – and reducing the number of income tax brackets and tax reliefs (OECD 1989; 1991). As a result, government revenue collected from direct taxation is expected to register a significant rise to a tax/GDP ratio of 7.6 per cent. According to OECD calculations, the exchequer received forty per cent more revenues under the new system than would have been collected under the old regime (OECD 1987). However, despite recent improvements, evasion is still widespread, particularly with regard to undeclared profits, delayed social security payments, non-declaration of income by the self-employed and the undervaluation of property deals (EIU 1991c).

### LABOUR LAW REFORM

Portugal's labour legislation has long been a target for reform by successive governments. Still seen by many on the left as one of the revolution's major achievements, the labour laws have come to be regarded as a structural rigidity and an obstacle to modernisation. The business sector complained that the inflexible labour laws prevented firms from dismissing workers and reducing the size of their workforce. As a result, they became burdened with inflated wage bills which discouraged investment in much-needed technological improvements. Indeed, such distortions in the labour market have undoubtedly encouraged the spread of unwelcome features in the Portuguese economy such as child labour, short-term contracts and wage arrears.

The majority PSD administration that assumed office in 1987 was pledged to bring the labour laws into line with European practice as part of the preparation for 1992. In the past, the twin barriers of trade-union and political opposition forced weak or unstable governments to shelve their reform plans. It was no surprise that the proposals aroused strong opposition from the Communist and Socialist parties, especially the labour package (*pacote laboral*) and the law on dismissals. It had to negotiate two major hurdles: first, a strong and vociferous opposition and trade-union protests that the bill had not been fully debated and was bulldozed through parliament, culminating in a general strike held in March 1989 which was generally regarded as the best-supported and most widespread for some time; and second, a declaration by the constitutional court that the bill violated the right to work and to employment. When the new law came into force in June 1989, it meant that employees, who in the past could only be dismissed for disciplinary reasons, could now be made redundant if the economic and commercial situation warranted it. An attempt was also made to clamp down on the use of child labour by raising the minimum age for employment from fourteen to sixteen years.

For some, however, the new laws did not go far enough. The Portuguese Industrial Association objected on the grounds that they remained inflexible and would encourage short-term fixed employment contracts, which grant workers fewer rights than permanent contracts, to be the norm rather than the exception. Recent evidence does bear out these fears: seventeen per cent of employees are on temporary contracts, and many new jobs are for women on short-term contracts.

### PUBLIC ENTERPRISES AND THE PUBLIC DEBT

The wave of nationalisations during 1975 concentrated ownership in the hands of the state. Resources were poured into public enterprises that continually turned in losses. The government found itself financing substantial pay increases and providing a panoply of subsidies across a whole range of goods and services. Non-financial public enterprises swallowed a fifth of total national investment yet produced only a tenth of the national value added and employed a mere four per cent of the workforce (EIU 1989). The criteria used in making investment decisions were more often taken on political and social grounds rather than commercial logic. It should not be forgotten that such priorities were underpinned by a general consensus among the leading political parties over the desirability of public enterprises. This was reinforced by the 1976 constitution, which protected their inviolability.

While a large public sector preserved the revolution's social achievements, it was clearly detrimental to modernisation and economic growth. The operating losses among the public-sector corporations and their reliance on often unjustified subsidies and state funding fuelled a mounting public debt. Moreover, government investment decisions were often ill-considered and wasteful in

*Table 5.10*:   Evolution of the Public Debt (percentage of GDP; selected years).

| | 1973 | 1976 | 1980 | 1982 | 1984 | 1986 | 1989 |
|---|---|---|---|---|---|---|---|
| | 18 | 41 | 47 | 62 | 76 | 80 | 70 |

*Source*: OECD 1991.

market terms (OECD 1986). Management and planning were made more difficult by the removal of most of the top and middle managers in state enterprises and their replacement by appointees, often inexperienced, of the incoming administration whenever there was a change in government. Also, the growth and protection of areas such as steel, chemicals and shipbuilding deflected much-needed investment away from woefully neglected tasks such as upgrading the country's infrastructure. The two stabilisation packages in 1978 and 1983 did cut public-sector losses but, significantly, never attempted to restructure. As a result, the general government debt, which had stood at eighteen per cent of GDP in 1973 (a very low ratio by international standards), expanded to seventy-four per cent in 1989 due to the accumulated stock of past deficits and higher interest payments (OECD 1991).

Although the debt/GDP ratio stood close to the EC average (seventy-four per cent), it was traditionally financed by compelling the banks to purchase the public debt. In order to eliminate the distortions caused by such requirements, the government aimed to reduce the public-sector deficit to half of its 1987 level and gradually to reduce the public debt in three ways: making advanced repayments to balance the large capital inflows in recent years; changing the way it is financed; and using proceeds obtained from privatisation.

As part of a more market-driven monetary policy, the central bank has greater independence than was the case in the past. Previously, the government compelled the banks to buy the public debt, thereby forcing them to lend to their customers at artificially high rates of interest. Interest rates on the public debt are to be gradually adjusted to market levels following the deregulation of lending rates in September 1988. Moves towards a more market-oriented financial system continued in 1990 when further autonomy was granted to the Bank of Portugal by outlawing direct lending to the government and credit ceilings were abolished.

THE SHAPE OF THE STATE ENTERPRISE SECTOR

Accurate and comprehensive information on the significance of public enterprises in the economy is unavailable, but it is estimated (EIU 1989) that sixty-eight enterprises (forty-five non-financial and twenty-three financial) are 100 per cent state-owned. In addition, eighty industrial and service companies come under the aegis of Instituto e Participações do Estado (IPE), the state holding company, along with three newspapers, Portucel, the pulp and paper company and the Pousada hotel chain.

The weight and scope of the public-enterprise sector can be gauged from the following list of industrial companies: Petrogal (oil-refining), Setenave (ship-building), Siderugia (steel), Cimpor (cement), Unicer and Centralcer (brewing), Portucel (pulp and paper), Tabaquiera (tobacco), Quimigal and CNP (petrochemicals). In addition, EDP and EPAL share a monopoly of electricity and water provision respectively. The state dominates non-financial services through control of transport companies such as Caminhos de Ferro Portugueses (railways), Rodoviário Nacional (coaches), CCFL (buses and trams in the capital), TAP (airline carrier) and other services such as Correios e Telecommunicações (post and telecommunications) and Enatur (tourism and hotels), as well as the nine largest public banks, two savings banks, an investment bank and eight insurance companies.

The contribution made by the state-owned manufacturing sector to total output actually declined during the 1980s due to financial cutbacks, the expansion of the private sector and the fall in demand during the 1983–5 recession. It made tackling the problem of loss-making state-owned industrial enterprises an urgent priority. In 1985, total net losses amounted to US$317,000,000. The chief loss-maker was CNP (US$194,000,000), followed by Quimigal (US$70,000,000) and Setenave (US$65,000,000) (EIU 1986). Restructuring become necessary if only to ease the public debt burden and rationalise investment allocation.

## 'MENOS ESTADO, MELHOR ESTADO'

The Social Democrats were determined to retrace the public- private-sector boundary. An ambitious privatisation timetable, envisaging one sale every month, was launched under the slogan 'less state, better state' and became the programmatic flagship of the Cavaco Silva administration. However, the process has been characterised by numerous delays and setbacks that fully justifies the eight-year time-span allotted to the programme by the government. In the initial stages, the slow pace can be explained by the constitutional constraints, the lack of experienced administrators to steer the sales through, the negative impact of the October 1987 stock-market crash and unforeseen external events. Then, as the programme began to gather pace during 1990, the Gulf crisis combined with the collapse of communism in eastern Europe to dampen the prospect of successful sell-offs. Further difficulties arose from the political uncertainty surrounding the 1991 general election, when defeat for the PSD could have foreshadowed the imposition of tough new privatisation conditions that would dampen foreign and domestic interest.

In 1988, a constitutional amendment made partial privatisation possible with the disposal of up to forty-nine per cent of the equity of state-sector companies. It took until June 1989, following lengthy negotiations between the PSD and the PS, before further changes to the constitution received the necessary two-thirds majority which allowed for 100 per cent privatisation. In April 1990, a boost was given to the process when a new privatisation law was placed on the statute books.

The Cavaco Silva government embraced privatisation for variety of motives. First, the sell-offs were seen as a means of raising much-needed funds which can be channelled directly into reducing the level of public debt and for use as cash injections to improve the balance-sheets of state-owned companies prior to their transfer to the private sector. The declared intention was to use eighty per cent of the capital raised through state sell-off to reduce the debt, which was regarded as a serious structural flaw in the economy. Unfortunately, expectations of a revenue windfall had to be scaled down once bad debt write-offs, compensation, cash injections and other hidden transfers were taken into account. In the case of the CNP, the state took over US$1.5 billion of the petrochemical company's debts prior to its sale to Neste from Finland, and it also wrote off over half Quimigal's debts (48,000,000 contos) in preparation for its privatisation in 1992. It also assumed US$670,000,000 of Setenave's debts as part of its *saneamento financiero* (financial restructuring). Such is the extent of the financial problems at the national airline, TAP, that the earliest envisaged date for privatisation is 1995. A further impediment to optimising any returns on the sales is the poor condition in which public-enterprise accounts have languished. This made an accurate valuation difficult if not impossible. Preparing state enterprises for flotation on the stock-market was necessarily a lengthy and complicated process. However, there remains a marked reluctance to disinvest completely in some key state enterprises, and the government has insisted on keeping a majority stake.

Second, the reprivatisation programme is regarded as a catalyst that will improve efficiency and competitiveness throughout the Portuguese economy. An overstaffed, bureaucratically-organised and inefficient state sector is to be replaced by efficient private-sector management. In addition, the involvement of foreign capital is expected to inject higher levels of investment and transfer technology which is expected to contribute to productivity gains. Third, the government hoped to promote *capitalismo popular à la portuguesa* (Portuguese popular capitalism), which would create a new and broadly-based shareholder class with priority given to specific groups: the workforce in the company, small shareholders and emigrants. The disposal of large amounts of capital was also expected to instil new life into Portugal's small and moribund Lisbon and Oporto stock-markets.

While the Cavaco Silva government declared its intention of either fully or part-privatising many of the sixty-eight directly state-owned and eighty IPE-run companies, it adopted a gradualist and pragmatic approach. In fact, there was no choice but to opt for a phased programme. The reasons were both political and practical: a headlong rush to privatise would have provoked stern opposition and thwarted plans to remove the constitutional constraints imposed by the forty-nine per cent ceiling on any sell-off, and Portugal's small stock-markets

*Table 5.11*:  Portugal: Reprivatisations.

| | Company | Sector | % sold | Value (Esc. bn) |
|---|---|---|---|---|
| **1989** | | | | |
| | Unicer | brewing | 49 | 9.5 |
| | BTA | banking | 49 | 28.5 |
| | Aliança Seguradora | insurance | 49 | 7.1 |
| | Tranquilidade | insurance | 49 | 25.7 |
| **1990** | | | | |
| | Unicer | brewing | 51 | 13.3 |
| | BTA | banking | 31 | 22.4 |
| | Tranquilidade | insurance | 51 | 18.9 |
| | Centralcer | brewing | 100 | 34.6 |
| | BPA | banking | 33 | 49.8 |
| | Transinsular | shipping | 51 | 1.8 |
| | Jornal de Noticias | newspaper | 82 | 7.5 |
| **1991** | | | | |
| | Aliança Seguradora | insurance | 51 | 6.8 |
| | SFP | banking | 100 | 16.5 |
| | Diario de Noticias | newspaper | 100 | 9.0 |
| | Bonança | insurance | 60 | 18.8 |
| | BESCL | banking | 40 | 60.9 |
| | Banco Fonsecas e Burnay | banking | 100 | |
| **1992** | | | | |
| | BESCL | banking | 60 | |
| | Mundial Confiança | insurance | 100 | |
| | BPA | banking | | |
| | UBP | banking | | |
| | BPSM | banking | | |
| | Companhia de Seguros | insurance | | |
| | Rodoviário Nacional | road transport | | |
| | Petrogal | oil | | |
| | Secil | cement | | |
| | Cimpor | cement | | |

*Source: Financial Times* 4 November 1991.

were incapable of absorbing large volumes of shares, particularly when the equity market had still not fully recovered from the October 1987 crash.

Fourteen years after the nationalisations took place in the wake of the revolution, the first reprivatisation operation took place. The first phase (April–December 1989) involved the part sale of Unicer, the brewery company, the Banco Totta e Açores (BTA), the country's fifth-largest bank, and two insurance companies, Aliança Seguradora and Tranquilidade. Unicer was chosen to start the programme because, with more than half the home market, it represented one of the most successful and attractive companies in the state sector. The issue was tailor-made for both national and overseas investors, as future growth prospects were good (beer sales grew by an annual average 9.7 per cent between 1980 and 1986), and the Unicer portfolio, which includes the Superbock, Cristal, Tuborg and Löwenbräu brands, was ideal to take advantage of future market expansion. Unicer's solid financial base and successful management team easily overcame any doubts generated by the partial nature of the privatisation.

The successful Unicer sale raised Esc 9.5 billion for the treasury and created 11,866 new shareholders. Twenty per cent of the shares were reserved for employees and small savers, and ten per cent were allocated to foreign investors. No single Portuguese entity was allowed to obtain more than ten per cent in the primary sale. The second privatisation followed in July when the government offered forty-nine per cent of the shares in Banco Totta e Açores (BTA), a bank with a ten per cent market share and 6,000 employees. It initiated the government's programme to dispose of state banking-sector interests with one exception – the Caixa Geral do Depósitos, the country's largest bank.

Interest in the BTA flotation, which was heavily oversubscribed, centred on a battle for control between two groups. The former, led by Belmiro de Azevedo and his Sonae group, gained a reported eleven per cent share, and the latter, headed by José Roquette, linked to the Spanish bank, Banco Español de Crédito. Foreign investors used a number of ploys to avoid restrictions by purchasing shares through local subsidiaries and going into partnership with local firms. A Spanish bank's involvement in the contest for control led to fears that BTA would lose its independence and be reduced to a mere affiliate of a larger Spanish bank. Similar fears were expounded when shares in Aliança Seguradora, the sixth-ranked national insurer with an 8.8 per cent market share, were offered for sale in late September 1989. It marked the first sale in a two-stage offer which would see another of Portugal's largest insurers, Tranquilidade, fourth-ranked with 9.9 per cent of the market, sold to the private sector. In the event, the offer was nearly six times oversubscribed, but claims were made that the Paris-based UAP had circumvented the ten per cent rule and, in fact, controlled thirty per cent of the stock.

The issue of foreign control figured prominently in the debate over the new privatisation bill that took place during the autumn of 1989. Two schools of thought emerged. The first was that the process would *desportugalizar* ('deportugalise') vital sectors of the economy and surrender the country's independence and national autonomy. The government was accused by some sectors of the press of putting 'the country up for sale' or being prepared to 'saldar as pratas de familia' (sell the family silver) for a quick killing. It ran the risk, according to some critics, of replacing excessive state control by too much foreign control, with the result that decisions affecting the Portuguese economy would be taken abroad and senior jobs awarded to foreigners. The issue was highlighted by news that a French company, UAP, had captured over twenty per cent of the shares in the Aliança sale, substantially exceeding the five per cent allowed, and that the Colombian Santo Domingo company had acquired important holdings in both the Centralcer (forty-six per cent at a cost of 17,500,000 contos) and the Unicer brewing businesses. The government was clearly sensitive to such criticisms and began to consider limits to the influence that could be exerted by foreign capital. One proposal suggested a pre-qualifying round in which the finance ministry would select a nucleus of Portuguese shareholders to ensure that key companies remained under domestic control.

The second controversial area focused less on the origins of capital investment and more on the potential growth and productivity that might result. It is accepted as inevitable that Portuguese capital has problems competing with foreign capital in an increasingly European and international economic system because of Portuguese companies' limited financial resources and their restricted access to credit. The effective response to such developments, it is argued, is to improve the competitiveness of national enterprises so that they are fit to compete in the European marketplace and to phase the privatisation process to allow for structural adjustments to take effect. The government has encouraged the formation of strong Portuguese groups (*núcleos duros*) to assume control of the privatised companies, but has been attacked for failing to discriminate in favour of national investors. Some critics warn that government intervention is undesirable and contrary to the public interest, preferring open competition to select the new owners. Others have asked where these consortia are to come from. One possible source is the former owners of nationalised companies. The re-emergence of the old business families was signalled in March 1990 when the de Mello family, in partnership with a Scandinavian consortium, acquired control of Lisnave, the important shipbuilding and repair company. The trend was confirmed when the pre-1975 owners of Tranquilidade, the Espírito Santo banking group, became the major shareholder in the reprivatised company. However, concern was expressed in some quarters that control was only won by paying an excessively high price for the privatised shares. The same group, along with Jorge do Mello and others, has formed a consortium which aims to acquire a major stake in Portugal's largest company, Petrogal, in which the state is to retain a 'golden share' equivalent to twenty per cent of the social capital.

The *Lei-Quadro da Reprivatizações* became law on 5 April 1990. The new law allowed the government to sell more than the previous forty-nine per cent maximum. A case-by-case approach was adopted and the rules on foreign ownership were tightened. The second stage in the privatisation programme differed in a number of ways from the first. A larger number and broader span of companies were to be sold off, ranging from Portugal's largest commercial bank, the Banco Português do Atlântico (BPA), to part-privatisations in TAP, the national airline, Centralcer, the second-largest brewer, and SNA, a fishing-fleet operator. The increased tempo of the sales (the declared aim is to return sixty public companies to the private sector) will generate new difficulties. Inevitably, the early candidates comprised companies in good financial shape and with a positive public image. The direct sell-off method was considered unviable in the case of loss-making industrial enterprises, such as CNP and Setenave, where management was put out to private contract and private capital injected. It was no surprise, then, when the debate began on a new privatisation law, that greater flexibility was emphasised. While the government regarded privatisation as the most appropriate and efficient way to modernise and restructure the economy, it was determined not to be limited to a single model. Apart from a stock-market flotation (*oferta pública*), other options in the government's privatisation armoury included an open or limited public bidding (*concurso público*), as well as direct negotiations with selected national or foreign interests. The last option was regarded as appropriate in the case of companies identified as strategic to the national economy. Foreign participation was to be restricted to ten per cent in full privatisations, but the government wanted the right to increase the percentage in the case of public enterprises with a 'very unfavourable' economic profile.

Concern that the 'national interest' might be in jeopardy shaped trade-union opposition to the proposals. The UGT General Secretary, Torres Couto, expressed no objection to privatisation in principle but voiced widely-held fears that Portugal would be transformed into a mere production platform for foreign operators. He stressed the need to equip Portuguese entrepreneurs with the financial resources to restructure in the face of international competition and argued for worker participation in the ownership of enterprises. The PS placed their own proposal before the National Assembly which would limit to twenty per cent the share that any individual or collective could obtain and suggested a ten per cent ceiling on foreign purchasers. In the Socialists' plan, future privatisations would be overseen by a Reprivatisation Commission in order to guarantee a wider dissemination of transferred capital and better safeguards against the concentration of ownership.

Although ostensibly committed to a full programme of privatisations, the government has been accused of lacking a clear policy on which companies should be candidates for sale. By mid-1990, the core of the public sector had been only marginally touched, and its future role and shape remained unclear. Further delays to the programme occurred during early 1990 caused, in part, by constitutional challenges to the new law and also by a government reshuffle which halted progress because the new finance minister and his advisers needed time to familiarise themselves with the details and the options.

The second phase fell into a number of clear stages: the first witnessed the disposal of the remaining fifty-one per cent shares in Unicer, BTA, Aliança and Tranquilidade, and the success of the financial-sector privatisations continued with the sale of thirty-three per cent sale of the Banco Português do Atlântico (BPA). The problems to be encountered during the second stage were signalled by the less-than-enthusiastic response to the offer of a majority stake in the

shipping company, Transinsular. In November 1990, the first major flop occurred when over a third of the shares in the flotation of the Centralcer brewery
business remained unsold. Although the BPA sale showed that investor demand
still existed when the right company was up for sale, the Gulf crisis and
subsequent stock-market downturn caused the privatisation schedule to become
becalmed.

The third phase commenced amid an improved financial climate in May 1991
with the sale by auction of an investment company turned banking concern,
Sociedade Financiera Portuguesa (SFP), the second tranche of the Aliança
Seguradora sale, and the sales of the insurer Bonança (fifty per cent) and the
shipping firm Portline (eighty per cent), which fetched only its reserve price.
Only one purchaser came forward with an offer for the Banco Fonsecas e Burnay
when bids were sought. The eighty per cent share went to the Banco Português
do Investimento (BPI) with a 36,000,000-conto bid that turned out to be a bargain
price, as 28,000,000 contos remained in the bank as part of its capital. Sales of
state-owned financial-sector companies spilled over into 1992. The remaining
sixty per cent of BESCL was privatised, followed shortly by Portugal's third-largest insurer, Mundial Confiança (the first 100 per cent privatisation at once, with
forty per cent disposed of by competitive tender). The next stage involved the
more problematic area of large industrial firms such as the oil company Petrogal,
the cement companies Cimpor and Secil, Siderurgia Nacional (steel) and
Telecom, the telephone company.

Criticism has focused on the disorganised and arbitrary nature of each
flotation. The underlying aims of the disposals have varied: some are sold direct
to the private sector while others are targeted at broadening the share ownership
base. When the first forty per cent tranche of the Banco Espírito Santo e
Comércio de Lisboa came to the market in July 1991, twenty-five per cent of
the stock was reserved for employees, small investors and emigrants and a
further twenty-five per cent for depositors. The remainder went on sale to the
public. For the sale of the national bus company, Rodoviário Nacional, foreigners were restricted to thirty per cent of the capital on offer, and, because of its
strategic importance as a supplier of energy, overseas investors were limited to
forty per cent of Petrogal's partial privatisation. In addition, the state reserved
the right to veto any bids that affected the national interest. The plan is for a
later sale of twenty per cent to employees and small investors.

It is not just the international economic climate and lack of stock-market
confidence that has slowed down the momentum of the privatisation programme. Former owners and shareholders dispossessed when their companies
were nationalised in 1975 have pressed for better compensation terms. When
the sale of state assets began in 1989, they accused the authorities of neglecting
the rights of former shareholders. They argued that the assets and shares of their
former companies have been undervalued and cite the Tranquilidade sale, when
only Esc 1.5 billion of the almost Esc 45 billion raised went on compensation

payments. Other critics have accused the government of concentrating on maximising its revenues rather than on ensuring that Portuguese groups are in a position to bid for the companies.

Has the privatisation programme lived up to the expectations of its proponents? Certainly, the state's role in the economy has been reduced and some of the proceeds raised – Esc 250 billion (US$1.8 billion) by the end of 1991 – used to pay off some of the accumulated public debt. Overall losses in the public enterprise sector stood at Esc 14 billion in 1990 after the government assumed substantial amounts of debt and improvements from restructuring were taken into account (EIU 1991d). There are also indications that the state-owned banks are becoming more efficient in response to the stimulus provided by competition from the private banks. On the other hand, share-ownership has not spread widely. By late 1991, a total of 102,000,000 shares had been put on the market, creating 213,000 new shareholders. This must be offset against the nearly US$4 billion of public-enterprise debts absorbed by the government and the far-from-generous compensation paid to the dispossessed owners. Moreover, the Lisbon and Oporto stock exchanges have only come to life when shares in financial-sector companies are on offer. This is largely explained by government-imposed restrictions on the sale of shares in newly-privatised firms within a year of their purchase, which eliminated any possible quick sale and profit. It has also been the case that share-ownership is not an attractive proposition for savers when inflation is at a high level. In practice, the limitations on foreign participation which are in theory restricted to between five and thirty-five per cent have proved impossible to enforce. The different limits set for different sales (ranging from thirty per cent for SFP to five per cent for BESCL) did not help matters. Centralcer fell into the hands of Colombian Bavaria brewing group, and the French insurer UAP gained control of Aliança amid suspicions that the government had turned a blind eye to the manoeuvres of foreign investors eager to circumvent the regulations. It may represent a tacit admission that foreign control is inevitable, given that the Portuguese do not dispose of sufficient capital to absorb the stock in such a wide-ranging programme, particularly when they are in competition with the often equally or more attractive privatisations initiated in Angola during 1991–2. A number of companies hope to regain control of their pre-1975 agricultural and industrial interests in the former Portuguese colony.

### A FESTA ACABO: THE END OF THE BOOM?

Portugal underwent an investment- and consumption-led economic boom in the years following entry into the EC. Indeed, the period of the second Cavaco Silva administration became known as the years of the *vacas gordas* (fat cows), which, according to critics of government policy, would inevitably be followed by *vacas magras* (thin cows). In fact, economic policy was based on a gamble that strong demand could be reconciled with low and decelerating inflation. It relied heavily on a continuation of the external deflationary climate and a unique confluence of factors that are unlikely to be repeated: the inflow of EC funds, the buoyant levels of foreign investment and favourable exchange rates. In future, growth will depend on improvements in productivity and quality upgrading. Yet, with incoming EC funds stoking up purchasing power, output failing to satisfy internal demand and recession in some of Portugal's principal export markets, the inevitable outcome was higher inflation and a worsening trade account. The government soon faced a dilemma: should it continue its expansionist policies in order to close the development gap with its European partners or give priority to the fight against inflation to ensure that the rate would not reduced to the EC average?

Cavaco Silva's insistence that austerity would not be necessary was motivated both by electoral considerations and by a belief that the battle against inflation could be left to monetary policy. The reverses sustained at the polls in the European and local elections held during 1989 could be attributed to a cluster of factors: mid-term blues (Gallagher 1989), voter apathy (abstention at around fifty per cent) and a warning to the government that the electorate did not approve of its confrontational tactics and its disinclination to enter into dialogue. Cavaco Silva was determined to go to the electorate with an optimistic and upbeat message in October 1991. He could point to an impressive set of statistics: a twenty per cent growth in disposable income between 1985 and 1990; an increase of twenty-seven per cent in private consumption over the same period; 400,000 jobs created, with unemployment at its lowest level since the 1970s; and one of the highest average annual growth rates in the OECD area.

Electoral considerations meant that measures to dampen an overheated economy were delayed and limited in scope. In March 1989, Cadilhe attempted to curb excessive consumer spending and tackle the worsening trade balance by imposing credit and foreign-exchange restrictions. His package (*pacote*) imposed limits on credit sales of specific goods, such as video recorders and motor cars. These proved necessary, as car sales had boomed, rising seventy-two per cent in 1986, sixty-five per cent the following year and sixty-three per cent in 1988. In addition, hire purchase for cars over 1,400 cc and for car leasing was banned, and buyers were obliged to pay fifty per cent on purchase and to repay the remainder within a year. Turning his attention to the banks, the finance minister tightened credit ceilings and imposed further controls on foreign borrowing amid private-sector complaints that it would inhibit their growth. The outspoken minister failed to survive the resignation of the Governor of the Bank of Portugal, José Alberto Tavares Moreira, who cited excessive bureaucratic intervention and a pro-public-sector bias as the reasons for his departure, and, above all, the failure to meet projected inflation targets. In January 1990, Cadilhe was replaced by a less controversial figure, Miguel Beleza.

By the end of 1991, it was clear that the brakes had not been applied firmly enough to the economy. There was a resurgence in domestic consumption fuelled by substantial real wage gains and a willingness to dip into savings in order to purchase consumer goods. Apart from electoral considerations, attempts to curtail domestic demand were hampered by progressive financial deregulation. Monetary management became more problematic following the deregulation of the financial markets, and capital inflows reached record levels after controls on international capital movements were removed. By leaning heavily on monetary policy (controls on the money supply principally through credit restrictions, high interest rates and a revaluation of the escudo), the danger is that Portugal's competitive position will suffer and more imported goods will be sucked in. The indications are that Jorge Braga de Macedo's appointment to the finance ministry in October 1991 presages a more single-minded effort to ensure that there is no return to the familiar stop-go pattern of the past.

# Conclusion

In a reminder of Salazarist propaganda which tried to picture the country as a peaceful oasis in the midst of a world menaced and corrupted by communism, social problems and war, Portugal's rulers in the early 1990s liked to claim a similar tranquility. In contrast to the upheavals in eastern Europe and the prolonged recessions afflicting some of the advanced industrial economies, Portugal began 1992 with the EC's highest growth rate, the lowest unemployment, a buoyant investment scene and a newly re-elected political majority promising four more years of stable government.

There are two contrasting perspectives on the current state and future prospects of the Portuguese economy. The first echoes the government line and takes a positive view of the changes set in motion. It asserts that substantial progress is being made towards removing some of the deeply-ingrained economic and psychological problems that resulted from decades of dictatorship and peripherality. It is argued that five years of strong growth have transformed the industrial and commercial landscape and created a more optimistic and outward-looking business culture.

The second perspective reserves judgement on the progress made because the full impact of competition is yet to be felt. It is argued that the restructuring process is still in its infancy and that whole swathes of uncompetitive domestic industry and agriculture will experience severe difficulties over the next decade. This 'pessimistic' scenario is encapsulated in the Fitzgerald report on the Portuguese economy presented to the European Parliament in 1991. The Irish conservative MEP cast a shadow over the euphoria usually associated with *cavaquismo*. In particular, the report criticised the limited regional specialisation, the failure to identify priority sectors for future investment and growth and the persistence of regional inequalities. Fitzgerald highlighted Portugal's continued peripherality as part of the group of satellite states outside the prosperous 'golden triangle' of advanced industrial economies, still hamstrung by a weak business culture, the legacy of a strong state interventionist tradition and persistent infrastructure and educational deficiencies. The imminent accession or closer integration of Austria, the Scandinavian countries and some eastern European states casts further doubt over Portugal's future in Europe.

Certainly, one thing is clear – the stability and progress enjoyed in the recent past should be tempered by the recognition that short-term difficulties and perennial structural problems are still to be overcome. Developments since 1974 can be interpreted as a dual catching-up process: the first phase involved public services such as education, health etc., following the neglect experienced under Salazar; the second phase saw a surge in consumer expenditure and acquisition of consumer durables during the post-1985 boom. Closing the gap with the rest of Europe could have begun earlier and been less frenetic if internal adjustments had not been postponed because of the constitutional straitjacket inherited from the revolutionary period and the unwillingness of the political leadership to confront difficult issues. The signs are that the Portuguese economy was entering a new cycle in 1991 in which development will be less dramatic, but the opportunity does exist for measured progress within a less favourable post-Maastricht external environment.

# Bibliography

Almeida Coutinho, R. M. de (1982) *The economic effects of external shocks: the case of Portugal*. Unpublished PhD. Yale University, New Haven.

Amaro, R. R. (1987) 'A economia nos primordiós do Estado Novo: estagnação ou crecimento?' In *O Estado Novo. Das origens ao fim da autarcia 1926–1959*, pp. 233–45, vol. 1. Editorial Fragmentos, Lisbon.

Anderson, P. (1962) 'Portugal and the end of ultra-colonialism', *New Left Review* 15, May–June, pp. 83–102; 16, Jul–Aug, pp. 88–122; 17, Winter, pp. 85–114.

Ashoff, G. (1980) 'The southward enlargement of the EC: consequences for industries and industrial policies', *Intereconomics*, Nov–Dec, pp. 299–307.

Bacalhau, M. (1984) 'Regional distribution of Portuguese emigration according to socio-economic context'. In Bruneau, T. C., Da Rosa, V. M. P. and Macleod, A. (eds) *Portugal in development: emigration, industrialization, the European Community*, pp. 53–63. University of Ottawa Press, Ottawa.

Bachtler, J. (1990) 'North versus south in European regional policy', *European Access*, 6 Dec.

Baklanoff, E. N. (1978) *The economic transformation of Spain and Portugal*. Praeger, New York.

Baklanoff, E. N. (1979) 'The political economy of Portugal's old regime: growth and change preceding the 1974 revolution', *World Development* vol. 7, nos 8–9, pp. 799–811.

Baklanoff, E. N. (1984) 'Changing systems: the Portuguese revolution and the public enterprise sector', *Comparative Economic Studies* vol. 26, part 23, Summer, pp. 63–76.

Baklanoff, E. N. (1986) 'The state and economy in Portugal: perspectives on corporatism, revolution and incipient privatization'. In Glade, W. P. (ed.) *State shrinking: a comparative inquiry into privatization*, pp. 257–81. ILAS, University of Texas, Austin.

Barata, L. (1991) 'Os fundos estructurais'. In *O Economista Anuário da economia Portuguesa*, pp. 33–38.

Barreto, A. (1988) 'O vinho do Porto e a intervenção do estado', *Análise Social* vol. xxiv, pp. 373–90.

Barreto, J. (1990) 'Os promodiós da Intersindical sob Marcelo Caetano', *Análise Social* vol. xxv, nos 105–6, pp. 57–117.

Bermeo, N. (1986) *The revolution within the revolution: workers' control in revolutionary Portugal*. Princeton University Press, New Jersey.

Bermeo, N. (1987) 'Redemocratization and transition elections: a comparison of Spain and Portugal', *Comparative Politics*, January, pp. 213–31.

Bliss, C. and Braga de Macedo, J. (eds) (1990) *Unity with diversity in the European economy: the community's southern frontier.* Cambridge University Press, Cambridge.

Bittlestone, M. (1989) *The southern enlargement of the* EEC, 2nd ed. European Documentation Centre, Polytechnic of North London, London.

Blume, N. (1975) Portugal under Caetano, *Iberian Studies* vol. 4, no 2, Autumn, pp. 46–52.

Braga da Cruz, M. (1988) *O partido e o estado no Salazarismo.* Editorial Presença, Lisbon.

Braga de Macedo, J. (1984) 'Portugal and Europe: the dilemmas of integration'. In Bruneau, T. C., Da Rosa, V. M. P. and Macleod, A. (eds) *Portugal in development: emigration, industrialization, the European Community*, pp. 211–38. University of Ottawa Press, Ottawa.

Braga de Macedo, J. and Sebastião, M. (1989) 'Public debt and implicit taxes', *European Economic Review* 33, pp. 573–9.

Braga de Macedo, J. and Serfaty, S. (eds) (1981) *Portugal since the revolution: economic and political perspectives.* Westview Press, Boulder.

Brandão de Brito, J. M. (1989) *A industrialização portuguesa no pós-guerra (1948–1965): O condicionamento industrial.* Dom Quixote, Lisbon.

Brassloff, A. (1991) 'Portugal, 1992 and all that', *Journal of the Association for Contemporary Iberian Studies* vol. 4, no 2, Autumn, pp. 25–36.

Bratenstein, R. and Fischer, M. (1975) 'Portugal. The causes of the economic crisis', *Intereconomics* vol. 10, no 11, pp. 344–8.

Brettell, C. B. (1984) 'Emigration and underdevelopment: the causes and consequences of Portuguese emigration to France in historical and cross-cultural perspective'. In Bruneau, T. C., Da Rosa, V. M. P. and Macleod, A. *Portugal in development: emigration, industrialization, the European Community*, pp. 65–81. University of Ottawa Press, Ottawa.

British-Portuguese Chamber of Commerce (BPCC) (1989) *Portugal: trade and investment opportunities 1990.* Caversham Press, London.

Bruneau, T. C. (1984) *Politics and nationhood: post-revolutionary Portugal.* Praeger, New York.

Bruneau, T. C. (1986) *Politics in contemporary Portugal. Parties and the consolidation of democracy.* Lynne Reiner, Boulder.

Bruneau, T. C., Da Rosa, V. M. P. and Macleod, A. (eds) (1984) *Portugal in development: emigration, industrialization, the European Community.* University of Ottawa Press, Ottawa.

Buckley, P. J. and Artisien, P. F. R. (1983) 'Investment legislation in Greece, Portugal and Spain: the background to foreign investment in Mediterranean Europe', *Journal of World Law* 17 (6), Nov–Dec, pp. 513–23.

Cabral, M. (1986) *Portugal: business partners in Europe.* Anglo-Portuguese Foundation: De Montfort Publishing, London.

Cassola e Barata, N. J. D. (1992) 'Portugal and the European Monetary System'. Gibson, H. D. and Tsakalotos, E. (eds) *Economic integration and financial liberalisation: prospects for southern Europe*, pp. 138–70. Macmillan/St Antony's College Oxford, London.

Castro, A. de (1983a) 'A dinâmica económica desde 1910 até à década de 1960'. In Saraiva, J. H. *Historia de Portugal*, pp. 643–51. Publicações Alfa, Lisbon.

Castro, A. de (1983b) 'Sentidos principais das "subestructurações" económicas de 1960–1961 a 1974–1975'. In Saraiva, J. H. *Historia de Portugal*, pp. 653–7. Publicações Alfa, Lisbon.

Chaney, R. (1986) *Regional emigration and remittances in developing countries: the Portuguese experience.* Praeger, New York.

Chislett, W. (1991) *Portugal: a new era.* Euromoney Publications, London.

Clarence-Smith, G. (1985) *The third Portuguese empire 1825–1975: a study in economic imperialism.* Manchester University Press, Manchester.

Clausse, G. (1984) 'Portuguese emigration to the EEC and the utilization of emigrants' remittances'. In Bruneau T. C., Da Rosa, V. M. P. and Macleod, A. (eds) *Portugal in development: emigration, industrialization, the European Community,* pp. 143–66, University of Ottawa Press, Ottawa.

Commission of the European Communities: see European Commission.

Corkill, D. R. (1988) 'Portugal's political transformation: the election of July 1987', *Parliamentary Affairs* vol. 41, no 2, April, pp. 247–57.

Corkill, D. R. (1991) 'Menos estado, melhor estado: Portugal's privatisation programme', *Journal of the Association for Contemporary Iberian Studies* vol. 4, no 1, Spring, pp. 41–7.

Corporate Intelligence on Retailing (1990) *Retailing in Europe: Portugal.* Corporate Intelligence and Research Publications, London.

Costa, C. S. (1991) 'Cinco anos e meio de integração de Portugal na CEE: das dúvidas de momento da partida á autoconfiança reencontrada'. In Rebelo de Sousa, M. et al. (eds) *Portugal em mudança: ensaios sobre a actividade do xi governo constitucional.* pp. 239–333. Imprensa Nacional-Casa da Moeda, Lisbon.

Cravinho, J. (1983) 'Characteristics and motives for entry'. In Sampedro, J. L. and Payno, J. A. (eds) *The enlargement of the European Community: case studies of Greece, Portugal and Spain,* pp. 131–48. Macmillan, London.

Cravinho, J. (1984) 'Structural adjustment in Portugal in the face of entry to the EEC'. In Bruneau, T. C., Da Rosa, V. M. P. and Macleod, A. (eds) *Portugal in development: emigration, industrialization, the European Community,* pp. 183–209. University of Ottawa Press, Ottawa.

Daltrop, A. (1982) *Political realities: politics and the European Community.* Longman, London.

Deubner, C. (1984) 'The paradox of Portugal's industrialization: emigrant labour, immigrant capital and foreign markets'. In Bruneau, T. C., Da Rosa, V. M. P. and Macleod, A. (eds) *Portugal in development: emigration, industrialization, the European Community,* pp. 167–82. University of Ottawa Press, Ottawa.

Duarte Silva, A. E. et al. (eds) (1989) *Salazar e o salazarismo.* Dom Quixote, Lisbon.

Duffy, J. (1962) *Portugal in Africa.* Penguin, Harmondsworth.

Eaton, M. (1990) 'Central Portugal's textile industry: depression or recovery on the road to international production', *Iberian Studies* vol. 19, nos 12, pp. 95–112.

Eaton, M. (1991a) 'Industrial assistance in Portugal: the role of the EFTA fund', *Tijdschrift voor Econ. en Soc. Geografie* 82, no 3, pp. 163–76.

Eaton, M. (1991b) 'The industrialisation of textile and clothing firms in Central Portugal', *Journal of the Association for Contemporary Iberian Studies* vol. 4, no 2, Autumn, pp. 47–57.

Economist Intelligence Unit (EIU) (1986) *Portugal to 1990: the challenge of modernization.* Special Report no 237 (written by Mark Hudson), London.

Economist Intelligence Unit (EIU) (1988) 'Portuguese textiles: living with EC membership', *Textile Outlook International* no 19, September, pp. 54–65.

Economist Intelligence Unit (EIU) (1989) *Portugal to 1993: investing in a European future.* Special Report no 1157 (written by Mark Hudson), London.

Economist Intelligence Unit (EIU) (1990) *Portugal: country report.* Quarterly, no 1 (1990a), no 2 (1990b), no 3 (1990c), no 4 (1990d), London.

Economist Intelligence Unit (EIU) (1991) *Portugal: country report*. Quarterly, no. 1 (1991a), no. 2 (1991b), no. 3 (1991c), no. 4 (1991d), London.
Economist Intelligence Unit (EIU) (1990e) *Portugal: country profile, annual survey 1989–90*. London.
Economist Intelligence Unit (EIU) (1991e) *North and central Portugal in the 1990s*. European Investment Region series. Special Report M604 (written by Jorge Gasper and Allan Williams), London.
*The Economist* (1972) *Between Africa and Europe: a survey of Portugal*, 26 February.
*The Economist* (1988) *Another new world: a survey of Portugal*, 28 May.
*The Economist* (1990) *Not quite kissing cousins*, 5 May.
*O Economista* (1991) *Anuário da economia Portuguesa* no 4, Lisbon.
Eisfeld, R. (1989) 'Portugal in the European Community 1986–1988: the impact of the first half of the transition period'. Paper presented at International Conference on Portugal, Durham, New Hampshire, 21–24 September.
*O Emigrante* (1991) *O sistema bancário em Portugal*, 8 November.
European Commission (1989) *Employment in Europe*. Commission of the European Communities, Luxembourg.
European Commission (1990a) *European economy: social Europe*. Commission of the European Communities, Luxembourg.
European Commission (1990b) *Community support framework 1989–93 for the development and structural adjustment of regions whose development is lagging behind (objective 1): Portugal*. Commission of the European Communities, Luxembourg.
European Commission (1991a) *Panorama of EC industries 1991–1992: current situation and outlook for sectors of manufacturing industry and services industries in the European Community*. Commission of the European Communities, Luxembourg.
European Commission (1991b) *European economy*, supplement A, no 6, June.
European Commission (1991c) *European Economy: annual economic report 1991–1992* no 50, December.
European Commission (1991d) *The regions in the 1990s: 4th periodic report on the social and economic situation and development in the regions of the Community*. Brussels/Luxembourg.
*Exame* (1991a) *Portugal em exame: edição especial*, June.
*Exame* (1991b) *Melhores e maiores: edição especial*, November.
*Expresso* (1991a) *Portugal está a envelhecer*, 22 June.
*Expresso* (1991b) *Nós gostamos da CEE*, 7 December.
Featherstone, K. (1989) 'The Mediterranean challenge: cohesion and external preferences'. In Lodge, J. (ed.) *The European Community and the challenge of the future*, pp. 186–201. Pinter, London.
Ferrão, J. and Jensen-Butler, C. (1986) 'Industrial development in Portuguese regions during the 1970s', *Tijdschrift voor Econ. en Soc. Geografie* vol. 77, no 2, pp. 132–48.
Figueiredo, A. de (1975) *Portugal: fifty years of dictatorship*. Penguin, London.
Financial Times Series (1990) *European finance and investment. Part 4: Portugal*, 30 April.
Financial Times Series (1991) *European finance and investment: Part 4: Portugal*, 23 April.
Financial Times Survey (1982) *Portuguese industry*, 29 September.
Financial Times Survey (1985) *Portugal: trade, industry, exports*, 23 December.
Financial Times Survey (1986a) *The Azores*, 15 April.

Financial Times Survey (1986b) *Portugal: the 600-year alliance*, 10 May.
Financial Times Survey (1986c) *Portuguese exports and industry*, 27 November.
Financial Times Survey (1987a) *Portugal: banking and finance*, 12 March.
Financial Times Survey (1987b) *Portugal*, 30 October.
Financial Times Survey (1989a) *Portuguese banking and finance*, 3 April.
Financial Times Survey (1989b) *Portugal*, 11 October.
Financial Times Survey (1990) *Portugal*, 24 October.
Financial Times Survey (1992a) *European finance and investment: Portugal*, 4 March.
Financial Times Survey (1992b) *Madeira*, 17 June.
Gallagher, T. (1982) *Portugal. A twentieth-century interpretation*. Manchester University Press, Manchester.
Gallagher, T. (1986) 'Twice choosing the unexpected: the Portuguese elections of 1985 and 1986', *West European Politics* vol. 9, no 4, October, pp. 233–7.
Gallagher, T. (1988) 'Goodbye to revolution: the Portuguese election of July 1987', *West European Politics* vol. 11, no 1, January, pp. 140–5.
Gallagher, T. (1989) 'Portugal', *Electoral Studies* vol. 8, no 3, pp. 317–21.
Gallagher, T. (1990) 'Conservatism, dictatorship and fascism in Portugal, 1914–45'. In Blinkhorn, M. (ed.) *Fascists and conservatives. The radical right and the establishment in twentieth-century Europe*, pp. 157–75. Unwin Hyman, London.
Gallagher, T. and Williams, A. (1989) *Southern European socialism: parties, elections and the challenge of government*. Manchester University Press, Manchester.
Georgel, J. (1985) *O salazarismo*. Dom Quixote, Lisbon.
Gibson, H. and Tsakalotos, E. (eds) (1992) *Economic integration and financial liberalisation: prospects for southern Europe*. Macmillan/ St Antony's College, Oxford.
Gillespie, R. (1990) 'The consolidation of the new democracies'. In Urwin, D. W. and Paterson, W. E. (eds) *Politics in Western Europe today: perspectives, policies and problems since 1980*, pp. 227–50. Longman, London.
Gladdish, K. (1990) 'Portugal: an open verdict'. In Pridham, G. (ed.) *Securing Democracy. Political parties and democratic consolidation in southern Europe*. Routledge, London.
Graham, L. S. (1975) *Portugal: the decline and collapse of an authoritarian order*. Sage, Beverly Hills.
Graham, L. S. (1990) *The state and policy outcomes*. Praeger, New York.
Graham, L. S. and Makler, H. (eds) (1979) *Contemporary Portugal*. University of Texas Press, Austin.
Graham, L. S. and Wheeler, D. (1983) *In search of modern Portugal*. University of Wisconsin Press, Madison.
Grayson, G. (1986) 'Portugal's new link with Europe', *Current History*, November, pp. 373–6.
Griffiths, S. (1990) 'A market too free'. *The Times Higher Education Supplement*, 7 December.
Hammond, J. (1988) *Building popular power: workers and neighbourhood movements in the Portuguese revolution*. Monthly Review Press, New York.
Harvey, R. (1978) *Portugal: birth of a democracy*. Macmillan, London.
Holland, S. (1979) 'Dependent development: Portugal as periphery'. In Seers, D., Schaffer, B. and Kiljunen, M. L. (eds) *Underdeveloped Europe*, pp. 139–60. Harvester, Sussex.
Hudson, R. and Lewis, J. R. (1984) 'Capital accumulation: the industrialisation of southern Europe'. In Williams, A. (ed.) *Southern Europe transformed: political*

*and economic change in Greece, Italy, Portugal and Spain*, pp. 179–207. Harper and Row, London.

Illeris, S. (1989) *Services and regions in Europe*. Avebury, Aldershot.

International Labour Office (1979) *Employment and basic needs in Portugal*. ILO, Geneva.

Kaplan, M. (1991) *The Portuguese: land and people*. Viking, London.

Kay, H. (1970) *Salazar and modern Portugal*. Eyre and Spottiswoode, London.

Kayman, M. (1987) *Revolution and counter-revolution in Portugal*. Merlin Press, London.

Keefe, E. K. (ed.) (1977) *Area handbook for Portugal*. American University, Foreign Affairs Studies, Washington.

King, R. (1984) 'Population mobility: emigration, return migration and internal migration'. In Williams, A. (ed.) *Southern Europe transformed: political and economic change in Greece, Italy, Portugal and Spain*, pp. 145–78. Harper and Row, London.

Korner, P. (ed.) (1986) *The IMF and the debt crisis: a guide to a Third World dilemma*. Zed Press, London.

Krugman, P. and Braga de Macedo, J. (1981) 'The economic consequences of the April 25th revolution'. In Braga de Macedo, J. and Serfaty, S. (eds) *Portugal since the revolution: economic and political perspectives*, pp. 53–87. Westview Press, Colorado.

Lains, P. and Reis, J. (1991) 'Portuguese economic growth, 1833–1985: some doubts', *Journal of European Economic History* vol. 20, no 2, Fall, pp. 441–58.

Leeds, E. R. (1984a) *Labour export, development and the state: the political economy of Portuguese emigration*. Unpublished PhD. Massachusetts Institute of Technology, MA.

Leeds, E. R. (1984b) 'Salazar's "modelo económico": the consequences of planned constraint'. In Bruneau, T. C., Da Rosa, V. M. P. and Macleod, A. (eds) *Portugal in development: emigration, industrialization, the European Community*, pp. 13–51. University of Ottawa Press, Ottawa.

Lewis, J. and Williams, A. (1981) 'Regional uneven development on the European periphery: the case of Portugal 1950–1978', *Tijdschrift voor Econ. en Soc. Geografie* 72, pp. 81–98.

Lewis, J. and Williams, A. (1985a) 'Portugal: the decade of return', *Geography* vol. 70, pp. 178–82.

Lewis, J. and Williams, A. (1985b) 'The Sines project. Portugal's growth centre or white elephant?', *Town Planning Review* 56, pp. 339–66.

Lewis, J. and Williams, A. (1986) 'The economic impact of return migration in Central Portugal'. In King, R. (ed.) *Return migration and regional economic problems*, pp. 100–28. Croom Helm, London.

Lewis, J. and Williams, A. (1988) 'Factories in fields: small manufacturing firms in rural southern Europe'. In Linge, G. J. R. (ed.) *Peripheralization and industrial change: impacts on nations, regions, firms and people*, pp. 113–30. Croom Helm, London.

Lewis, J. and Williams, A. (1989) 'A secret no more: Europe discovers the Algarve', *Geography* vol. 74, no 2, April, pp. 156–8.

Lewis, J. and Williams, A. (1991) 'Portugal: market segmentation and regional specialization'. In Williams, A. and Shaw, G. *Tourism and economic development: West European experiences*, 2nd ed., pp. 101–22. Belhaven Press, London.

Lister, P. H. (1988) *Foreign aid and economic development in Portugal: the nature, causes and growth of external capital dependency*. Liverpool Papers in Geography, working paper no 1, Liverpool.

158 *The Portuguese Economy since 1974*

Livermore, H. V. (1967) *A new history of Portugal*. Cambridge University Press, Cambridge.

Lizana, A. G. and Alcudia, P. (1990) 'The evolution of the Spanish and Portuguese economies and labour markets since the 1970s', *Iberian Studies* vol. 19, nos 1 and 2, pp. 84–94.

Logan, J. R. (1985) 'Democracy from above: limits to change in southern Europe'. In Arrighi, G. (ed.) *Semiperipheral development: the politics of southern Europe in the twentieth century*, pp. 149–77. Croom Helm, London.

Loureiro, J. (1991) *Economia e sociedade: indústria no após guerra, anos 50 e 60*. Edições Cosmos, Lisbon.

Lygum, B., Ottolenghi, D. and Steinher, A. (1988) 'The Portuguese financial system', *European Investment Bank Papers*, December, pp. 8–66.

Machado, D. P. (1987) 'A critique of Thomas C. Bruneau's "Politics and nationhood: post-revolutionary Portugal" '. *Iberian Studies* vol. 16, nos 1 and 2, pp. 115–34.

Machado, D. P. (1991) *The Structure of Portuguese Society. The Failure of Fascism*. Praeger, New York.

Machado Pais, J. (1978) 'O fascismo nos campos em Portugal – a campanha do trigo', *Análise Social* vol. 14, no 2, pp. 321–89.

MacKay, R. D. J. (1983) 'The Portuguese economy', *Barclays Review* vol. lviii, no 1, February, pp. 15–18.

Makler, H. M. (1979) 'The Portuguese industrial elite and its corporative relations: a comparative study of compartmentalization in an authoritarian regime'. In Graham, L. S. and Makler, H. M. (eds) *Contemporary Portugal: the revolution and its antecedents*, pp. 123–65. University of Texas Press, Austin.

Makler, H. M. (1983) 'The consequences of the survival and revival of the industrial bourgeoisie'. In Graham, L. S. and Wheeler, D. L. (eds) *In search of modern Portugal*, pp. 251–83. University of Wisconsin Press, Madison.

Marques, A. (1988) *Política económica e desenvolvimento em Portugal (1926–1959)*. Livros Horizonte, Lisbon.

Marques Mendes, A. J. (1990) 'Economic cohesion in Europe: the impact of the Delors Plan', *Journal of Common Market Studies* vol. xxix, no 1, September, pp. 17–36.

Marques Mendes, A. J. and Thirwell, A. P. (1989) 'The balance of payments constraint and growth in Portugal 1951–1984'. In Yannopoulos, G. N. (ed.) *European integration and the Iberian economies*, pp. 21–39. Macmillan in association with the Graduate School of European and International Studies, University of Reading, Basingstoke.

Martins, A. (1987) 'Industrial policy in Portugal'. In Beije, P. R. et al. (eds) *A competitive future for Europe? Towards a new European industrial policy*, pp. 178–90. Croom Helm, London.

Maxwell, K. (1976) 'The thorns of the Portuguese revolution', *Foreign Affairs* 54, January, pp. 250–70.

Maxwell, K. (ed.) (1986) *Portugal in the 1980s: dilemmas of democratic consolidation*. Greenwood Press, New York.

Miguélez Lobo, F. (1990) 'Irregular work in Portugal'. In European Commission, *Underground economy and irregular forms of employment*. Programme for research and actions on the development of the labour market, Brussels.

Mónica, M. F. (1990) *Os grandes patrões da indústria portuguesa*. Dom Quixote, Lisbon.

Morrison, R. J. (1981) *Portugal: revolutionary change in an open economy*. Auburn House, Boston.

Mullin, J. R. (1992) 'The implementation of regional industrial policies in the European Community: a case study of Setúbal, Portugal', *Portuguese Studies Review* vol. 1, no 2, Fall Winter, pp. 44–61.

Murteira, M. (1979) 'The present economic situation: its origins and prospects'. In Graham, L. S. and Makler H. M. (eds) *Contemporary Portugal: the revolution and its antecedents*, pp. 331–42. University of Texas Press, Austin.

Nataf, D. (1987) *Social cleavages and regime formation in contemporary Portugal.* Unpublished PhD. University of California, Los Angeles.

Nataf, D. and Sammis, E. (1990) 'Classes, hegemony, and Portuguese democratization'. In Chilcote, R. et al. (eds) *Transitions from dictatorship to democracy: comparative studies of Spain, Portugal and Greece*, pp. 73–130. Crane Russak, New York.

Naylon, J. (1987) 'Iberia'. In Clout, H. D. (ed.) *Regional development in western Europe*, 3rd ed., pp. 383–417. David Fulton, London.

Neto, A. M. (1991) *Industrializaçao de Angola. Reflexão sobre a experiencia da administracão portuguesa (1961–1975).* Escher, Lisbon.

Nunes, A. B., Mata, E. and Valerio, N. (1989) 'Portuguese economic growth 1833–1985', *Journal of European Economic History* vol. 18, no 2, Fall, pp. 291–330.

*The Observer* (1977) *Portugal: an* Observer *extra*, 13 February.

OECD (1966) *Mediterranean regional project: Portugal.* OECD, Paris.

OECD (1976) OECD *economic surveys: Portugal.* OECD, Paris.

OECD (1977) OECD *economic surveys: Portugal.* OECD, Paris.

OECD (1978) *Regional problems and policies in Portugal.* OECD, Paris.

OECD (1980) OECD *economic surveys: Portugal.* OECD, Paris.

OECD (1981) OECD *economic surveys: Portugal.* OECD, Paris.

OECD (1982) OECD *economic surveys: Portugal.* OECD, Paris.

OECD (1986) OECD *economic surveys: Portugal 1985/6.* OECD, Paris.

OECD (1988) OECD *economic surveys: Portugal 1987/8.* OECD, Paris.

OECD (1989a) *Industrial policy in* OECD *countries: annual review 1989.* OECD, Paris.

OECD (1989b) OECD *economic surveys: Portugal 1988/9.* OECD, Paris.

OECD (1991) OECD *economic surveys: Portugal 1990/1.* OECD, Paris.

OECD (1992) OECD *economic surveys: Portugal 1991/2.* OECD, Paris.

Pais, J. M. (1978) 'O fascismo nos campos em Portugal – a campanha do trigo', *Análise Social* 14, no 2, pp. 321–89.

Parry, J. (1991) 'Sustaining Europe's poorer regions', *International Management*, September, pp. 39–54.

Passos, M. C. (1991) 'Resistências e desfasamentos num processo de modernização e desenvolvimento: os reformadores no governo de Marcello Caetano', *Sociologia* 10, pp. 21–42.

Patrício, M. T. (1990) 'Industrialization and communism: The Portuguese Communist party confronts the Sines growth pole', *Journal of Communist Studies* vol. 6, no 3, September, pp. 44–63.

Patrício, M. T. (1991) 'A estratégia política e económica do estado português num pólo de crescimento: o projecto industrial de Sines', *Sociologia* 10, pp. 9–19.

Pereira, B. F. (1986) 'Portugal and Spain'. In Maxwell, K. (ed.) *Dilemmas of democratic consolidation*, pp. 63–87. Greenwood Press, New York.

Pimlott, B. (1977) 'Socialism in Portugal: was it a revolution?', *Government and Opposition* vol. 12, no 3, pp. 332–50.

Pintado, X. (1964) *The structure and growth of the Portuguese economy.* EFTA, Geneva.

160 *The Portuguese Economy since 1974*

Pinto, M. (1990) 'Trade union action and industrial relations in Portugal'. In Baglioni, G. and Crouch, C. (eds) *European industrial relations: the challenge of flexibility*, pp. 243–64. Sage, London.

Pires de Lima, M. (1987) 'Contribuição para uma história de organização racional do trabalho em Portugal no contexto da economia sob o Estado Novo'. In Rosas, F. et al. *O Estado Novo: das origens ao fim da autarcia 1926–1959*, vol. 1, pp. 325–31. Fragmentos, Lisbon.

Pitta e Cunha, P. (1983) 'Portugal and the European Economic Community'. In Graham, L. S. Wheeler, D. (eds) *In search of modern Portugal*, pp. 321–38. University of Wisconsin Press, Wisconsin.

Porch, D. (1977) *The Portuguese armed forces and the revolution*. Croom Helm, London.

Porto, M. (1984) 'Portugal: twenty years of change'. In Williams, A. (ed.) *Southern Europe transformed: political and economic change in Greece, Italy, Portugal and Spain*, pp. 84–112. Harper and Row, London.

Raby, D. L. (1988) *Fascism and resistance in Portugal*. Manchester University Press, Manchester.

Robinson, R. A. H. (1979) *Contemporary Portugal: a history*. George Allen and Unwin, London.

Rocha, E. (1985) 'Crecimento económico em Portugal nos anos de 1960–73: alguns aspectos', *Análise Social* vol. xx, no 84, pp. 621–44.

Romão, A. (1983) *Portugal faceà* CEE. Livros Horizonte, Lisbon.

Romão, A. (1985) 'A inserção da economia portuguesa na economia mundial: evolução recente e perspectivas'. In Sousa Ferreira, E. and de Opello, W. (eds) *Conflict and Change in Portugal, 1974–1984*, pp. 269–79. Teorema, Lisbon.

Rosas, F. (1986) *O estado novo nos anos trinta: elementos para o estudo da natureza económica e social do salazarismo (1928–1938)*. Editorial Estampa, Lisbon.

Rosas, F. (1987) 'A crise de 1929 e os seus efeitos económicos na sociedade portuguesa'. In Rosas et al. (eds) *O Estado Novo: das origens ao fim da autarcia 1926–1959*, pp. 249–58. Fragmentos, Lisbon.

Rosas, F. (1989) 'A indústria portuguesa durante a segunda guerra mundial'. In Carrilho, M. (ed.) *Portugal na segunda guerra mundial*, pp. 49–89. Dom Quixote, Lisbon.

Rosas, F. (1990) *Portugal entre a paz e a guerra 1939–1945: estudo do impacte da guerra mundial na economia e na sociedade portuguesa*. Imprensa Universitaria – Editorial Estampa, Lisbon.

Rother, B. (1988), 'Socialist economic policy in the crisis. The case of Portugal', *International Journal of Political Economy* vol. 17, no 4, Winter, pp. 88–105.

Sammis, E. P. (1988) *The limits of state adaptability: the formation, consolidation and breakdown of the Portuguese dictatorship (1926–1974)*. Unpublished PhD. University of California, Los Angeles.

Saraiva, J. H. (1983) *História de Portugal*. Publicações Alfa, Lisbon.

Schmitt, H. O. (1981) *Economic stabilization and growth in Portugal*. Occasional paper no 2, IMF, Washington.

Schmitter, P. (1975) *Corporatism and public policy in authoritarian Portugal*. Sage, Beverly Hills.

Schwartzman, K. C. (1989) *The social origins of democratic collapse. The first Portuguese republic in the global economy*. University Press of Kansas, Lawrence.

Smith, D. (1990) *Portugal and the challenge of 1992: an assessment of the European Community's most vulnerable partner in the run-up to the 'single market' of 1992*. Camoes Center/RIIC, Special Report 1, Columbia University, New York.

Sousa, M. R. de et al. (eds) (1991) *Portugal em mudança: ensaios sobre a actividade do XI governo constitutional*. Imprensa Nacional-Casa da Moeda, Lisbon.

Stallings, B. (1981) 'Portugal and the IMF: the political economy of stabilization'. In Braga de Macedo, J. Serfaty, S. (eds) and *Portugal since the revolution: economic and political perspectives*, pp. 101–35. Westview, Boulder.

Stuart, B. C. (1981) 'Stabilization policy in Portugal, 1974–78'. *Finance and Development*, September, pp. 25–9.

Synek, C. (1991) 'Balanço da política económica de 1987 a 1991'. In *Anuário da Economia Portuguesa*, pp. 67–74. Associação Portuguesa de Economistas, Lisbon.

Telo, A. (1987) *Portugal na segunda guerra mundial*. Perspectivas e realidades, Lisbon.

Thormann, P. H. (1969) 'Employment and earnings in Portugal, 1953–1967', *International Labour Review* vol. 99, Jan–June, pp. 589–602.

*Time* (1985) *Enlarging the Community*, 23 December.

Torres, A. and Veloso, L. (1984) *Estudos de economia portuguesa*, vol. 1. A Regra do Jogo, Lisbon.

Tsoulakis, L. (1981) *The European Community and its Mediterranean enlargement*. Allen and Unwin, London.

United Nations (1974) *Economic Survey of Europe*. United Nations, New York.

Weingardt, N. (1987) 'Portugal's accession and integration into the European Economic Community', *Denver Journal of International Law and Policy* 15 (2–3), Winter–Spring, pp. 317–36.

Wiarda, H. J. (1973) 'The Portuguese corporative system: basic structures and current functions', *Iberian Studies* vol. 2, no 2, Autumn, pp. 73–80.

Wiarda, H. J. (1977) *Corporatism and development: the Portuguese experience*. University of Massachusetts Press, Amhearst.

Williams, A. (1984) *Southern Europe transformed: political and economic change in Greece, Italy, Portugal and Spain*. Harper and Row, London.

Williams, A. (1987) *The western European economy: a geography of post-war development*. Hutchinson Educational, London.

Williams, A. (1989) 'Socialist economic policies: never off the drawing board?' In Gallagher, T. Williams, A. (eds) *Southern European socialism: parties, elections and the challenge of government*, pp. 188–216. Manchester University Press, Manchester.

Williams, A. (1991) 'The Portuguese economy in transition', *Journal of the Association for Contemporary Iberian Studies* vol. 5, no 2, Spring, pp. 30–9.

Williams, A. and Shaw G. (1991) *Tourism and economic development: western European experiences*, 2nd ed. Belhaven Press, London.

Williamson, P. J. (1985) *Varieties of corporatism: theory and practice*. Cambridge University Press, Cambridge.

Wise, M. (1984) *The common fisheries policy of the European Community*. Methuen, London.

World Bank (1978a) *Portugal: current and prospective economic trends*. World Bank, Washington.

World Bank (1978b) *Portugal: agricultural sector survey*. World Bank, Washington.

World Bank (1989) *Trends in developing economies 1989*. World Bank, Washington.

World of Information (1989) *The Europe review: the economic and business report 1989*. Saffron Waldon.

Yannopoulos, G. N. (ed.) (1989) *European integration and the Iberian economies*. Macmillan in association with the Graduate School of European and International Studies, University of Reading, Basingstoke.

## NEWSPAPERS, MAGAZINES AND NEWSLETTERS

*Diário de Noticias* (daily)
*Económico Semanario* (weekly)
*The Economist* (weekly)
*O Emigrante* (weekly)
*Exame* (monthly)
*Expresso* (weekly)
*Financial Times* (daily)
*O Jornal* (weekly)
*Portuguese Focus* (monthly)
*Público* (daily)
*Sábado* (weekly)
*Tradewinds Newsletter* (Portuguese UK Chamber of Commerce)

## JOURNALS

*Análise Social*
*Banco de Portugal* (Quarterly Bulletin)
*Cadernos de Ciências Sociais*
*Economia*
*Economia* EC
*Economia e Socialismo*
EFTA *Bulletin*
*European Industrial Relations Review*
*International Currency review*
*Portuguese Studies Review*
*Revista Crítica de Ciências Sociais*
*Sociologia: Problemas e Práticas*

# *Index*

166                                    *The Portuguese Economy since 1974*

*see also* unemployment
energy
  costs, 73, 108
  industry, 86–7: economic dislocation, 44;
    public works programme, 9;
    Second World War, 12
entrepreneurs, 68
entry of firms, 68
environmental concerns, 83
Espírito Santo, 144
*Estado Novo*, 3, 4–10
Estaleiros de Viana de do Castelo (ENVC), 73
eucalyptus plantations, 74–5
Europe
  immigrants, 22
  links with, 15–17
  Portuguese attitude, 27
European Agricultural Guidance Fund
    (FEOGA), 95
European Community (EC)
  Eastern Europe, 109–10
  economic growth, 49
  funds, 95–103, 109, 148
  investment, 131, 134
  Iberian market, 105–9
  membership, 27, 52, 88–95, 110–11
  monetary union, 113–15
  presidency, 115–16
  single market, 111–13
  textiles industry, 69
  trade, 16, 103–5
European Economic Space (EES), 109, 116
European Free Trade Association (EFTA), 15–
    17
  and EC, 92–3
  Industrial Fund, 99–100
  membership, 27
  textiles industry, 69
  and UK, 92
European Investment Bank, 89
European Regional Development Fund
    (FEDER), 95, 102
European Regional Frontier Association, 109
Europeanists, 19, 27
Exchange Rate Mechanism (ERM), 113–14
exchange rates, 48
exile, 19, 23
exports
  AD government, 51
  balance of payments, 124
  child labour, 57
  decolonisation, 36
  EC, 16, 91, 103–5, 110: single market, 113
  economic dislocation, 44
  EFTA, 15–16
  *Estado Novo*, 8
  fishing industry, 78

increase, 18
industrial policy, 64
minerals, 79
proto-liberalisation phase, 13
'restorationist' phase, 4
Second World War, 12
Socialist ascendancy, 47, 48, 49
Spain, 106
textiles industry, 69, 70
wine industry, 76

Fábrica de Borracha Continental Lda, 7
failures, business, 49, 68, 113
fascism, 3
fecundity, 54
Fiat, 132
Financial and Economic Recovery Pro-
    gramme, 51
financial concentration, 20–1
financial markets, 136–7
financial sector
  investment, 108, 131
  liberalisation, 134–6
Finland, 79
First Republic, 2–3
First World War, 3
fishing industry, 77–9, 94, 102
fixed-term contracts, 56
flour industry, 7
footwear industry, 57, 70
Ford, 131, 132–4
foreign exchange
  reserves, 40, 47
  tourism, 24–5
foreign investment, *see* direct foreign invest-
    ment (DFI)
Foreign Investment Code, 46, 129
foreign ownership of firms, 67
foreign participation in privatisation, 142,
    145, 147
foreign trade patterns, 103–5
forestry industry, 74–6
Foznave, 73
fragmentation
  of industry, 65–6
  of land, 63
France
  EC, 89, 104
  immigrants, 22
fraud, 102–3
Freitas do Amaral, Diogo, 51, 119

GAPIN, 132
gas, natural, 87
General Agreement on Tariffs and Trade
    (GATT), 15, 102
General Confederation of Portuguese Workers